Peasant Icons

PEASANT ICONS

Representations of Rural People in Late Nineteenth-Century Russia

CATHY A. FRIERSON

New York   Oxford
OXFORD UNIVERSITY PRESS
1993

Oxford University Press

Oxford   New York   Toronto
Delhi   Bombay   Calcutta   Madras   Karachi
Kuala Lumpur   Singapore   Hong Kong   Tokyo
Nairobi   Dar es Salaam   Cape Town
Melbourne   Auckland   Madrid

and associated companies in
Berlin   Ibadan

Copyright © 1993 by Oxford University Press, Inc.

Published by Oxford University Press, Inc.,
200 Madison Avenue, New York, New York 10016

Oxford is a registered trademark of Oxford University Press

Library of Congress Cataloging-in-Publication Data
Frierson, Cathy A.
Peasant icons : representations of rural people in
late nineteenth century russia /
Cathy A. Frierson.
p.   cm.   Includes bibliographical references and index.
ISBN 0-19-507293-6 (cloth).—ISBN 0-19-507294-4
1. Soviet Union—History—Alexander II, 1855–1881.
2. Peasantry—Soviet Union—History—19th century.
3. Peasantry in literature.
4. Peasantry—Soviet Union—Public opinion.
5. Stereotype (Psychology)—Soviet Union.
I. Title.   DK222.F73   1993   947.08—dc20   92-7783

Chapter 3 contains some material previously published in "Rural Justice in Public Opinion : 'The Volost'
Court Debate, 1861–1912," *The Slavonic & East European Review* 64 (October 1986): 526–45. Reprinted
by permission of the editors. Chapter 8 contains some material previously published in the following
sources: *Land Commune and Peasant Community in Russia,* ed. Roger Bartlett (1990), pp. 303–20, reprinted with permission of St Martin's Press, Inc.; "Razdel: The Peasant Family Divided," *The Russian
Review* 46 (January 1987): 35–51, and is reprinted with permission, copyright © 1987 by *The Russian
Review,* all rights reserved.

2 4 6 8 9 7 5 3 1

Printed in the United States of America
on acid-free paper

To the memory of my mother,
Annie Bond Short Frierson

Preface

When I began this project, I was very much under the influence of the conceptualization of late Imperial Russia through modernization theory and of the approach to its study through the history of ideas. My initial question, typically broad for a student formulating a dissertation topic, was: What role were the peasants expected to play in Russia's industrial development in the late nineteenth century? As I began my research, I was struck by the fact that all of the figures whose discussions of the peasants' role I read seemed to be talking about a different "peasant." This led me to explore the various images, one may even say models, of the peasant that had entered public debate about Russia's course of development by the 1880s. Delving further into that more specific question, I realized that the first three decades of the post-Emancipation period were a crucible for the development of those images, and that, furthermore, the distinctive feature of that crucible was its admixture of moral and economic concerns in educated Russia's articulation of images of the newly freed peasantry. This led me to focus on the narrower subquestion within the larger peasant question of the search for the peasant soul.

Since I began this project, historians of Russia have turned increasingly to the study of the peasantry. Early on, such scholars as David Macey, Jeffrey Brooks, Thomas Pearson, Frank Wcislo, and Ben Eklof examined the peasantry from the vantage point of policy makers, educators, and publishers who acted in some way on peasant culture. More recently, such scholars as Barbara Engel, Stephen Frank, Steven Hoch, Carol Leonard, Timothy Mixter, and Christine Worobec have studied the peasantry from below. I have also taken this approach in my research on questions of rural concepts of justice, the break up of patriarchal households, and fire and arson in rural Russia.

As we have moved in the direction of social history to balance political and intellectual history, however, we continue to confront the legacy of that first post-Emancipation generation of observers of peasant culture who did so much to define the dominant images of the peasant for educated Russians. Their images, in turn, shaped the research agenda of their successors and established the nature of the questions more sophisticated ethnographers, statisticians, and economists would take to the village. When the men and women who provided our sources for the study of social history formulated questions about village culture, wrote ethnographic surveys, and designed commission programs, they were operating within the framework of models of peasant behavior that had been constructed during the search for the peasant soul. Their emphasis on material culture, economic relationships, and the potential for exploitation in the village resonated with images of the rational peasant, the grey *muzhik*, and the *kulak* as village strongman. This study, then, takes us back to the fundamental concepts of the peasantry that influenced not only the way educated Russians of the late nineteenth century would approach their rural compatriots, but also the filters through which we examine the rural culture of late Imperial Russia a century later.

Durham, N.H.   C. A. F.
September 1992

Acknowledgments

I began this project as a graduate student at Harvard University, where I enjoyed generous support from the Department of History and the Russian Research Center. The opportunity to study at Harvard under these circumstances came to me largely because of the guidance and high expectations of Samuel H. Baron, who taught me as an undergraduate at the University of North Carolina at Chapel Hill, and who has continued to be a part of my scholarly development ever since. Richard E. Pipes served as my dissertation advisor at Harvard and encouraged my interest in the peasant question in Russia and my investigation of the specific question of the construction of images of the peasant in public discourse. His insistence on a readable text of manageable size did much to shape this project. Abbott Gleason also read sections of the dissertation and welcomed me into the profession during these years. At the dissertation stage, certain individuals offered support of a more general but equally crucial kind. Chief among these were Suzan K. Burks, Wayne K. Ishikawa, and Paul R. Josephson. Beyond this close circle, the faculty members, fellows, staff, and other graduate students at the Russian Research Center provided a supportive and friendly atmosphere that is the stuff of graduate student dreams.

As I moved from the dissertation to this book, I solicited and received criticism and advice from Jane Burbank and Laura Engelstein. Daniel Field, Melissa Stockdale, Christine Worobec, Steven Hoch, Monika Greenleaf, Ronald LeBlanc, Elizabeth Frierson, and Barbara Engel read the manuscript in part or in entirety and offered their comments. Elizabeth Ransome and Elizabeth Blackmon worked as research assistants and contributed beyond their work in the Harvard libraries and the Library of Congress.

Rutgers University offered support in a number of ways. While I taught in the Department of History at Camden College, I received research funds and leave time as a Henry Rutgers Fellow. My chairman, Allen Woll, ensured that I worked steadily toward completion of the manuscript. Joan Coward welcomed me in the department and offered collegial advice, as did Andrew Lees, who also gave the manuscript a close reading in the final stages of revision.

I also received financial support from the International Research and Exchanges Board, the Fulbright-Hays fellowship program, and the Kennan Institute for Advanced Russian Studies. I am grateful to the librarians and archivists at the New York Public Library, the Library of Congress, the Harvard University libraries, the Lenin Library and Central State Archive of Art and Literature in Moscow, the Saltykov-Shchedrin Library and Pushkin House in St. Petersburg, and the State Archive of the Smolensk Region in Smolensk.

I prepared the manuscript for production as a new member of the Department of History at the University of New Hampshire. The university contributed directly to this project by paying for the reproductions of paintings included as illustrations. Beyond financial support, the community within my department and through the office of Dean Stuart Palmer provided a supportive environment for my work as a scholar.

By the time I turned to writing this book, I had become a mother. Having discovered the particular challenges of teaching, writing, and mothering, I developed an appreciation for the struggle of my mother, who combined these responsibilities in a less generous era than mine. In recognition of the effort it cost her to ensure that her four daughters had opportunities beyond hers, I dedicate this book to her in the hope that it is a partial fulfillment of the vision for us to which she gave her life.

Contents

Peasant Icons

What could be more terrible than to live in alienation from one's own people?

A. N. ENGELGARDT, 1881

Introduction

On the occasion of the twenty-fifth anniversary of Gleb Ivanovich Uspenskii's writing career in 1887, a large crowd of between two and three hundred people gathered at a literary evening where he planned to read his
most recent sketch. When he stepped onto the stage, the audience stood up
and applauded loudly. Overwhelmed, he hesitated, and opened his note-
book only to close it again and walk away. Brought back forcibly, he
consented to read his piece only if a friend sat by his side. The crowd fell
silent and listened intently as he barely whispered his way through the
sketch. When he closed the book and rose to leave, the crowd burst forth
with even more enthusiastic applause.[1]

Uspenskii's fame in 1887 grew out of his contributions to a public
debate following the emancipation of the Russian serfs in 1861 that consumed the interests of educated Russia, dominated the pages of literary
and journalistic publications, and informed the most important school of
Russian painting of the period. In salons of luxurious urban residences, in
libraries of state functionaries, in damp and cold rooms of university and
institute students, in parlors of gentry estates, in studios of Itinerant painters, at meetings of state commissions, in sessions of scholarly societies, and
above all else, in editorial offices of major literary-political journals of the
day, Imperial Russia's educated society was wrestling with the question,
Who is the Russian peasant?

For most of the people posing this question, the answer was drawn from
texts—from eyewitness accounts, literary-journalistic sketches, reports of
state commissioners, and paintings created by individuals who lived among
the peasantry. Separated from the peasants by physical and cultural distance, men and women of position and education relied on the writings of
such figures as Uspenskii, who went to the countryside to address the
question directly and send back their conclusions to be published by the
editors of major journals, displayed at exhibitions, and devoured by the
educated public. This book is an exploration of those texts, of the various
images of the Russian peasant they produced, of the sources and morphol-

ogy of those images, and thus of the larger debate or discourse that took on
a life of its own in post-Emancipation Russia. It is a study, as it were, of the
iconography of the free peasantry in late Imperial Russia. Just as early
Russian iconographers had striven to reveal the truth of the divine incarnation in man through the lives of Jesus Christ, disciples, and saints, so
iconographers of the peasantry strove to reveal the truth of rural man and
woman as the incarnation of Russian culture.[2]

As such, it is a study in intellectual history which aims to examine
texts within the context that informed their creation, structure, and meaning. These contexts include those identified by Dominick LaCapra as
problematic when examined individually or exclusively, but illuminative
when perceived as part of a highly dynamic whole: the relation between
the author's intentions and the text; the relation of the author's life to the
text; the relation of a text to the corpus of a writer; the relation of society
to texts; the relation between modes of discourse and texts.[3] In the case of
educated Russia's fascination—one may even say obsession—with the
peasant during these years, each of these relations bore on the images
that authors and painters created in their search for definitions. Of particular importance were the intellectual and social climates which both established the types of questions to be asked about the peasant and the
requirements for authority or legitimacy for anyone purporting to answer
those questions. In this work, then, I am engaged in the search for origins: the origins of a set of images of the peasant in a society where the
peasantry made up the vast majority of the population and came to be
seen as the decisive element in the culture's future. Beyond origins, I
have sought to describe and analyze the elements that entered into each
image and the sources for those elements in the context of the relations
LaCapra outlined. I have also sought to explain how each of these images
played off the others, and how that interplay or contest both generated
the debate and emerged from it.

This was not the only debate concerning the peasantry or the village
that was taking place during these years. The debate over the "agrarian
question" emerged by the mid-1870s;[4] the proper role of the commune in
Russia's social and legal system was the subject of its own public discussion;[5] questions of public health and education for the rural community
occupied bureaucrats and professionals alike;[6] and debates about and proj-
ects for reforming local governance of the peasant population continued
from the Emancipation through the end of the century.[7] The search for an
answer to the question, Who is the Russian peasant?, was in many ways
more basic and less obviously a part of the political domain than these
debates, for it established the challenge of figuring out who the peasant was
as the first step in defining his role in Russia's future development.

Contexts and Sources

LaCapra has insisted on both a more contextualized approach to the study of texts and a questioning of the goal of establishing unity, conformity, or synthesis in evaluating the meaning of a text or set of texts.[8] I find his challenge to be particularly appropriate to the debate about the Russian peasant, perhaps because that debate was part of the atmosphere that ultimately informed LaCapra's own vision of the nature of discourse, literature, and history. His insistence on the failings of a search for unity or synthesis grew out of the influence of Mikhail Bakhtin's notions of dialogism and polyphony, the "multiplicity of voices" that Bakhtin identified as the distinctive feature of Dostoevsky's poetics.[9] Bakhtin's conceptualization of the dialogue, interplay, and contest between independent voices and consciousnesses in Dostoevsky's novels impressed upon LaCapra the tensions that inhere in all complex texts, and between texts and contexts. Bakhtin himself had linked the polyphony of Dostoevsky's texts, his novels, with what he called "the multi-leveledness and contradictoriness of social reality" in the context of post-Emancipation Russia.[10] Having himself changed ideological camps, living himself in the highly charged atmosphere of a society in rapid flux, Dostoevsky became sensitized to the power of contradictions in life and turned to "an objective visualization of contradictions as forces coexisting simultaneously. . . ."[11]

What Bakhtin found distinctive in Dostoevsky, and LaCapra incorporated in his search for a redefinition of intellectual history, was equally true of the debate over the nature of the Russian peasant that pervaded intellectual life in Russia at the time Dostoevsky was writing his novels and made its way into Dostoevsky's work as well. Although the texts studied here were not complex either in the authors' intention or in their final form, they displayed much the same polyphony and intertextuality. Every text that appeared, whether a piece of fiction, a work of journalism, or a painted canvas, was a response to another text once the debate took off in the mid-1860s. Bakhtin wrote that in Dostoevsky, "almost no word is without its intense sideward glance at someone else's word."[12] The same can be said of the words that came to make up the contradictory declarations on the nature of the Russian peasant. This study, then, is a study in contradictions, the contradictions within educated Russian society's elaboration of the character and meaning of the Russian peasant. It is a study that may demonstrate certain unities of predisposition and goals among the authors of texts on the Russian peasant, but it is ultimately an account of a highly contentious, fractious debate in which authors disagreed with each other and with their own words on the peasant. Returning to the metaphor of the icon, we can say that the debate produced not one definitive icon, but a

collage of images—an iconostasis—in which the individual images conformed to a canonical articulation in form but diverged in their disparate
message of the truth about rural man and woman. The process of constructing that collage of images was one of contested truths, of individual iconic
images of the peasant which were the product of educated society's search
for comprehension.

This debate is, furthermore, an example of discourse in the sense that
Hayden White used the term in *Tropics of Discourse.* For here was a group
of educated members of society confronting something they found unset-
tling and strange—the peasantry—and they set out to conquer that unknown territory through description, through language, through texts that
would facilitate understanding. White's definition of tropes, the agents that
drive discourse, applies fully to the images or metaphors that seekers of the
Russian peasant employed, as "deviations from literal, conventional or
'proper' language use, swerves in location sanctioned by neither custom
nor logic. Tropes generate figures of speech or thought by their variation
from what is 'normally' expected. . . ."[13] Through their texts on the peasant, participants in this debate constantly engaged in a dialogic redefinition
of terms and reversed the expected meanings of words and labels in an
effort to settle on images that were "realistic" and "true." The debate over
the nature of the Russian peasant, emancipated and a potential fellow
citizen, was precisely a mediation between educated Russia's "apprehen-
sion of those aspects of experience still 'strange' . . . and those aspects of it
which we 'understand' because we have found an order of words adequate
to its domestication."[14]

In that sense, the story is one with a beginning and an end, a progression from alarm over confrontation with something unknown and strange
to confidence in understanding and familiarity. The beginning coincided
with the emancipation of the Russian serfs in 1861 when the so-called
peasant question thrust itself with full force on the consciousness of would-
be reformers and activists. The end came around 1890 when educated
society retreated from the iconostasis of images their search had generated
and redefined the proper approach to the study of the peasant and his
world. This marked the closure of one discourse and the opening of another. Within this thirty-year span, a generation of writers, publicists, painters, critics, ethnographers, economists, and legal scholars selected the peasant as the subject of their life's work. Writers placed their stories in the
village, ethnographers reported the peculiarities of local mores, legal scholars examined the shape and significance of peasant customary law, local
petty officials published their experiences in the major journals of the day,
and landowners across the empire offered their eyewitness accounts of life
"in the countryside." They found a ready audience of readers who were
searching for guideposts in a period of social and economic change, private

individuals as well as state specialists and bureaucrats who were committed to overcoming Russia's backwardness and to living a civilized life as they imagined it.[15]

The question, Who is the Russian peasant?, was deeply embedded in the larger questions, What is Russia? and What will Russia be?, in a period of broad cultural self-definition. Of the various contexts out of which the texts in this study emerged and with which they interacted, the context of social and economic transformation was particularly important. The imperative behind the exploration of village culture was the sense of rapid development and change, an awareness of a great cultural shift. It was a "transitional epoch," which demanded that fundamental elements of Russian culture be identified as a prelude to action.[16] For the post-Emancipation generation of Russian intellectuals there was little, if any, doubt that they lived in exceptional times. They viewed the emancipation of the serfs as "the greatest event in the domestic history of the Russian people since the time of Peter the Great."[17] A reform that redefined the legal, social, and economic status of one third of the population heralded a new era. The series of further reforms that followed the Emancipation and altered such major national institutions as the military, the judicial system, universities, and local admin-istration served to reinforce the sense of new beginnings, possibilities, and directions.[18] Although it seemed obvious that a new Russia was unfolding, it was not at all clear what shape it would take and what roles the various elements of the new social order would play in its design. It was a time of both heightened expectancy and disturbing uncertainty. As one witness ob-served, "Our time, being a time of universal reconstruction [*perestroika*] in Russia, is also a time of extreme confusion of ideas, mutual misunderstand-ings, intensified expectations and exaggerated fears."[19] It was a time when there seemed to be very few givens, when almost every aspect of the culture was on unstable ground, when any proposition or prediction was likely to be contested, when contradictions reigned, when the dominant intellectual posi-tion was one of questioning and criticism. LaCapra observed that "most modern writers of note have seen their period as revolutionary or at least as 'transitional.' "[20] It was that consciousness of being in a state of change and new possibilities that tended to provoke the search for new definitions and understandings that moved educated Russia during these years. This exag-gerated sense of new beginnings was also characteristic of what Iurii Lotman and Boris Uspenskii have identified as the polarity of Russian culture.[21] As in previous moments in their cultural development, educated Russians con-ceived of their historical position according to a binary division between the old world (here, that which predated the Emancipation) and the new one that would emerge after it. Binary elements also shaped the primary con-cerns of educated society in this moment of heightened consciousness of newness.

No entity pressed more firmly or more constantly on the unsettled consciousness of post-Emancipation educated Russian society than the village and its inhabitants. As early as August 1861, six months after the announcement of the Emancipation, the liberal journal *Notes of the Fatherland* pointed to the irruption of the village onto the cultural scene. Whereas St. Petersburg had long been the center and arbiter of all Russian life, bit by bit "onto the stage the village [was] stepping forward, village life, village interests, upon which Petersburg used to look down from on high." The usual questions about life in St. Petersburg were being replaced by the single, compelling question, What are the *muzhiks* doing?[22]

This shift of focus for educated society was, on one level, a response to the peasantry's newly defined presence in the Empire. Altogether the peasantry constituted more than 80 percent of the population, the keystone reform of the Reform Era had been on their behalf, and Russia's economy was dominated by agriculture, which in practice meant peasant farming. Products of the Reform Era, such new institutions as trial by jury and the local organs of self-rule—the *zemstva*—drew peasant citizens directly into national life as jurors and *zemstvo* delegates. Peasants had become more than a large presence in the rural world: they had become potential partners in Russia's progress. This passive majority seemed suddenly to be the key to Russia's future during a period of transformation, yet the traditionally more active, educated elements of Russian society who were known as *obshchestvo*[23] confessed virtual ignorance of the peasant. This confession both troubled and inspired them to get to know the Russian peasant and to discern the defining elements of his mentality and morality.

Getting to know the peasant was also a process of cultural self-definition. While those individuals who engaged in the effort to explore and describe village culture consciously and explicitly referred to it as a separate and strange culture, they also judged the world they discovered in terms which revealed they were searching for an acceptable image of Russia that issued from the seedbed of her past and future. In this they were echoing a widely held sentiment, expressed explicitly in Alexander Herzen's anticapitalist, anti-Western declaration of 1856, "We are not bourgeois, we are peasants . . . we are poor in towns and rich in villages."[24] In a less polemical tone, the liberal journalist Grigorii Eliseev reminded his reading public in 1868, "[i]t is obvious that Russia, both in the composition of its population, its residence and population, is a state that is predominantly rural, a state of peasants."[25]

White has argued that the fascination with "wild" or primitive peoples or elements within a culture occurs "in times of socio-cultural stress, when the need for positive self-definition asserts itself, but no compelling criterion of self-identification appears," and especially when educated elements of society are "uncertain as to the precise quality of their sensed humanity. . . ."[26] This was indeed the case in post-Emancipation Russia when legal, social, and economic definitions of one's place in the world were in question, or under assault if one were part of the privileged class of former serf owners. Unlike those who were fascinated with "wildness" in White's analysis, however, the educated Russians who set out to describe and analyze the Russian peasant after 1861 were not initially appealing "to the concept of wildness to designate an area of subhumanity that was characterized by everything they hoped they were not."[27] On the contrary, they were seeking alternative moral definitions of Russian culture through the peasantry, they were hoping to find a moral spring from which they could draw, they were seeking not distinction from the peasants, but some kind of identification with them.

A distinguishing feature of the exploration of the peasantry in the thirty years after the Emancipation was an emphasis on the moral and mental makeup of the peasant, which was labeled the "peasant soul." Although no simple or clear definition of this term ever appeared, its meaning took shape through the accumulation of individual definitions in various works of journalism, fiction, and art. The peasant soul encompassed first and foremost the peasant's morality. Second, it represented the peasant's psyche. Third, it referred to the peasant's system of beliefs, which were manifest in his actions within his family and community. Furthermore, the search for the peasant soul was understood to be a search for the Great Russian peasant soul, the soul of the Orthodox believer at the center of Imperial Russia. Educated society's use of this term as the frame for the question, Who is the Russian peasant?, was a product of two further contexts that shaped the textual construction of peasant images.

First was the prominence of the sense of moral responsibility and guilt toward, and perception of dreadful separation from, the vast majority of the population of Russia. Many of the authors who went to the countryside to decipher the peasant soul were seeking redemption through rapprochement with the peasantry. In the village they hoped to find some kind of moral or spiritual healing to close the national wound of serfdom and individual wounds of alienation within a profoundly divided culture.[28] Distressed over the state of their souls as members of privileged Russia, they were anxious to determine the state of the peasant's soul as an alternative moral anchor in transforming Russia. Tainted in one way or another by the sin of exploitation inherent in the pre-Emancipation social and economic order, participants in the debate over the peasant soul were particularly attuned to this feature of man and society which they hoped very much not to find in untainted, native rural Russia.

The issue of exploitation and the filter of moral judgment it imposed on the definition of the Russian peasant were all the more pressing because of two challenges from Western Europe confronting educated Russians as

they envisioned their nation's economic and social development in the
Reform Era: capitalism in the economy and the Darwinian model of struggle and competition in biology. The prospect of stepping onto a path of
economic development that moved toward the economies of Western Europe, and of Germany and Britain in particular, alarmed Russians who
feared the corrosive effects of the urge for profit at the expense of paternalism and collectivism. The gentry had already proved themselves capable of
this form of exploitation through generations of serfdom. Was it not possible to hope that peasant Russia was either immune or allergic to exploitation in economic relations? The search for the peasant soul was an effort to
answer that question in the affirmative.

The challenge of Darwin's theory of natural selection was twofold.
First, it carried the authority of scientific truth in a time when educated
Russian society was entering a phase of utter infatuation with science; faith
in the power of objectivity, empiricism, and realism, the approaches associated with scientific truth; and an urge to take these scientific principles and
use them in developing a science of society, with peasant culture the specific case study.[29] The second aspect of Darwin's challenge was its fundamental assumption of the inevitability of struggle and competition: struggle
with the material conditions of the environment and competition between
and within species for survival in that struggle.[30] This was a provocative
challenge to the self-image of collectivist Russia that was a legacy of
Slavophilism for intellectuals across the spectrum of attitudes and still central for such neo-Slavophiles as I. S. Aksakov, editor of the journal *Rus'*. It
generated a specific set of questions about the peasant that wound back to
the issues of morality and psychology: Was the peasant naturally collectivist
or communal in his attitudes? Did the peasant display tendencies toward
individualism? Did village culture function primarily through competition
or through systems of mutual aid? The fact that Darwin was so much a part
of the discourse in public opinion prompted the creators of peasant images
to address these questions, and equally prompted those who responded to
those images to judge them through a Darwinian filter.

The influence of biological methods was also evident in the taxonomic
approach that characterized the development of peasant images. Authors
and painters created peasant types who were presented as both empirical
and representative. Taxonomy intersected with morality when types assumed various positions in a hierarchy of acceptability for the self-
definition of Russia that the question, Who is the Russian peasant?, would
provide.

The obvious paradox was that public opinion was demanding a scientific approach and borrowing from the science of biology through the Darwinian metaphor to identify, define, and catalogue such a nebulous concept
as the peasant soul. Science was expected to provide the tools for under-

standing morality. Yet the figures who strove to meet this expectation were not scientists by any definition, nor were they experts or specialists. In a word, they were not professional students of the peasantry. Very few of them would have claimed the label ethnographer, sociologist, statistician, economist, or juridical scholar. Professions had not yet fully emerged in Imperial Russia, although they were developing rapidly in a process that ran parallel to the search for the peasant soul.[31] During the 1860s, the 1870s, and the first half of the 1880s, one did not have to bear the imprimatur of a profession to be an authority on the peasantry. One had simply publicly to avow loyalty to the principles of science and to have personal knowledge of the village based on residence in the countryside. This absence of rigor in defining the sources of information on the peasantry allowed the vagueness of the subject itself. By the end of the 1880s, specialists in ethnography, statistics, jurisprudence, and economics would be more stringent in their requirements, and their professionalization would in turn redefine the subjects of inquiry on the peasantry. No longer would the peasant soul be a legitimate subject of investigation. No longer would fictional accounts of the village serve as reliable information on the peasantry. No longer would amateurs have the authority that they did in the twenty-five to thirty years after the Emancipation. No longer would morality and psychology be considered the key that would unlock the mystery of the village.

By 1890, that mystery was considered "solved." The peasant types or images that had emerged from the previous generation's explorations served as the set of templates that established the patterns of investigation taken up in a more truly scientific or professionalized manner. The progression from the iconographic *narod* to the equally iconographic *kulak* in the debate and in the order of the chapters in this study reflects that trend. One might be tempted to use the word *evolution* to describe the shift from the original, expected meaning of the shared concept of the peasantry connoted by the word *narod,* which is explored in the first chapter, to the concept of the *kulak* which sat at the other end of the spectrum. *Narod* was a broad concept, with fluid boundaries, which referred not to individual peasants but to the peasantry as the simple folk, the mass, the group, the cultural mainspring of Russia. It was a word and a concept that was related to the essential qualities of the people, their spirituality, morality, and their cultural distinction from educated Russia. *Kulak* was a term that came to denote the peasant individualist par excellence, a single and singular figure, an independent actor and agent in the village. It was also a term that primarily referred to the function of the figure so named as the manipulator of cash and credit in the rural economy. Definitions of the peasant thus moved away from the nebulous and spiritual, the essential or inherent, to a more environmental explanation, as it were, which defined the peasant within the social and economic systems of the village. The *kulak* would continue to be a subject of study and a referent for more specialized, professionalized analysis of the countryside through statistics, economics, demography, and full-blown ethnography into and beyond the 1890s. The *narod* would not.

As tempting as it is to present this process as an evolution and to describe it as an unbroken narrative, such an approach would violate the contentiousness of the debate, and the jostling between competing images that continued at the end of the story. It is possible to say, however, that there was a shift, a progression away from the very nebulous images of the *narod* and the communal peasant as those most highly invested with morally desirable qualities toward images which affirmed the concepts of the struggle for existence and the adaptations to environment, with particular stress on the physical environment of climate and soil and the economic environment of a nascent money economy. The latter images would continue to inform study of the peasant as an economic actor well into the twentieth century and contribute to the emphasis on material culture in the village as the key to sociological and ethnographic methodology and understanding.

The process of exploring, describing, and defining the peasant and his world in the post-Emancipation era began with individual experience, the experience of an educated man or woman who observed village life and recorded his or her impressions and conclusions. The individual experience became a societywide phenomenon through the publication of their accounts—fictionalized, journalistic, or scholarly—in serious journals of the day and in separate volumes, often collections of previously serialized articles or literary works. The individual experience of entering the mysterious and unknown village thus became a national experience through the public repetition of the encounter and broad participation in assessing its significance. This process created a circular relationship encompassing public opinion, the individual, his or her experience in the village, the text he or she produced, the editorial decisions of those who made that experience available to the educated public, and, finally, the response of public opinion.

The individual investigator or observer carried the context of educated society's expectations into the village and approached peasant culture with the intellectual predispositions described. Once in the village, however, he or she encountered another context—the physical, social, and spiritual world of the given place and time. This the authors would have termed "reality," and they set as their task describing that reality as accurately, objectively, and empirically as possible. Given their taxonomic approach, they found the village a frustrating reality indeed. For there was no one village any more than there was one peasant soul. Various village communities displayed various characteristics depending upon their location, economic basis, proximity to the railroad, pre-Emancipation status, the terms of the Emancipation land agreements worked out with their local gentry, the level of labor out-migration to other agricultural areas or to factory towns and cities, the ethnic composition of the population, and any number of other factors. Not only did villages vary across space, but also across time, so that even one village defied the static assumption underlying the search for peasant types.

This changeability of the setting which framed the urban, educated investigators' encounters with the peasantry contributed to the contested nature of the images they created. Within individual texts, between texts created by the same author, and certainly between texts created by different authors, the debate over the peasant soul exemplified the "threshold where seeming opposites entered into an exchange and possibly coexisted, often in tensely charged relationships."[32] Most major authors such as Uspenskii, Zlatovratskii, and Engelgardt contributed at some point in their career to the development of more than one image, and even of images which seemed to contradict each other utterly. This was a reflection of the fact that these authors usually moved about to various villages, or lived in one community at various points in time or over a long expanse of time, or themselves came to develop different perspectives on the world they were witnessing and describing. The contest of images appearing before the public provided the drama and tension of the debate and led to the hardening of the edges around each image as it was juxtaposed with others. The drama was heightened, in turn, by editors of the serious journals of the day, who often published texts side by side in the same issue offering opposing views on the peasant. This was particularly true of *Notes of the Fatherland*, which established itself as the main arena for this contest.

Editors of different journals also played off articles or series of articles against each other. This rivalry was particularly keen between *Notes of the Fatherland* and *Rus'*, journals which represented the opposite poles of public opinion. *Notes of the Fatherland* was the premier progressive journal of the day, recognized as the organ of the Populist and highly critical intelligentsia, and subsequently almost constantly in hot water with the censors because of the radical tendencies they perceived there.[33] Beginning in the 1860s and through the 1870s, nearly every issue carried some article or piece of fictional writing about the nature of the peasant, with the writings of Gleb Uspenskii and Aleksandr Nikolaevich Engelgardt serving as the mainstay of the journal. Engelgardt's views so raised the hackles of government censors that the editor, M. E. Saltykov-Shchedrin, had to pull two of his articles in March 1880 under the censor's threat to stop publication of the issue.

Rus', on the other hand, was clearly a neo-Slavophile journal, edited by Ivan Sergeevich Aksakov and devoted to promoting both positive images of the simple Russian folk and a suitably paternalistic approach to them by educated society. In obvious response to and clearly with a "sideward glance" anticipating response at *Notes of the Fatherland,* beginning in January 1881 *Rus'* published the series "Letters about the Russian Peasantry" by Dmitrii Kishenskii, who challenged the conclusions of the "pseudorealists" at *Notes of the Fatherland.* Aksakov and his agricultural editor, Sergei Sharapov, were willing to engage in a bit of reversal themselves, however, and tried to convince Engelgardt, whose views were very closely associated with the progressivism of *Notes of the Fatherland,* to write something for *Rus'* as well.[34]

Each of the journals had a political or philosophical position that was established and recognized in public opinion. In the 1860s, *The Contemporary* was the home of radical writers of the newly emerging "third element," edited by the poet of Russia's "new people," N. G. Chernyshevsky, who also set the terms of scientific realism in literature. The *Russian Herald* promoted liberal views in the 1860s but shifted to become an organ of conservatism, following the philosophical journey of its editor, Mikhail Katkov. *Herald of Europe* was consistently the voice of liberalism in Russia and the organ where Western literature appeared in translation and Emile Zola served as a correspondent from Paris. When the government closed down *Notes of the Fatherland* once and for all in 1884, two journals continued its role, although less successfully and with considerable internal dissension: *Northern Herald* and *Russian Wealth.*[35] *Russian Thought* also published the work of some of the so-called Populist writers, notably Nikolai Nikolaevich Zlatovratskii, promoting a generally positive and romanticized view of the peasantry.

It was largely through these journals that public opinion in post-Emancipation Russia was formed, especially in the early years of the reform. Together they made up one of the most important forums of civil society, a region of mediation between state and society, an area where government censors might impose a heavy hand but where editors, writers, critics, statisticians, and journalists could still hold authority, provide information, and present views on issues of national concern. They reached a broad audience, reaching as many as 100,000 readers in the case of *Notes of the Fatherland.* Readers ranged from impoverished students to the Minister of the Interior and, one may surmise, the Tsar himself.[36] They included many bureaucrats who belied the notion of sharp division between state and society as members of both who served the state while engaging in the common intellectual pursuits of society.[37] Furthermore, many of the journals published synopses of state commission reports and analyses of those reports, adding to the crosscurrents in post-Reform Russia. Although the serious political-literary journals of the day were not the sole forum for the emergence of public opinion, they were arguably the one with the broadest participation if one includes readership in participation. And they were certainly the most important one for sorting out the definition of the peasant soul.

Given the fact that the main sources for this work are texts produced by and for educated Russians, I would like to say a few words about its nature as a study of elite attitudes or elite culture. I find LaCapra's caveat useful here. "High or elite culture is an equivocal term . . . ," he reminds us. "It is misleading simply to conflate hegemonic with elite culture because this conflation occludes the problematic degree to which there may be critical or contestatory tendencies in elite culture itself."[38] One problem with the term *elite* is that it invites that very conflation with hegemony, of privilege with power, of property with political influence, of a layer of society that somehow stands above the masses and, by implication, controls and exploits them. In terms of post-Emancipation Russia, it sets up a false division which ultimately assumes the presence of clear-cut classes, and of the desire and ability of those identified as elite to determine the fates of those who are not.

What would *elite* mean in post-Emancipation Russia if it were applied to the various voices examined here? Ultimately, it would have to mean "not peasant." It is certainly true that these are not peasant voices. Indeed, the thrust of the study is to identify what nonpeasants thought about peasants and how their conceptualization both drew on the existing culture and informed its future development. But to be "not a peasant" did not mean necessarily to have privilege or power in this setting. To identify a discourse as a discourse of elites invites the urge to unmask the participants in this debate in a search for their ulterior motives, which are already assumed somehow not to be laudable.

This label fails on several counts. First, the authors in this discourse were hardly a homogeneous group in their social and economic status. Some were very privileged indeed and could reasonably expect to have considerable influence within the culture. A. N. Engelgardt and L. N. Tolstoy immediately come to mind. Both were propertied. Both lived among the peasants, but in their gentry houses. Both lived primarily by writing and did not share the sweat and toil of the peasantry in the most intimate way for any extended time or under any compulsion other than their curiosity. Sergei Sharapov, editor at *Rus'* and a major landowner in Smolensk Province, was similarly privileged, similarly a notable. Some continued to move among the circles of Russia's most privileged and powerful, such as Ivan Nikolaevich Kramskoi, who was both the most important painter of the peasant psychological portrait and portraitist of the nobility and Russia's men of arts and science. Others, however, including Uspenskii, Zlatovratskii, and P. N. Zasodimskii, lived modestly at best, and in penury at worst and most typically. They could not, in fact, support themselves, but lived on a combination of their meager incomes from writing, gifts from the grant-in-aid society for needy writers, and loans from their wealthier friends and patrons. Certainly these figures were not of the *narod*, they were not of the masses, but neither were they privileged, secure, or even stable for most of their lives. They lived on the edge, sometimes slipped over, and one can argue that this financial tenuousness in their lives attuned them to the fragility and search for equilibrium that informed the peasant soul.

Second, their audience was not made up of the elite in the broad meaning of the term. Many of their readers were students at technical institutes or universities in the capitals and provinces. Others were lower-level bureaucrats, living in the sparseness and want that characterized the world of the petty clerk. Still others were living the life of impoverished rural schoolteachers, doctors, lawyers, and clerks. They were separated from privilege and power as much as wealthy urbanites were from the village. There is even evidence that some of these works made their way into the hands of the peasants through lending libraries set up by these schoolteachers, doctors, and clerks.[39] To lump all of these figures into one group—the elite— obscures this diversity, and obscuring this diversity, in turn, diminishes the intensity of the debate. For the interest that the debate over the peasant soul held for members across educated society marked the urgency of the era, the combination of sincerity and passion in the search for the peasant and for cultural definition. It was a common enterprise, an enterprise that could prompt a wealthy hostess with a home in Moscow large enough to seat two to three hundred guests to invite the modest writer Gleb Uspenskii to share his latest views on Russia and her people. It was a drama that drew in a wide audience sharing the conviction of K. D. Kavelin, who explained, "Everyone for whom the fates and interests of the Russian state and people are dear knows and understands very well that our entire existence depends on the economic, mental and moral condition of four-fifths of the population. The condition in which the peasantry finds itself will inevitably be that of the educated classes as well."[40]

This drama lasted roughly from the mid-1860s to the mid-1880s. When the action began, there was an enthusiastic audience, curious, optimistic, excited by the prospect of familiarity and possible intimacy with the peasant. One can also say that they entered the theater with a certain sympathy for the characters they expected to meet there. But as the drama wore on, as peasant figures began not only to dominate the stage but also to take on features that disturbed, disappointed, and ultimately frustrated their educated suitors, advocates, and critics, the audience turned away, the theater emptied, and by the late 1880s the directors of Russian intellectual life— the editors and critics of the major journals, newspapers, and publishing houses—called for an end to the show.

The curtain call for these peasant characters, however, remained in the public consciousness. As the curtain closed on the village, a very small number of peasant types lined up, each one familiar to the educated witness of their character development over the last twenty years. In the end, there were five male characters and three female characters. The men ranged from the ill-defined but likeable member of the *narod,* the simple man of the simple folk, to the highly defined, sharply featured, individualistic and exploitative *kulak,* the village strongman. The peasant woman was restricted to three roles: virago, shrew, or victim. The transition in the definition of male peasant types from vagueness to precision and from the collective to the individual was part of both increasing sophistication of approaches to the village and disillusionment upon discovery of indications of indigenous exploitation there. The triad of female peasant types exhibited little development and revealed the static patriarchalism of most of the outsiders who took it upon themselves to describe peasant women and their lives.

Historiography of the Question

Before turning to the first forays into the village after the emancipation of the serfs in 1861, I should say a bit about my own backward and sideward glances at the studies of this period which have preceded or appeared during my work on this book. The thirty years which constitute the focus of this study have been the subject of considerable study, with an early emphasis largely on either the radical movements or the politics of reform and counterreform.[41] More recently, developments in social and economic history have yielded works on the village itself and on institutions of cultural exchange between educated society and the peasant.[42] Biographies of individuals who figure prominently in this work have also been written in the Soviet Union and the West.[43] They focus on the "life and work" of these figures, however, seeking developments and trends in the individual's life without exploring the complexity of the concepts they produced. The three studies which deal most closely with questions of the cultural encounter I am describing and the images of the peasants they produced have been written by Richard Wortman, Daniel Field, and Andrew Donskov.[44]

Wortman's prosopography of the Populists concentrates heavily on the psychology of Engelgardt, Uspenskii, Zlatovratskii, and Vorontsov and thus becomes a study of their psychic similarities, rather than of the connections among their peasant images or the significance of their conclusions. He explores the emotional and psychological needs that drove these men to the village, explains the pathology of their disenchantment, but dismisses any historical interest in their thought or observations on village culture.[45]

Thus, he provides our best analysis of the mentality of these four Populists but does not explore the models of peasant behavior that they contributed to public discourse. Because three of the figures in his study—Uspenskii, Engelgardt, and Zlatovratskii—were prime agents in the discourse on the peasant soul, my work follows closely on his in those chapters where these three authors contributed to the construction of the given image. My goal has been to go beyond the contexts he explored, however—the relationship of the life of the writer to the text and of the author's intentions and the text—to explore the various other contexts that gave shape to the images of the peasant soul they helped to create. These writers were a major part of the story, but Wortman's focus on Populism did not explore the societywide discourse that I have tried to convey here.

Daniel Field's investigation of two events shaped by the peasants' myth of the Tsar does refer to the attitudes of the major actors toward peasants as reflected in their behavior and description of the incidents at the communities of Bezdna and Chigirin. As an exercise in the historiography of events, his work addresses the topic of this study directly only in his conclusion, "The Myth of the Peasant." There he briefly describes a commonly held patronizing attitude among literate Russian society, which enabled edcuated Russia to justify its paternalism, whether the paternalism of radical Populists or of Slavophiles and monarchists.[46] He detects various descriptions of the peasant as childlike, innocent, and bestial within that frame, but he does not explore the images in any depth. Donskov's study in literary history examines the shift from positive to negative peasant characters in Russian plays but does not discuss images in prose works, scholarly studies, or publicistic writing. His is primarily a textual analysis, but within that frame, he discerns a shift in mood that is consonant with the one examined here. His study and mine thus complement each other.

More recently, Esther Kingston-Mann's study of Lenin's views on the peasantry briefly discusses Slavophile and Populist images of the peasantry and the turning away from the village that Populists experienced in the 1870s. As a background to the focus of her work—the development of Lenin's views of the peasant—this discussion includes Populist and Marxist images but does not explore the larger discourse from which they emerged or examine the elements of the images in any detail.[47] Even so, her conclusions about Lenin point to the force that the final three images of the male peasant discussed here—the peasant as rational economic actor, the peasant as victim, and the peasant as exploiter—held for students of the peasantry in Russia at the end of the nineteenth century and the beginning of the twentieth.

This is even more true of Teodor Shanin's two-volume study of Russia as a developing country and his earlier, seminal work on the peasantry as "the awkward class."[48] In the latter he draws heavily on the teachings of the agricultural economist A. V. Chaianov, who identified the peasant household as the fundamental unit of the national economy and was one of the first to elaborate the full model of subsistance agriculture and the peasant as a rational economic actor. Here we find one of the victorious images of the contest over the peasant soul in the 1870s and 1880s incorporated as the keystone of agricultural economics in the first decades of the twentieth century. Chaianov's conclusion that the peasant was not a natural capitalist and that his household economy could serve as the basis for a national economy through the establishment of agricultural cooperatives carries strong echoes of the conclusions of A. N. Engelgardt, one of the chief architects of the images of the peasant in post-Emancipation Russia. Shanin's work thus both illustrates the tenacity of the images that grew out of the debate over the peasant soul in the Reform Era and challenges us to identify the original models that still resonate in our approaches to the peasant and his world.

Structure of This Text

This text opens with a chapter describing the stage set for the drama of the debate over the peasant soul. It focuses on the 1860s, when the terms and genres of the discourse were established. During these years, standards were defined for what types of knowledge or information would be considered legitimate and authoritative in the debate, and the genres that would present that information took shape. Each of the remaining chapters, with the exception of Chapter 3, is devoted to one of the images that appeared in the debate over the peasant soul. Chapter 2 analyzes the concept of the *narod* as the prevailing image of the peasant held by educated society at the beginning of the search. It includes a discussion of the experience of the "Going to the People" movement as an extreme, but important example of confrontation and redefinition. Chapter 3 explores two debates in public opinion about the role of the peasant in the judicial world of reformed Russia which were critical in fueling the discourse about the peasant soul. These debates ran simultaneously with the early disintegration of the concept of the *narod* and offered both alternative approaches to and definitions of the peasant. Chapters 4 through 8 trace the full development of the images that had emerged in the discussions about the peasant from the perspective of law and justice. The final chapter explores the triune image of the Russian peasant woman. I have not placed this chapter at the end of the study because I consider it least important. On the contrary, the construction of the image of the *baba* was climactic and revealed many of the developments that informed the images of the male peasant described in the preceding chapters. Equally important, concluding this study with the images of the peasant woman that had come to dominate public opinion toward the end of the nineteenth century highlights the distance between the sentimental images of A. N. Radishchev and N. M. Karamzin at the end of the eighteenth century and the harsh, even repulsive images of Tolstoy a century later. The images of the *baba* thus offer a potent distillation of the process explored here.

1

The 1860s:
Setting the Stage

By the time of the Emancipation in 1861, it was already a commonplace of Russian intellectual life that Russia was a divided culture: educated and uneducated, Westernized and native, urban and rural, landlord and peasant. Interest in the peasant and the use of the peasant as a symbol of Russian culture were by no means new. The emergence of national consciousness in Russia in the eighteenth century had rested on a similar focus on the village, as Hans Rogger so skillfully demonstrated thirty years ago.[1] The post-Emancipation portrayal of the peasant as symbol of untainted, unadulterated Russian culture was already evident in literature in the late eighteenth century and in the first half of the nineteenth century. The most famous reference points for the literary image of the peasant in the late eighteenth century were A. N. Radishchev's Aniuta in his *Journey from St. Petersburg to Moscow* and N. M. Karamzin's "Poor Liza." These two female figures were the sentimentalists' version of the Russian peasant, more *paysanne* than Russian *baba* in that they were as much, if not more, products of the influence of French sentimentalism as they were reflections of the Russian reality. As Donald Fanger has explained, they marked an important step in the process in humanizing the Russian peasant in literature by endowing her with noble virtues.[2] In these two examples, the ability to love, coupled with rural purity, made them worthy symbols of the sentimentalist ideal.

    I. S. Turgenev and D. V. Grigorovich continued the tradition of presenting the peasant as the embodiment of noble sentiment in the 1840s and 1850s. They were innovators in their creation of literary works which focused entirely on the Russian peasant, but their peasant heroes were the vehicle for presenting moral ideals rather than the psychological types they would become in their post-Emancipation treatment. Grigorovich especially strove to establish the peasants' setting by including ethnographic detail in sociological "physiological" sketches which both anticipated and served as a model for the writers of the 1860s forward. He similarly incorporated peasant speech in his effort to present the peasant's point of view.[3] Critics in the 1870s and 1880s would contrast the more "realistic" and thus more "illuminating" literary treatments of the peasant in their time with these earlier efforts and conclude that Turgenev and Grigorovich came up short. Turgenev was faulted for failing to penetrate the "peasant's soul."[4] He was accused of being too concerned in *A Huntsman's Sketches* with the political ideal of Emancipation and thus unable to explore fully the personality or even the material reality of the peasant. Here, as in M. A. Markovich's *In the Backwoods,* the peasants became noblemen and ladies in rustic dress.[5] Even so, Turgenev set an important precedent for the post-Emancipation search for the peasant by setting up a fundamental contest of images in *A Huntsman's Sketches* through his juxtaposition of differing peasant "types," from the first sketch on two very dissimilar peasants— Khor and Kalinych—through the entire volume, where distinct images of noble peasant souls appeared, while Grigorovich prepared the way for the literary-journalistic sketches of the 1860s. This focus on the peasant within his community, as in the works of Nikolai Gogol and other writers of the Natural School, although not immediately recognized as legitimate art, began the process of bringing the peasant to the reading public before the Emancipation.[6]

The Literary Sketch

The pendulum swung in the opposite direction in the years immediately following the Emancipation. In an effort to spare no detail in their realistic description of peasant life, a group of authors of modest nongentry social origin, known as the *raznochintsy* writers, focused predominantly on male peasants. They stripped the romanticized peasant of all his features as ideal and presented him instead as brute. In the writings of such authors as N. V. Uspenskii and F. M. Reshetnikov, peasants began to emerge as objects of scientific study in an extreme and clumsy expression of what the authors understood to be the goals of realism in literature according to the standards of N. G. Chernyshevsky and N. A. Dobroliubov. This search for unembroidered realism encouraged the dominance of the genre which would dominate writing on the peasant for twenty-five years, the sketch. True to the philosophy of literature espoused by Chernyshevsky, editor of the journal *The Contemporary* where most of the *raznochintsy* works appeared, these authors aspired to convey reality by piling one detail on top of another in a concentrated short piece of writing which seemed appropriately photographic. Loyal to the concept of empiricism, they hoped to present a portrait of peasant culture by describing the bits and pieces of daily life in the village.

N. V. Uspenskii's "Sketches of the Folk's Daily Life" (January and April 1861) included such scenes as two peasant deacons' wives chatting about the rye and the cattle, a quarrel between two women, peasant wives gathered to weave in the evening as they wait for their husbands' return, and conversations among peasants as they stand outside the offices of the local administration.[7] The writing is prosaic and utterly soporific. If the inclusion of detail in Pushkin's *Onegin* was an element of his mastery, where, as Edward J. Brown concludes, "little feet" in a digression become "synecdochically, the whole poem,"[8] the fat legs of peasant women standing by the river in Uspenskii's "Sketches" are lost in a deadly profusion of the minutiae of peasant life. Sketches by these authors in the early 1860s were also relentlessly dreary. The following passage in Uspenskii's sketch of a St. Petersburg traveler's stay in the village was typical of the genre's tone.

> I was recently in a peasant izba: they talked about work, they wove, they argued; chicks wandered about on the floor. The entire family reproached each other about who ate how much bread; one sick woman was moaning on the benches; the young man in the family told his old mother that there was no money for the soul tax, that the granary was falling down; the old woman said that they were out of grain. And this is probably what happens every day![9]

I. Selivanov's more dramatic "Two Murders" presented an equally bleak picture of village culture in a tale populated by characters who were either thoroughly evil individuals or thoroughly dehumanized victims. Here, the patriarch has a hawklike face, the kind of face that makes one want to turn away, and the matriarch is so beaten down that "it is hard to decide whether this is a human being or a workhorse."[10] Both tormenter and tormented are more animal than human. Peasants also appeared as dull-witted, ignorant, and superstitious.[11] The most powerful and influential example of this approach to the village was F. M. Reshetnikov's "Podlipovtsy: An Ethnographic Sketch," which began to appear in *The Contemporary* in March 1864 and would later be published as a separate volume.[12] I will discuss this work in Chapter 6; at this point, it is important to note that all of Reshetnikov's characters were beastlike, and recognized as such by the critics. As one student of this trend has concluded, "The common and distinctive attribute of these writers was their unwillingness to romanticize or idealize the peasant in any way. In fact, they often deliberately chose to perceive and portray only the most dismal features of peasant life and character."[13]

The shift in literary treatments of the peasant from feminine repository of moral or social ideal to hyperrealistic male brute was characteristic of the first moment of confrontation with the freed peasant, who had suddenly been transformed from the object of sympathy and advocacy as a younger brother en route to Emancipation into an unfamiliar fellow citizen. Suddenly thrust into the shared space of citizenship, he was not only alien, but also threatening, especially to the *raznochintsy*, whose own lack of noble pedigree made them particularly insecure about their humanity in the new Russia. At this moment in post-Emancipation Russia, we see the closest approximation of the process White described in terms of the "fetish" of wildness and of the fear that is common in such moments of cultural confrontation.[14]

It would necessarily also be a moment of disillusionment and loss of the former romantic myths about the village and the peasants, as the liberal critic and author M. E. Saltykov-Shchedrin realized as early as 1863. He explicitly identified images of the village with images of Eden and warned his readers against this illusion in any romanticized picture of rural life.

> In the very word, "the countryside," there is the sense of something innocent; you are somehow carried away by the thought of those pleasant . . . places where our forefathers wandered until they tasted the knowlegde of good and evil from the tree. . . . But let the viewer not be too carried away by this charming picture, let him once and for all convince himself that his eyes lie, that the artist who painted the picture is also doing something false, and that in rural life there are neither splendid landscapes, nor entrancing tableaux de genre, but hard and ugly labor.[15]

New contacts would bring new "realities" and the old myths would have to yield to greater accuracy in describing the rural world.

A contributor to the Slavophile journal *Day* was one of the first to recognize the emerging tendency to speak of the peasantry in terms of universal moral absolutes in November 1861. "Is the Russian peasant good or evil? Here is one of those very strange questions which, despite their total strangeness, not only have a constant place in conversations, but are also maintained everywhere in society and even in literature, and are decided by each in his own fashion and lead to serious polemics." Was it not absurd, the author continued, to ask whether an entire population was good or evil? But this was the manner of the question, demanding proof, "at whatever cost, only it had to be one of two: either absolute goodness or absolute evil. . . ."[16] He called, in an early summons, for a more measured examination of the nature of the Russian folk. "We will look at the question more simply, and we will begin to explore it with that impartiality which is always possible in any question, as long as there is no room for personal sympathy and antipathy."[17] Here we see the early stages of the blending of questions of morality and an insistence on objectivity, impartiality, the signposts of scientific truth.

Detail alone did not veracity make, and by the end of the 1860s, the hyperrealism and one-sided depiction of rural life in the sketches of the *raznochintsy* writers came under attack as being both uninformative and untrue. As one observer of the village concluded:

> Recently, when literature and its practitioners turned to the depiction of reality alone, with all of its ugliness and banality, there appeared tens of writer-photographers, whose entire task consisted in noting the most shocking and banal aspects of the life of the gentry, peasants, and clergy and in adorning the pages of some journal with all of this filth. . . . But I have come to doubt that there is a whole world inhabited only by fools and idiots. . . .[18]

In a more measured tone, a major critic at *Notes of the Fatherland* explained that the first step in the study of any new phenomenon must be observation and the description of concrete details and facts, and that this was the stage that the *raznochintsy* had reached in their study of the peasants' life. But it was time to move to a higher plane, a more sophisticated stage in literature on the peasant.[19] The conviction was gathering that familiarity with the village would have to go beyond the convention of the sketch-exposé and that the peasant and his world would have to be studied more intensively, following the principles of science.

The Eyewitness Account

The first antidote to the extremism of the images of the peasants in *raznochintsy* sketches was the eyewitness account as a means of introduction to the village. In the early years of the enactment of the Emancipation, there were numerous reports from the countryside in which landowners and local officials described their interaction with the newly freed peasantry. Some articles focused almost exclusively on economic aspects of the Emancipation, but many explored the peasant mentality as they described negotiating Emancipation settlements with peasants in their area. Two themes were predominant in these accounts: peasant mistrust of the terms of the Emancipation and the agents who tried to introduce them, and the cultural divide and miscomprehension between the peasants and educated Russians.[20] In his report from Samara Province, Dmitrii Samarin described the mystification that shrouded discussions with peasants about the economic ramifications of the Emancipation.

> Any time you discuss the shift from corvée to quit-rent with the peasants, it becomes clear to you that it is not economic considerations that push the peasants away from the advantage you are offering; you will sense that some kind of idea that even they are not capable of communicating stands before them, an idea which draws them unwillingly toward this economic incongruity, which, just like a cherished secret, is rarely expressed by them, but directs them in all of their actions.[21]

It was becoming apparent to those who went to the village that quick and easy characterizations of the peasant would not hold on face to face contact. The peasant could be a baffling and frustrating enigma.

> It is not nearly as easy as it seems to understand what the peasant wants, what he is thinking; what he says at first is not really what he means, he almost always speaks in such a way that it is possible to understand him to mean just the opposite, or, probably, to accuse him, to refuse his request,—which almost always seems illegal in its external exposition and completely respectable in its inner meaning; but for the unaccustomed, it is even difficult to grasp this meaning.[22]

Although eyewitness accounts such as these did not dehumanize the peasant as in the image making of the contemporary literary sketches, they did underscore the peasant's separation from the culture of the manor house and the state in the form of the local administrator. The combined effect of the sketches of the *raznochintsy* writers and the eyewitness accounts of gentry and local officials was to reinforce the sense of cultural division and to make the peasant seem further removed, more strange, more thoroughly "other" than he had been on the eve of the Emancipation.

The Ethnographic Sketch

Ethnographic sketches were the third source of information on the peasant in the 1860s. They presented the peasant as both peculiar and typical of Russian culture. During the 1860s, ethnography entered a period of active development as a field of scholarly study and an arena for amateur enthusiasm.[23] The Imperial Russian Geographic Society had an Ethnographic Division which included surveys about peasant culture as part of its mandate. It sponsored such monumental efforts as A. N. Afanas'ev's collection of Russian folktales.[24] The government had dipped into ethnography through an ethnographic expedition of writer-ethnographers under the jurisdiction of the Ministry of the Navy in the late 1850s. As Catherine Clay has explained in her work on the expedition, the effort was part of a search for an appropriate Imperial identity in an empire of vast cultural differences.[25] Abbott Gleason has described the adventures of Pavel Ivanovich Iakushkin as a young amateur ethnographer who dressed in peasant costume and wandered among the peasants in the 1860s.[26] Iakushkin was one of a number of students who went to the village to learn about peasants as a prerequisite for radicalizing them. Ethnographic forays were not limited to young students of this ilk. Ethnographic sketches and reviews of ethnographic collections were welcomed by serious journals across the political spectrum. Three major publications were reviewed in *Notes of the Fatherland* in July 1861.[27] Ethnographic sketches and fiction heavy in ethnographic detail appeared in the liberal *Russian Herald*[28] and the Slavophile *Day*.[29] *The Contemporary* published the reports of Iakushkin and others.[30] When some of the sketches published in *The Contemporary* came under attack as sensationalist because they described nudity and promiscuity, A. N. Pypin (who would become one of the most important figures in the history of sponsoring and institutionalizing ethnography as a discipline in Russia) offered a definition of ethnography which was consonant with the emerging insistence on clear-eyed objectivity in approaching the peasant and his world. To be an effective ethnographer, he explained, one had to accept the fact that "in the life of the folk (*narod*), as in the life of educated society (*obshchestvo*), there are dark sides which may be explained in one way or another, but with which one may not, probably, feel any sympathy,—one cannot hide these dark aspects of ethnography in any way, if one wants only to remain conscientious."[31] Pypin went on to say that ethnography was in its infancy in Russia and that studies tended to consist of all facts, and little or no analysis. In this, ethnographic sketches resembled the *raznochintsy* sketches and the eyewitness accounts of the period. Each of these three genres would continue to contribute to image making of the peasants in the 1870s; their form in the 1860s provided the outline for what would become fuller, more intentional, and more analytical efforts in the following decade.

The Standard of Scientific Truth

The maturation of these genres was nourished by the dominance of science as a model of intellectual endeavor. The characteristic approach of the authors discussed in this study was a commitment to what they understood to be scientific principles: rationalism, empiricism, and objective realism. Their sideward glance was directed at romanticism as an inadequate mental attitude that failed to penetrate "reality" and thus did not offer useful guidance on the pressing concerns of transforming Russia. Scientific metaphors ran throughout their fictional accounts of the village, their eyewitness accounts, their criticism of each other, and their entire effort to dissect and define peasant culture. The structure of their accounts of village life, whether fictionalized in the literary-journalistic sketch or reported as unmediated observation, bespoke their effort to appear scientific. Each typically opened with a description of the physical setting of the report or sketch, thus establishing the major features of the geographic, climatic, and economic environment. They were striving for what was essentially a positivistic definition of peasant society.

In his study of the birth of sociology in Russia, Alexander Vucinich addressed the impact of the positivist or scientific attitude on the men of this generation. As he explained, they shared an anticipation of social progress, as well as "the exaltation of science" as "the most distinctive feature" of this period.[32] Chernyshevsky, Dobroliubov, and D. I. Pisarev became the Russian interpreters of Comte, Moleschott, Buchner, and Vogt and set the standard for the young men and women who matured during the 1860s. P. L. Lavrov and N. K. Mikhailovskii built their systems of sociology on similar principles. Lavrov hailed the use of Comtean positivism and the scientific method to study society objectively.[33] Mikhailovskii may have added the subjective element to the study of society, but he insisted equally on a rational, objective approach.[34] Both these men recognized that even as late as the 1880s, sociology was an "infant science" still in search of "sound scientific foundations."[35] Still, it was a powerful model for all those seeking the peasant soul.

The authors discussed here were not sociologists by profession but were caught up in the mood of positivist philosophy, evolutionary biology, and a general enthusiasm for science among educated Russians.[36] A. N. Pypin captured this mood in 1870 in his characterization of research at that time: "What was early on the personal work of people attracted to peasants is now a scientific endeavor with more sophisticated results."[37] One major figure in this endeavor, Aleksandr Nikolaevich Engelgardt, was himself a prominent chemist. Before he was forced into internal exile to his country estate and began to write articles on village life, he had established his reputation as a public figure who disseminated scientific knowledge in public lectures and popularized articles on recent scientific discoveries and through his position as rector of the St. Petersburg Agricultural Institute. When he took up his pen to enter the discourse on the peasant soul in 1871, he brought his scientific training to the texts, insisted on the objectivity and empiricism of his reports, set a standard for others who followed his lead, and consequently held virtually unquestioned authority in the discourse.

The qualities these figures most stringently demanded of themselves and each other were sincerity and truth. Virtually all reporters or analysts of peasant culture in the post-Emancipation period opened with an oath of allegiance to these principles, assuring readers that they reported or depicted only what they knew to be true. They conflated objectivity with sincerity and empiricism with truth. They also stressed the limited nature of their observations, pointing out that they described the specific case example on the basis of what they had seen and heard themselves; they confessed that their material was anecdotal; and they often explicitly disavowed any intention of generalization.[38] Any writer, such as Markovich, who failed to follow these prescriptions and strayed from the inductive method was susceptible to attack for lack of knowledge of the village and false representation of the peasant and his world.[39] The requirements for authority on the peasant verged on the canonical, and the perceived proximity of an author's approach to science was the criterion which determined its inclusion in or exclusion from the discourse.

This all added up to an urge to depict reality as directly as possible. The increasing availability of data from commissions sponsored by the state, professional societies, and the local organs of self-government (*zemstva*) strengthened the sentiment that this was a time of realistic objective study of the countryside, which subsequently contributed to confidence that discoveries and conclusions were trustworthy and true.

If each report were indeed a conclusive representation of reality, however, there would have been no contest, no discourse, no debate over the nature of the peasant soul. That a debate did emerge reflects a truism about "realism" as a genre which White has described in this way: "On analysis, every mimesis can be shown to be distorted and can serve, therefore, as an occasion for yet another description of the same phenomenon, one claiming to be more realistic, more 'faithful to the facts.' "[40] A persistent declaration of greater realism and knowledge of the peasant drove the discourse on the peasant soul.

Publicism

The combination of the influence of science with the sense that these were extraordinary times encouraged the dominance of publicistic writing as the mainstay of publishing houses and the serious literary-political journals in St. Petersburg and Moscow. Publicism as a mode of discourse had characterized public opinion in Russia from its beginnings in the eighteenth century. It employed writing as a means of entering the public arena, carving out space for influence, perhaps authority, within autocratic Russia.[41] Thus, it focused on issues of public or national concern and tended to favor the essay or regular column as a form. In the post-Emancipation era letters from the country on the peasantry, reminiscences of experiences in the countryside, essays on transformations perceived in the village, analyses of government reports or publications of statistical bureaus, and book reviews all fell under the heading of publicism for they all afforded an opportunity to express an opinion and to offer a prediction about Russia's future. Publicism also swallowed up fiction through the sketch, or literary-journalistic sketch, as it was often called. Public concerns largely displaced private concerns in the face of the evident enormity of social and economic transformation. Furthermore, the atmosphere of rapid changes called for fresh impressions, current information, and quick responses to developments and events. The emergence of newspapers and popular journalism, as well, placed editors at the weightier journals of the day under pressure to publish similar reporting from the countryside.[42] This was manifest in the popularity of the sketch as the preferred genre of most young writers. The sketch was also appropriate for many because of their poverty and the need to produce quickly and consistently.[43] Such figures as G. I. Uspenskii, N. N. Zlatovratskii, and P. N. Zasodimskii were under constant financial pressure and, thus, largely limited to this genre in their literary efforts. They also buttressed their authenticity in the spirit of scientific realism by writing strictly journalistic articles on peasant life; Uspenskii's *From a Village Diary* and Zlatovratskii's *Rural Daily Life and the Mood in the Countryside* were the finest examples of this trend. This is not to say that publicism was the only type of writing appearing before the Russian reading public. Serious journals continued to publish the novels of Tolstoy, Saltykov-Shchedrin, Turgenev, and numerous Western authors in translation. But publicistic writing was in its heydey, and the peasant was its primary subject.

A Multileveled Discourse

I am tempted to say that there were two levels of discourse in Russian society, the first dominated by the sketch, the eyewitness account, the statistical report and the ethnographer's study; the second dominated by the psychological novel, the poem, and the play. Such a tidy division would obscure the reality that each of these genres was a part of the societywide search for cultural and moral anchors. Thus, whereas the search for the "peasant soul" was largely confined to publicistic writing, Tolstoy's Pierre Bezukhov and Levin find moral redemption and self-knowledge through the agency of peasant characters in *War and Peace* and *Anna Karenina*. The peasant characters in his play *The Power of Darkness* are drawn at the end of the debate on the peasant soul from the template cast by Uspenskii, Zlatovratskii, and other contributors to literary journalism. Engelgardt's letters "From the Country" respond to characterizations of the peasant in

Tolstoy, F. M. Dostoevsky, and N. A. Nekrasov; Kavelin's exposition of "The Peasant Question" takes up concepts and images from journalism and belles-lettres alike; scholars of customary law treat the peasant figures in Zlatovratskii's "Peasant Jurors" as real types, and literary critics appraise the success of the work according to its consistency with the reports of members in the judicial system; writers take reported events and court cases as the sources for their plots; the image of the peasant woman emerges from debate about the phenomenon of the breakup of patriarchal households; and the all-important figure of the peasant strongman, the *kulak,* enters the public consciousness primarily through fictionalized accounts only to become an accepted, "known" sociological and economic type. Participants in this discussion crossed boundaries of political persuasion, class, discipline, and genre to talk to each other in common recognition that "[u]ntil definite, clear concepts of the peasantry and the peasant question are worked out in Russia, until then we will, as we have until now, reel from corner to corner, exposing the masses to a most arduous and undeserved ordeal, and exposing our entire existence to the most serious danger."[44]

This study explores the texts that aimed to establish those "clear concepts of the peasantry," texts that fell under the rubric of publicism: literary-journalistic sketches, eyewitness accounts, studies of customary law and the peasant household division, literary criticism, editorial remarks, and the visual images of the Russian peasant that constituted the focus of the Itinerant school of painting. I have also drawn on some of the major prose fiction works of the period and Tolstoy's *Power of Darkness.* These were the works which contributed to the formulation of the image of the peasant as a cultural and moral entity, which set as their task the discovery and description of the "peasant soul," which offered evidence on the morality of the rural community. These were the works which brought the drama of individual confrontation into the public arena and constructed the small group of peasant figures who stood staring educated Russia in the face when the curtain fell.

2

Narod: Passive, Benighted, and Simple

We all, lovers of the *narod*, regard them as a theory, and it seems that none of us really likes them as they actually are, but only as each of us has imagined them. Moreover, should the Russian *narod*, at some future time, turn out to be not what we imagined, we all, despite our love of them, would immediately renounce them without regret.

F. M. DOSTOEVSKY, *Diary of a Writer*

When Dostoevsky published this observation and prediction in 1876, he captured the contradictions that had become apparent in the relationship between educated society and Russia's simple folk, the *narod*. He began with the assumption of a distinction between those who loved the folk and the folk themselves; he identified the contradiction between the imagined and the real folk; and he coupled two apparently irreconcilable reactions, love and renunciation. By juxtaposing the imagined and the real, he pointed to the fact that the concept of the peasantry wrapped up in the image of the *narod* was just that, a concept, a social construction as we would say today, which did not necessarily bear any resemblance to the reality of the village or the people who lived there. He was engaging in his wonted dialogism, questioning both an established image and an assumption of general, sincere beneficence as a given among those who were searching for the soul of the peasant. This chapter describes the early, established image of the *narod* and the questioning of that image as educated society moved away from the concept to approach the real. Thus it explores the archetype and the leads toward new images that grew out of the contested nature of the archetype by the mid-1870s.

The Archetypal Image of the *Narod*

When educated Russians turned their attention to the village, they shared an understanding of the rural population which found its expression in the concept of the *narod*. Like the German term *Volk* and the French *le peuple*, *narod* carried with it an immediate connotation both of "the other" and of the people as nation. This duality was evident in the most neutral of definitions of the term in two major nineteenth-century dictionaries. The 1814 edition of the dictionary of the Imperial Academy of Sciences distinguished the *narod* as the peasantry from the *narod* as the nation through the definition "*Prostoi narod. Chern'. Prostoliudiny.* [Simple folk. Common people. Common folk.]"[1] Vladimir Dal' 's definition in 1881 referred to the *narod* as nation, national group, those who lived in the same territory and spoke the same language, and offered as the fourth meaning the *narod* as other: "*Chern', prostoliud'e, nisshie, podatnye sosloviia* [Common people, simple people, the lower, taxable classes]."[2]

This conflation of meanings is an apt expression of the fact that whenever educated Russia set out to investigate the *narod*, they were also invariably engaged in a process of national self-definition. Hans Rogger's study of the development of national consciousness in the eighteenth century indicated that both larger meanings of the word merged in the minds of educated Russians who "discovered the folk" en route to acquiring a national consciousness in a process similar to that in Germany in much the same period.[3] This discovery of the folk arose in the urban-rural dichotomy in which rural society represented native Russia, while urban Russia (St. Petersburg and Moscow, primarily) represented a spoiled or tainted, Westernized, and thus alien culture. Fascination with and admiration of the people were evident in the popularity of folk motifs in literature, as well as the collection and recording of folktales, songs, sayings, and myths. In its eighteenth-century form, the folk, or *narod* became a positive entity, carrier of national integrity and exceptionalism, the result of what Rogger described as the intellectual process of the "conversion of the contemptible serf into the symbol of national pride. . . ."[4]

The emergence of the self-conscious division of Russia between educated society or *obshchestvo* and *narod* in the nineteenth century was essentially an extension of the urban-rural dichotomy of the eighteenth century. Abbott Gleason included the notion of national participation in his description of *obshchestvo:* "[T]he term was often employed to indicate those active in the life of the nation: men of affairs, artists, thinkers, and even rebels. . . ."[5] By contrast, the *narod* represented the passive layer of Russian culture. Those who were to become active participants in the high culture of the nation were likely, indeed almost inevitably, to take on or absorb elements of the Petrine world of Westernized education and bureaucracy.

The *narod* as a symbol of national pride by virtue of its cultural integrity persisted in the philosophies of Slavophiles and Westerners alike. Although A. I. Herzen and V. G. Belinsky may have disagreed vehemently with K. S. Aksakov, A. S. Khomiakov, and I. V. Kireevskii about the nature of the Russian peasant, they agreed that the *narod* were distinct from other Russians, that the peasants were somehow separate culturally from *obshchestvo*. We need examine only two statements from prominent intellectuals in the Slavophile-Westerner debate to see that a fundamental aspect of the concept of the *narod* was separateness from Westernized Russia. When Konstantin Aksakov wrote that the Russian people were apolitical, he explained that they, "long removed from any contact with history in the making, take part in it only by paying taxes and furnishing recruits for the army. They alone have largely preserved the essence of the Russian tradition in all its purity."[6]

In his famous letter to Jules Michelet of 1851, Alexander Herzen drew a sharp line between *le peuple russe* and their government as he responded to Michelet's diatribe against Russia's oppression of Poland. In this essay he described two Russias: "the official Russia, the Russia of the Tsar," and "the unknown Russia, the Russia of the people."[7] The people, whom he identified as communal peasants, had remained distinct because "they have remained outside all political movements, and for that matter, outside European civilization . . ."[8] and retained their integrity because "[t]he peasant never defiles himself by any contact with the world of cynical officialdom. . . ."[9] The people's opposition to the impure culture of society in the form of officialdom, in Herzen's view, had been "one long, mute, passive opposition to the order of things."[10]

In the now familiar scheme of a divided Russia of two cultures the *narod* consistently represented the passive population that was untouched by urban, Western civilization. Returning to the definitions offered previously, the components of *chern'* and *prostoi* conveyed these meanings. Whereas the meaning of *prostoi* as simple is straightforward, *chern'* is a rich word that summons images of darkness because it is the root for the adjective *chernyi:* black or dark. *Prostoi* also carried the connotation for members of educated and peasant society of stupid. These elements would persist in the post-Emancipation image when the peasants were referred to alternatively as the *prostoi narod* or as the *chernyi narod*. As the simple people or as the untainted folk, the *narod* also held a special position of moral strength which largely derived from their distance from the corruption of the Westernized city and from their very simplicity and lack of consciousness. These features were common to the image of the *narod* held by individuals as diverse as the Slavophile I. S. Aksakov, the liberal jurist D. A. Rovinskii, the radical Populist Ekaterina Breshko-Breshkovskaia, and the two great moralists of the post-Emancipation era, Tolstoy and Dostoevsky.

In the lead editorial in his Slavophile publication *Day* for March 10,

1862, Ivan Aksakov addressed the question, What is the *narod?* He offered an answer that not only was obviously true to the teachings of the Slavophiles, but also delineated the chief features of the *narod* that would be common to the image as it appeared in the writings of most educated Russians on the brink of acquaintance with the Russian peasant. His first definition identified the *narod* as inhabitants of a nation, all inhabitants of a country in the general sense. He then continued:

> But in the narrow and stricter sense, it is the simple *narod* who are called the *narod,* that popular multitude who live a spontaneous life and who, like a seed, hold in concentrated form all of the organic force, all of the development of the organism. . . . But this type, this specificity is manifest in the *narod* on the level and with the character of a spontaneous force—of course, not in the physical, but in the spiritual sense, a spiritual force that has not yet, however, become conscious.[11]

Aksakov thus selects the *narod* as the source of national character and of exceptionalism but stresses that the folk occupy this position unconsciously. It was this combination of cultural force and unconsciousness that endowed the *narod* with such great potential in the minds of virtually all those engaged in the first stage of discourse on the "peasant question." Aksakov went on to state explicitly what would prove to be a critical requirement in positive images of the peasant: "The *narod* is made up of separate entities, each of whom has his own rational life, activity and freedom; each of them, taken separately, is not the *narod,* but together they make up that integral phenomenon, that new character who is called the *narod* and in whom all separate individuals vanish."[12] Oneness, integrity, undiluted unity, submission of the individual to the whole as desirable attributes in the *narod* were the desiderata not only for Slavophiles of Aksakov's type. As the following discussion will demonstrate, not only this most nebulous of the constructs of the peasant image but indeed every peasant image would be evaluated in moral terms according to the degree of individualism exhibited in the type. Those deemed most individualistic were also deemed most destructive and immoral by almost all writers except contributors to the classically liberal journals, *Russian Herald* in the 1860s and *Herald of Europe* throughout the period.

The attribution of cultural homogeneity was important for the *narod* as nation, just as unity was important for the *narod* as the simple folk. This was particularly clear in articles in *Day* that addressed the Polish question in 1863, where the *narod* were identified as "our civic strength" and moral force in Western Russia.[13] Similarly, one N. Pirogov asserted in his observations as an arbiter of the peace that the peasants from various regions of Russia displayed remarkable resemblance in their attitudes and expres-

sions: "It seems to me that this unity is worthy of attention to the highest
degree, and that it shows how strong the spiritual and moral bond is that
unites all the members of the broad Russian family, despite some local
differences and nuances."[14]

Among the features of that moral and spiritual unity incorporated into
the image of the *narod* were patience in suffering and sympathy for the
suffering of others. Although this attribution was most evident in the writings of Dostoevsky (see Chapter 2, pp. 47–50), F. P. Elenev placed it at the
heart of his description of the *narod* in his eyewitness account in 1868.
Traveling through a famine-stricken region, he reported the passive endurance, the strength which had saved the *narod* in all its misfortunes, which
"compensated for the inadequacies of many other qualities which nature
and history have denied them."[15] He continued, "[T]his strength is the
inexhaustible endurance of our *narod*, their ability to endure every possible
deprivation and misfortune without falling into despair and without giving
up the struggle with the circumstances that oppress them to their last
breath."[16] Even more amazing than the *narod*'s endurance was their capacity for sympathy even in their own want. "The other equally famous trait
which distinguishes the Russian *narod* . . . is their compassion," which
they exhibited by giving whatever they could to anyone in need.[17] Both
their endurance and their compassion stemmed from their sense of community and oneness with the great mass of their brethren.

Tolstoy's Platon Karataev as an Illustration of the Concept

All of these features of the *narod*'s morphology found their way into the
character of Tolstoy's Platon Karataev in *War and Peace*, the fullest and
ultimately most famous literary image of the *narod* of the 1860s. Despite
the fact that the novel did not describe contemporary Russia but the Russia
of the era of the Napoleonic invasion, its main peasant character entered
public discourse and served writers in the 1870s and 1880s as a reference
point in the definition of the peasant soul.[18] Here, as in his other works of
the period under study, the focus of Tolstoy's work was not rural Russia,
but the search for spiritual peace and salvation. The portrayal of the peasant soul in the person of Platon Karataev was one element in the larger
themes of self-knowledge and redemption. One can argue that these
themes in Tolstoy's fiction were an expression in belles-lettres of the same
concerns of publicistic writing on the peasant as the cultural and moral
anchor for Russia. In that sense, his works were very much a part of the
societywide discourse that had the peasant at its center.

The figure of Platon Karataev in *War and Peace* appeared as a critical element in the development of Pierre Bezukhov's search for a sense of purpose in his life. The encounter between these two men in the setting of the guardhouse provided the stage for a juxtaposition of an authentic son of the Russian people with a bastard, Westernized son of the French-speaking aristocracy. *Narod* and *obshchestvo* thus met face to face as captives of the French forces in Moscow. Pierre's history up to his capture had been dominated by many false starts and disappointments in his effort to break out of the cycle of superficial social activity. The event immediately preceding his encounter with Platon Karataev was the execution of fellow prisoners. The horror of these deaths precipitated Pierre's total loss of faith—faith in an ordered world, in his soul, in God. In sum, "[h]e felt that it was not in his power to return to belief in life."[19]

Platon Karataev would bring him back to that belief. Physical sensations and basic needs first restored to Pierre a consciousness of life as he sat in the prisoners' barracks. The first was the smell of Karataev's sweat, the second the potatoes Karataev had saved from dinner and offered him. The peasant's direct speech and simple faith and understanding of his world acted on Pierre's disturbed sensibilities as a gentle agent of renewal. At the end of their first evening together, Karataev fell fast asleep, while "Pierre did not sleep for a long time and lay on his spot in the darkness with open eyes, listening to the even snoring of Platon, having lain down beside him, and felt that the world that had been destroyed before was now stirring in his soul with a new beauty on some kind of new and firm foundations."[20]

The foundations of life exemplified by Platon Karataev were the attributes of the *narod:* simplicity, truth, essential community with a larger group rather than individual expression, natural occupation, and a spontaneous, rather than a reasoned approach to life. These traits were apparent in his speech and song. One expression of his innocence was that he never thought ahead about what he said; words seemed to fly out of his mouth and this lack of artifice lent an unusual air of conviction to all he said.[21] Platon Karataev was not so much an individual man as he was one piece of a larger structure, as was clear from this description, "But his life, as he himself viewed it, had no meaning as a separate life. It had meaning only as part of the whole, which he constantly felt. . . . He could understand neither the value nor the significance of a man's individually-taken action."[22]

The total of these characteristics merged in Pierre's memory of Karataev as the "personification of everything Russian, good, and strong."[23] Only through his experience of four weeks of confinement was Pierre able to come to terms with himself and to see meaning in his life. Thus, closing the gap of estrangement between the artificial world of *obshchestvo* and the unspoiled life of the *narod,* this son of the aristocracy finally found his peace and renewal.

From various angles during his life, he had long searched for this calm, for this peace within himself, . . . he had sought it in philanthropy, in Masonry, in the distractions of social life, in wine, in a heroic feat of self-sacrifice, in romantic love for Natasha; he had sought it through reason, and all of these searchings and attempts had always deceived him. And, not thinking about it himself, he received this calm and peace with himself only through the horror of death, through deprivation, and through what he understood in Karataev.[24]

In the character of Platon Karataev, then, and equally in his impact on the central character in the drama, Pierre, Tolstoy captured both the essence of the image of the *narod* that stood before *obshchestvo* at the end of the 1860s and the all-important function that the image in that construction served for a society searching for expiation of the sin of exploitation in the past and for strength to define a more moral future.

Images of the *Narod* in the Going to the People Movement

Redemption and rapprochement were also the primary impulses of the most dramatic of this generation of explorers of the village, the radical Populists, the *narodniki*. Their assault on the village was an attempt at cultural and national redefinition undertaken with a perception permeated with the element of division. They were themselves active participants in the nation. As rebels, they aimed to bridge the gap between educated society and *narod* to serve both entities through either defending or inciting the latter. They were heirs to the traditional concept of the *narod* as it had developed in the eighteenth-century discovery of the folk and in the Slavophile and Westerner paeans to rural culture. An analysis of their preconceptions of the *narod* and of their post-Emancipation rediscovery of the folk illustrates the extent to which the image of the *narod* was available to them as they set out to penetrate village culture and engage the peasants. In explaining their experiences to each other, to their accusers in court once arrested, and in their reminiscences of the movement, these radical suitors of the peasantry employed the image of the *narod* much as other members of educated society did.

Daniel Field has argued convincingly that we should not accept the radical Populists' various forms of testimony as ingenuous, as most historians have, but as skillfully contrived to protect themselves and each other from prosecution.[25] Even if this is the case, their descriptions of their preconceptions of the peasantry as the *narod* and their confessions of revelation concerning the true nature of the peasantry offer evidence of the function of the image in their experience and in the experience of educated society more generally. For by appealing to the shared concept of the *narod* in their accounts of their activities, they confirmed the force that the image held for their audience of either accusers or sympathizers. Similarly, the skepticism toward the image of the *narod* that marked the conclusion of their movement reinforced the process of the image's diminution for observers across the political spectrum.

The narrative of the "going to the people" movement is so well known that there is no need to repeat it here. One should only keep in mind that the two large waves of movement to the village occurred in 1874–1875 and 1876–1878 after a prelude of discussion and initial forays in the period 1870–1874. Walicki dates the birth of Populism in 1869, after the publication of V. Bervi-Flerovskii's *Position of the Working Class in Russia,* P. L. Lavrov's *Historical Letters,* and N. K. Mikhailovskii's *What Is Progress?* Most historians recognize 1881 as the end of the period, although Norman Naimark's recent study indicates that the eighties were not as politically inactive a decade as we have assumed. Although the history of the aims and tactics of the radicals need not detain us, it is appropriate to pause over the question of the novelty of the movement, for its resolution hinges on the radicals' view, first, of their relationship to the Slavophiles, and, second, of their relationship to the *narod*.

The Populists clearly considered themselves to be a distinct and novel phenomenon, separate both from the Slavophiles of the thirties and forties and from their contemporaries, the liberals. In his statement to prison authorities in 1877, A. D. Mikhailov explained that the movement had taken on the label *narodnichestvo* only in 1876 when he and his fellow *narodniki* formed the all-Russian organization Land and Liberty.[26] In so doing, they were simply confirming the central aspect of their activity and that of their more or less radical fellow travelers: identification with the *narod*. When Populists explored the definition of their movement, they almost always wound their way back to the issue of proximity to the people. By proximity they meant more than simple infatuation; they insisted on life-and-blood experience among the people as essential to true knowledge and true communion. For them, this was the test for distinguishing their attitude and their actions. In their view this goal divided them from the Slavophiles. As an achievement of their experience, they believed, it divided them from the liberals.

They recognized that they shared the Slavophiles' positive view of the people and that they were equally enamored of the peasantry. Veterans of the movement often described the infatuation that characterized their first steps. A. O. Lukashevich recounted his departure for the village in 1873, "With a smile I now recall with what platonic love I looked at this journey in the train to Nizhnii . . . imagining the *narod*—this dear unfamiliar *narod*, whom I had wanted to get to know for so long."[27] From fifty years' distance, S. A. Viktorova-Val'ter described her attitude as nothing less than sinful: "Time later showed that idealization of the *narod* played a large role in our worldview, but . . . such idealization was the shared sin of our generation. . . ."[28]

There was no small amount of wishful thinking in the Populists' early images of the peasantry as they described it. They found the *narod* raised to the pedestal of moral perfection in the journalism that inspired them. N. A. Morozov described the image of the people he found in Lavrov's journal, *Forward*, to be "always the ideal of perfection."[29] In the fresh bloom of his new love, he drank in the nectar of idealism.

> It seemed to me that a whole new world had been opened before my eyes, and how many wonderful and unexpected things there were in it! . . . Upon reading these sections, I involuntarily wanted to forget my own eyes and ears which—alas! could not help me extract from chance encounters with peasants any high ideas, except for a few worthless phrases, involuntarily catching my ears as a result of universal applicability. . . . I passionately wanted to believe that everything among the simple *narod* was as good as the authors of these articles said, and that it was not necessary for the *narod* to learn from us, but us to learn from them. So . . . for several days I walked around like a drunken man.[30]

This desire to think the best of the *narod* allowed the Populists to develop their second characteristic attitude toward the people, which was obvious to contemporaries and historians alike: unbounded faith in the ideal. Morozov explained that for the Russian radical, socialism was his faith and the *narod* his god.[31] Another contemporary, S. F. Kovalik, highlighted this link to Slavophilism.

> Populist youth . . . had one trait which also belonged to the Slavophiles: they worshipped their people, and from the people and only from the people did they expect a new revelation. Like the Slavophiles they also did not know exactly what they should do among the people. . . . They closed their eyes and hoped that their faith in the people would tell them what they should do.[32]

The Populists thus explained that they adopted a faith based on an idealization of the *narod*, who were, furthermore, to be the source of "a new revelation," a revelation which the Populists would experience through their own action. They were determined to act on their faith, and they consciously set themselves apart and above others infected by *narod-oliubie* (love of the people) through action and knowledge. The Populist ethnographer Aleksandra Efimenko stated plainly, "We turn to . . . the *narod* with the hope of renewal, with belief in its power of resurrection;

we try to merge with the *narod*. . . . The chief preparatory work will consist of study of the *narod* from all angles. . . ."[33] Morozov described this as their willingness to sacrifice themselves in search of the ideal,[34] while A. I. Zheliabov explained it as the shift from dreamy metaphysics to positivism and a search for interests that were fundamental and recognized by the *narod*.[35]

One contributor to *The Cause* set the tone for the decade in an article in 1871. He assessed the use of the term *narod* as one of "enormous, yet imprecise meaning." He considered it as abstract in 1871 as it had been for the Slavophiles who idealized the *narod* through the prism of German transcendentalism for their "goodness, happiness and progress." For the Slavophiles, the *narod* were a fantasy, he continued, as familiar to them as Japanese culture.[36] By contrast, in 1871, because of the Emancipation ten years earlier and the possibility of the shift away from the customs of the commune, such ignorance had become a dangerous luxury because the fate of Russia was now inseparably bound up with the fate of the *narod*. "Thus it is necessary to know its actual situation down to the smallest details. . . ."[37] The Populists were thus conscious that they held an idealized image of the *narod* but were determined both to define it more clearly and to serve it more truly through personal knowledge and sacrifice. Their experience in seeking the idyll, only to lose it, held a singular position in Russia's cultural development. The very fact that the Populists' image of the *narod* was so distorted and idealistic makes the dissipation on impact of that image all the more interesting as the major example of the debunking of one mythical concept to make way for more concrete and self-confident image making.

Three features dominated the image of the *narod* employed by the Populists: homogeneity, simplicity, and ignorance or moral darkness in the form of spiritual weakness. Simplicity usually carried with it the idea of the child, that the *narod* was made up of childlike adults whose naïveté or lack of artifice made them both trusting and malleable. These characteristics enabled the Populists to view the peasants as vulnerable children who both needed their guidance and would be receptive to their teaching. One of the clearest statements of this assumption appeared in the 1874 manifesto of the Dolgushin circle, "To Critically Thinking People," which summoned educated youth to action with the challenge "Do you no longer want to be exemplary fathers of the family and concern yourselves with the upbringing of your children so that they may become people with new outlooks? . . ."[38] Ekaterina Breshko-Breshkovskaia reinforced this image in her favorable reports on her activity in the village. In 1878 the émigré journal *The Commune* published her reminiscences, in which she presented a rosy picture of her success among the *narod*, who, she said, loved her and accepted her with "that childish trust of the simple man

who is himself so far away from all kinds of artifice and deception . . .
that it would never occur to him to suspect another. . . ."[39] By 1882, this
tendency drew criticism from the editors at *The Week,* who urged readers
to abandon "the habit of thinking of grown people as children."[40]

The Populists were confident that the simple *narod* would generally
exhibit the childlike trust which Breshko-Breshkovskaia described and that
they would welcome their defenders and teachers. Bervi-Flerovskii clearly
perceived that it was his function to be the champion of an otherwise
defenseless peasantry. He described the peasants as unjustly accused of
"laziness, ignorance and poverty" and proclaimed that they were ignorant
only of the means of their own salvation.[41] It was the Populist's responsibility to liberate the peasant from that ignorance, from the dark oppression
that confined him. The *narod* was perceived to be a dark mass awaiting
illumination. As one radical reminded another in 1873, "[D]o not forget
that when a man has learned how to read, when he has learned how to
distinguish the evil from the good—on him rests the responsibility of en-
abling the dissemination of light among other ignorant people. In your
hands you have many ignorant people—enlighten them, teach them what
you yourself know. . . ."[42]

For the Lavristy more than for the Bakuninists, education and enlightenment were crucial. During the Trial of the One Hundred and Ninety-
three, when they were able to declare their goals publicly, the defendant
Andreeva was accused of having "expressed the notion that . . . if one gave
the *narod* education, then they would understand . . . and themselves by
means of an uprising escape their difficult position. . . ."[43] Breshko-
Breshkovskaia described her service and sacrifice when she declared that
she "had been arrested for the *narod,* for whom she spread literacy, hoping
to free them."[44] A. D. Mikhailov described the *narod* as dually oppressed,
bound "by an economic yoke" and kept in the dark by their own prejudices
and ignorance.[45]

The peasantry was benighted not only by ignorance, but also by a
tenuous morality. Some Populists saw their mission to be not only political
and intellectual but moral enlightenment. The *narod*'s spirit was in as much
need of protection as its material life. The conjunction of these missions
was evident in the testimony of G. F. Zdanovich at the Trial of the Fifty.
"My goal was the liberation of the *narod* so that their labor would not be
exploited in any way whatsoever, so that the *narod*'s consciousness would
not be darkened by the prejudices of ignorance, engendered by inescapable
poverty, and so that the morality of the *narod* would not decline, which is
inevitable given the murderous conditions of their life."[46]

The *narod* ideal was thus made up of simple people, childlike, ignorant
peasants whose liberation would come from the *narodniki,* who, as loving
fathers and teachers, would defend and enlighten them. It is worth noting

that these aspects of the image also dominated the speeches of the prosecutors at the Trials of the Twenty, Fifty, and One Hundred Ninety-three where the Populist activists who had been arrested and brought to trial faced the state. One need only read the detailed indictment to find frequent references to the simple (*prostoi*) and dark (*chernyi*) *narod,* here portrayed as unwitting victims, dupes of the insidious propaganda of the conspiratorial radicals. Prosecutor and defendant alike shared the basic concept of gullibility or malleability as a defining feature of the passive *narod.*

Homogeneity completed the trilogy of the *narod*'s makeup. Idealization rarely allows for differentiation or qualification within the ideal. The Populist vision of the *narod* took in one great mass of humanity whose very lack of definition provided much of its appeal, thus retaining this essential aspect of Aksakov's and Tolstoy's positive image making. Drawing on the two dichotomies of the urban versus rural and active (*obshchestvo*) versus passive (*narod*), the image of the *narod* in the 1870s as simple, ignorant, and oppressed rested on little concrete knowledge. The lack of sophistication that the radicals exhibited in their approach to the countryside was later cause for much chagrin and hand-wringing.[47] Letters, prison statements, and memoirs bear witness to the fact that their most significant discovery was that the *narod* consisted of individual peasants whose outlook not only was at variance with the Populists' expectations but also revealed unanticipated diversity in rural culture.

One of the most obvious indications of the Populists' vision of uniformity among the peasants was their early strategy of dressing as poor peasants. In their scheme of things, all peasants were poor and oppressed; therefore, it was logical to dress as a poor peasant if one hoped to "pass" as a peasant. Furthermore, they were confident that all peasants shared a resentment of their oppressors and, by extension, sympathy with any fellow sufferer. Thus, the surest access to the *narod*'s trust was to dress as a similarly impoverished and burdened peasant.

"With what equanimity the *narod* met them, history has already shown," one participant later wrote.[48] Dressed as beggars, the radicals were met by cautious suspicion and became sensitive to a distressing respect among the *narod* for hierarchy in society.[49] A. I. Ivanchin-Pisarev was one of the first to adjust to the peasant's hierarchical view of the world and advised newcomers to discard their peasant dress immediately and to return to their usual city attire. Morozov recalled his advice:

People foolishly think—he said about this—that for work among the *narod,* it is essential to dress like a *muzhik.* In their element, the peasants listen with respect only to the elders, and fathers of families. If a young, unmarried, and especially, beardless man begins to tell them about new ideas, they will only laugh at him and say, "What does he understand? The

egg doesn't teach the hen." It is completely different when a man stands a
little above them in social position, then they will listen to him attentively.[50]

As early as 1874, reports came back from the village that the *narod* was
not as cohesive a unit as expected. "The first thing I noticed among the
peasantry was the lack of solidarity among them," one veteran advised a
novice to the village.[51] Not only did the peasants fail to display the predicted solidarity among the oppressed; they also did not share the Populists' condemnation of serfdom and its remnants. Instead, peasants frequently expressed nostalgia for the days of serfdom. James C. Scott has
described this phenomenon in his study of Vietnamese peasants, explaining
that the nostalgia resulted there from the sense of the loss of the security,
the guarantee of food and shelter, which arose from the relationship with
the landlord under serfdom.[52] Much the same seems to have been the case
in Russia in the post-Emancipation period. Kavelin emphasized this unnatural rupture in landlord-peasant relations in his series of articles on the
peasant question in 1881.[53] Among the *narod*, nostalgia for the days of
serfdom took the form of complaints about the high cost of living as a free
man and the longing for guarantees against the vagaries of nature. In
addition, the old people considered the breakdown of patriarchal authority
to be a result of the young people's need to leave the village to earn the
cash required to meet all of the post-Reform tax obligations.[54] The radicals
expected to find resentment of high taxes; they were shocked by the often-
expressed desire to return to the days of serfdom.

Another indication of the Populists' image of the *narod* as an undifferen-
tiated mass was the type of propaganda they planned to use in the village.
Most of it reflected their division of Russian society into two great group-
ings: oppressors and oppressed. I. N. Myshkin explained at his trial in 1877
that he "knew from my early years that there were two classes of people in
the world: one, the peasants, always toiling, always suffering, the other,
benefitting from that toil."[55] Projecting their diagram of Russian society
onto the *narod*'s perception, the Populists were confident that one had only
to appeal to their sense of injury and to make them conscious of the source
of their hardship to engage them in a transformation of the society. They
had no doubt that the unvariegated mass of the folk would have similarly
unvariegated interests.

Several subjects of discussion seemed to promise a positive response
among the peasants. The first, most general one was to discuss their material conditions, then to contrast them to those of the wealthy landowners
and state officials. It was considered important in this discussion to explain
to the peasant that "it was not the laws of nature that sent this evil to
him."[56] The radicals also hoped that invoking the names of the great peasant radicals Stenka Razin and Emilian Pugachev would remind the peas-

ants that their ancestors had rebelled and that descriptions of peasant rebellions in Europe would encourage them to act.[57] A more immediate topic of discussion was the famine in Samara,[58] which provided the opportunity to point out the "heartlessness of the tsar, the indifference of *zemstvo* men, and men in the state councils."[59] Finally, they went to the village loaded down with illegal literature to read to and distribute among the peasants. The most popular were pamphlets printed in Switzerland in the early period (1872–1874) and on illegal presses in Russia during the height of the movement. The pamphlets included descriptions of peasant uprisings of the seventeenth and eighteenth centuries and of the socioeconomic position of the peasantry and translations of works deemed suitable, of which the most popular was "The Story of One French Peasant."[60]

The common theme was the exploitation of the peasants as a class; the hope was that making peasants aware of peasant rebellions in the Russian past as well as more recent uprisings in Europe would contribute to a sense of belonging to a broad oppressed group, to a consciousness that would break the pattern of passivity. Striking the chord of shared concerns would surely provoke united action.

As late as 1880, the stubbornly Populist journal *The Week* published the editorial "What Is *Narodnichestvo?*", which reiterated the notion that one of the major virtues of the *narod* was its homogeneity: "The *narodnik* does not love the *narod* only because they are unfortunate . . . ; he respects the *narod* as a collective whole, constituting in itself the highest level of justice and humanity of our time. . . . [S]ome individual spirits may be fine, but the collective spirit of the *narod* is always superior."[61] S. M. Kravchinskii also included this as a cardinal feature of the peasants when he introduced them to the West: "But through all the varieties of types, tribes and past history, the millions of our rural population present a remarkable uniformity in those higher general, ethical, and social conceptions. . . ."[62]

One element in the morphology of the *narod* was less certain: the level of religious belief. Most of the radicals believed that religion itself was a repressive force, thereby following the program of *Forward,* which had declared one of its two major struggles to be that of science against religion. Faith in a god as much as faith in the Tsar constituted one of those prejudices which kept the *narod* in darkness. They certainly rejected this crucial, one may say primary, element in the Slavophile definition of the *narod.* Even so, some of the radicals recognized that one of the best ways to approach the peasants would be through religious themes. One of the more impressive examples of success among the *narod* was that of Osip Aptekman, who gained his peasants' trust through religious discussions. He himself converted from Judaism to Russian Orthodoxy in order to be closer to the *narod.*[63] A. O. Lukashevich was also careful to observe religious ritual in his effort to gain acceptance among the peasantry.[64] Mikhailov described a family of sectarians he met during his later work among the peasants of the Volga region who had gone through several conversions to different sects, each time with total commitment and deeply held faith, thus indicating religious belief, if not Orthodox belief.[65] Kravchinskii maintained that, in fact, the Orthodox Church meant little to the Russian peasant. "The Orthodox Church," he wrote, "has no hold over the souls of the masses. The *pop,* or priest, is but an official of the bureaucracy and deprador [*sic*] of the commune."[66] Another radical, N. Bukh, found during his journey on foot in the Samara region that the peasants reacted negatively when he criticized the Tsar but gave him a sympathetic hearing whenever he described the priests and the Church as enemies of the *narod.*[67] Contradictory reports on the religiosity of the Russian peasant would continue throughout the post-Emancipation period, but it is understandable that radicals committed to the principles of science would emphasize any evidence they could summon of the peasants' skepticism toward formal and official religion.[68]

The Populists' modification of their methods to suit the peasants' attitude toward religion and the Church reflected their recognition that rapprochement would result from their interaction with the peasants rather than from simple imposition of their views. The fundamental discovery of the first wave of those who "went to the people" was that the *narod* may have been benighted, but it was neither a homogeneous nor a simple and passive mass of malleable peasants. They encountered a distinct culture which was separate from theirs not only by virtue of rural isolation from Westernization and the city or by virtue of passivity, but more so by a system of logic and needs which shaped the peasants' worldview. The outsiders had arrived with ideals to translate into action, only to realize their inapplicability in the face of the *narod*'s much more specific, practical needs.

Morozov's account of his efforts at propaganda provide a humorous and poignant example of the realization that reading aloud to peasants about ideas or events that were beyond their immediate world was useless. He described one positive relationship he shared with a peasant who attentively joined discussions on the problems of the peasants, the economy, and the state. His comprehension inevitably vanished, however, whenever Morozov attempted to read to him from his store of books. One evening, he felt as though he had broken through at last. While reading one especially moving passage, he looked up to discover, to his joy, "an expression of serious observation, almost desire" on the peasant's face. "What is it?" he asked the peasant with anticipation. "What good boots you have," the peasant said, pointing to Morozov's feet. "Did they cost a lot?"[69]

This type of reaction produced one great lesson the radicals took with them back to the city. Peasants were not interested in discussing the overthrow of autocracy or the ideals of socialism. They were interested in their daily needs, which could be as basic as a pair of good boots. The larger interests were lowering taxes and receiving more land; here were the points of appeal. It was clear that rewards of revolutionary activity would come only after long years of getting to know the peasants and working to develop their specific, material concerns into platforms for action.

The idealized *narod* had turned out to be a baffling mystery, a complicated phenomenon—a self-contained separate culture in Russia. The experience of the Populists who had sought rapprochement with the *narod* both to be close to their ideal and to understand it more clearly had left them with a new set of questions and uncertainties. As the following letter of one radical indicated, the confrontation with the reality of the village had made the initiative of this segment of society little more than an illuminating reconnoiter.

> Have all questions been answered and is there no room for doubt? Can it really be that experiences do not tell us anything? What is the *narod?* The answer to the first two questions is negative. The questions have not only not been resolved, but indeed have been posed incorrectly, and experience should lead to doubt. . . . That Russian radicalism knows neither man in general nor the Russian man in particular is an indisputable fact. That it wants to impose on the Russian man a form of reason and ideals which he cannot master, this is known without acquaintance. Radicalism promises him two birds in the bush when *a priori,* even from general understanding of human nature, it is possible to conclude that for every ignorant and undeveloped man, more than anything else, his own life is dear to him. The circle of his needs is limited by bread and wife, and everything that is higher than these needs is inaccessible to him until they are satisfied. After this, you develop in him human qualities and thoughts.[70]

The simple, homogeneous, benighted *narod* of the Populists' early vision had disintegrated on contact into "ignorant and undeveloped" individuals, not yet capable of "human qualities and thoughts." Here we see the interplay of various contexts bearing on the dissolution of one image and the reversal of the expected in a dialogic twist from positive ideal into subhuman. But that twist ultimately struck the radicals themselves, who knew "neither man in general nor the Russian man in particular."

The Image of the *Narod* in Dostoevsky's *Diary of a Writer*

During the same period when the experience of the radical Populists was suggesting a diminution of the heroic qualities of the *narod* and the image itself seemed to be metamorphosing into a frustrating and depressing icon of Russia's backwardness, F. M. Dostoevsky offered a contrary opinion which exemplified his dialogism at its best. His publicistic observations on the Russian *narod* in his *Diary of a Writer* between 1873 and 1881 offered a conservative alternative to the radical idol. Dostoevsky's image of the *narod* was similar to that of the Populists on several points. First and foremost, his *narod* were as much an ideal as were theirs, equally reflecting his projection of his own ideals, in his case, Christianity and universal communion among men. Second, he incorporated homogeneity in his concept of the *narod*, praising the distinctive singularity of profound religious belief as one of the *narod*'s salient features. He also characterized them as dark in the sense of ignorant, but he did not include moral vacillation in his morphology of the folk.

He diverged most directly from the radical image in his description of the *narod* as almost innately spiritual and Christian, and as consciously patriotic. For Dostoevsky, the connotation of *narod* as the nation and root of *narodnost'*—nationalism or nationhood—was as important, perhaps more so, as the concepts of simplicity and darkness. This perception of the folk as the essence of the nation shaped his vision of Russia's dividedness. He agreed with the radical position that the division of Russia into two cultures weakened the educated class and that only through reconciliation with the *narod* would *obshchestvo* find salvation. The urge for rapprochement and redemption thus found another expression in Dostoevsky's image of the *narod*.

The concept of the *narod* as the embodiment of the Christian ideal ran as a continuous theme through the *Diary*. The *narod*'s belief, in Dostoevsky's formulation, was both conscious and innate. It was not necessarily tied to the official Orthodox Church, although he did assign the Church some role in framing the *narod*'s understanding of Christ. The very name peasants chose for themselves, Dostoevsky argued, reflected their self-image: "They called themselves '*krest'ianin*', that is, 'Christian', and this is not only a matter of words; this comprises the idea of their whole future."[71] The key to the *narod*'s Christian faith was suffering: having suffered long they took to heart the suffering of Christ, his disciples, and the saints who followed to sacrifice themselves. Central to the *narod*'s Christian belief, then, was the sympathy of sorrow, an attribute equally stressed by advocates of the suitability of peasants on juries in criminal cases, a topic I will explore further in the following chapter. In this sympathy, they had a distinct advantage over the educated believer in Dostoevsky's view.[72] The *narod* manifested their faith in their traditions and in courageous actions. Of their traditions, Dostoevsky wrote, "I believe that the most important and most fundamental spiritual need of the Russian *narod* is their desire for suffering, constant and insatiable suffering everywhere and in everything. It is as if they have been affected by this thirst for suffering from time immemorial."[73]

The shining example of the strength of the *narod*'s faith was found in the action of one Foma Danilov, a peasant recruit from Samara who died under Turkish torture while fighting with his Slavic brethren rather than foreswear his faith. Dostoevsky hailed the martyrdom of this simple peasant who demonstrated the quintessential spiritual strength of the *narod*. Although cultured Russians may have found Danilov's sacrifice curious as a contradiction of the common view of the *narod* as spiritually weak, Dostoevsky believed that the people themselves would not find it surprising at all. "There we have . . . as it were, the portrait, the complete portrait of the Russian *narod*. . . . Our *narod* love the truth for truth alone and not for glory. Let them be coarse and ugly and sinful and undistinguished, but when their time comes, and a cause of national truth arises, then you will be astounded by the degree of spiritual freedom they will reveal. . . ."[74] In a characteristic juxtaposition, Dostoevsky here sets up the ugliness and capacity for sin among the folk with their superior love of truth for truth alone. Furthermore, unlike the others at whom Dostoevsky's sideward glance is cast in this passage, the simple man of the people loves his nation and its goals not for the sake of glory but out of essential sincerity. It was this moral strength, consciousness of basic truth, and natural sympathy for suffering that made the Russian *narod* superior to educated society, even in its ignorance, even in its darkness.

Dostoevsky went much further in this dialogic treatment of the *narod* by highlighting visible evidence of the peasants' most brutal inclinations and actions. Early entries of the *Diary* included graphic descriptions of the *narod*'s capacity for inhumanity, including one of the most chilling scenes of a peasant beating his wife to be found in writings of the period.[75] In that passage he used the words "our good little *muzhik*" to refer to the peasant husband who flays his wife as his evening's entertainment. Thus he used educated society's fond, almost diminutive term for the peasant male when he was analyzing one of the most disturbing, repulsive types of behavior peasant men exhibited. He played on the expected meaning of the word and the anticipated sympathy toward the *narod* to give more force to the impact of his description of the peasant's brutality. Having shocked the reader, he pursued further the underlying question, Who is the real peasant; who are the *narod*? He refused to concede that such cruelty was inherent; rather, it was imposed, and thus only a superficial layer over the *narod*'s fundamentally spiritual nature. Even rampant drunkenness did not ultimately besmirch the *narod*'s virtue in Dostoevsky's appraisal. "Yes, there is much bestiality in the *narod*, but do not point at it. This bestiality is the slime of centuries; it will be cleansed."[76] More important, "is not Christ's spirit in our people, dark but good, ignorant but not barbarian?"[77] In the face of contradictions in the *narod*'s life and behavior, contradictions he himself emphasized, Dostoevsky extracted the pure from the slime, the core from the superficial, the inherent from the imposed. This Christian essence of the *narod* distinguished it from educated society and made any enlightenment from above senseless. "I maintain frankly that we have absolutely nothing to teach such a people."[78] Not only could society not enlighten the simple folk; indeed they should seek enlightenment from them: "It is we who have to bow before the *narod* and await from them everything—both reason and expression; it is we who must bow before the *narod*'s truth and recognize it as such."[79]

The final component of Dostoevsky's image of the *narod* was conscious patriotism and sympathy for fellow Slavs in their struggles against the Ottoman Empire in the second half of the 1870s. The source of that patriotism was both the *narod*'s sympathy for fellow sufferers and a sense of union with their Christian Slavic brothers under the oppression of Islam. Perhaps no other prominent figure was as confident of the peasants' comprehension of and commitment to the cause of Slavic brotherhood. He described their spontaneous movement as early as the summer of 1876, when "Russians are taking their staffs in crowds of hundreds, escorted by thousands of people, are going on some novel crusade. . . ."[80] That these peasant volunteers were the heart of the national organism was clear. "Of Russians, of real Russians, there proved to be an infinitely greater number than had been estimated even by genuine Russians."[81] In sum, the *narod* was a wellspring of natural patriotism to be tapped by those who sought the strength of real Russia.

Tolstoy Reconsiders

Tolstoy offered a more skeptical opinion of the *narod's* patriotism during the war and generally shifted his view on the peasant in *Anna Karenina.* In the decade since the appearance of *War and Peace,* he had moved to a more equivocal description of the peasant as a man of the simple folk. Through his depiction of Levin's relations with the peasants on his estate and with his Populist brother, Sergei Ivanovich, in *Anna Karenina,* Tolstoy entered the general discussion of the peasant's mentality and of outsiders' ability to understand it. He used both sets of relations to hightlight the naïveté of any wholesale vision of the Russian people through the image of the *narod.*

Tolstoy answered Dostoevsky's claim of the peasants' conscious and deep patriotism directly in one of the final scenes in the novel. There, Levin argues with his brother who has just declared that the phenomenon of peasant volunteers en route to the Balkans was a reflection of the will of the *narod* who sympathized with their Slavic brothers. Levin replies: "This word '*narod*' is so indefinite . . . *volost'* clerks, teachers, and one of a thousand *muzhiks* perhaps know what it [the war] is all about. The remaining eighty million . . . not only are not expressing their will, but do not even have the vaguest idea what it is they should express their will about. So what right do we have to say what the will of the *narod* is?"[82] Here Tolstoy contested three currents of thought swirling around the concept of the *narod*. First he challenged the concept itself, by saying it was indefinite. Then he challenged the concept of the *narod* as conscious patriots. Finally, he challenged the ability of educated society to identify the general will of the indefinite *narod*. These were challenges that ran throughout the novel, especially in the relationship of Levin and his brother.

Although Sergei Ivanovich loved the countryside and the peasants, his understanding of both was a product of his vision of Russia as a country divided into two cultures, urban versus rural, educated society versus *narod*. Thus, he loved the countryside and rural inhabitants for everything that distinguished them from the city and educated society. When he visited Levin's estate, he was the consummate outsider who delighted in vignettes of country living and spoke with affectionate paternalism about the peasants, never changing his opinion about their distinctive culture.[83]

Levin, on the other hand, dismissed the existence of the so-called *narod*. He saw the peasants not as "the people," but as individual characters, some of whom he liked and others he disliked. Whereas his brother's vision of the people was static, Levin's changed constantly the more he knew and worked with them on his estate.[84] Two themes dominated Tolstoy's treatment of the peasant through Levin's experiences: the healthy release of manual labor beside simple, strong men and women, and the stubborn recalcitrance of the peasants whenever Levin proposed any innovation in the system of agriculture on his land. The former theme was most clear in the description of Levin's day of mowing in the second volume of the novel. Here the peasants appeared as skilled, physically strong, cheerful, and patient. Much of the appeal of society through labor came from the contrast Levin perceived between this community and his artificial existence in "society." When he sought the company of his peasants, he did so to escape the trivial world of *obshchestvo* through contact with "this working, pure, and common, splendid life."[85] In this setting, the *narod* served their function of the sought-after other, distinct from urban Westernized Russia, and Levin was very much a man of his social and intellectual milieu, indeed his brother's double.

Whenever Levin attempted to direct, as well as share, the labor of his peasants, however, he met an impenetrable wall of silent mistrust. Several scenes in the novel revolved around his efforts to promote rational farming on the estate and emphasized the certain frustration of anyone who hoped to shake the Russian peasant out of his desire to live peacefully, following the methods of his ancestors. Although Levin's peasants might patiently listen to his plans for reform, the expression on their faces revealed their conviction that he had other goals in mind and their determination not to be taken in by his schemes.[86] Through these scenes, Tolstoy was able to convey some of the disenchantment of the first forays to the village that had been described in the eyewitness accounts of the early 1860s. He was drawing equally on the eyewitness account of one of his most formidable contemporaries, Aleksandr Nikolaevich Engelgardt, who was reporting on his agricultural experiments and relations with the peasants on his estate in his letters "From the Country," which were appearing in *Notes of the Father-land* at the same time *Anna Karenina* was being published. Within the frame of the novel, these encounters undermined Levin's infatuation with the peasant's strength and simplicity and reminded him of the peasant's potential for drunkenness, lies, and slovenliness.[87]

Like Pierre Bezukhov, however, Konstantin Levin found self-knowledge and redemption through an exchange with a peasant. Levin's discovery of peace was quite similar to Pierre's. During a conversation with the peasant Fedor about other peasants on the estate, Fedor remarked that one of them was a good man because he lived for his soul and honored God. Levin demanded, "But how can one honor God?" The peasant's simple reply was that one should live not for one's own needs, but for God, and that one should respect other men; that one should not take, but give.[88] This straightforward moral vision of the world seemed the answer to all of the questions which had tormented Levin, and he walked away renewed, redeemed.

Fedor—man of the people and simple peasant—thus served as the mouthpiece for the moral message: think not of your own needs but of those of others and of God. Tolstoy's image of the *narod* in this novel of the late 1870s was equivocal and highly contradictory. It included both slovenliness and knowledge of important spiritual truths. The spiritual truth of the *narod* as voiced by Fedor was that common to all definitions of the concept: unity, self-sacrifice, and absence of individualism. Tolstoy thus joined in the general discomfort with a tidy definition of the *narod* and offered instead the possibility of baffling contradictions among the peasants. In so doing, he added to the weakening of the image as a force that could answer the question, Who is the Russian peasant?

Conclusion

Slavophiles, Populists, neo-Slavophiles, and moralists alike created an image of the peasants in the form of the *narod* as the repository of their ideals and as the other side of Russian culture, their very opposite. As such, it represented the most positive and the most general and ill-defined of the images of the peasantry. Dostoevsky himself recognized this when he wrote, "And yet, to all of us, the *narod* are still a theory and they continue to loom as an enigma."[89] The theory encompassed the elements of simplicity, homogeneity, and darkness for most outsiders; for the conservative, the *narod* were also believers and patriots. The image of the *narod* represented society's expectation of what lay beyond the capitals. The radical Populists realized the inaccuracy of their vision through their experience in the village and began the process of redefining of the peasant image. Dostoevsky sensed the tenuousness of the concept, as well as the personal investment in and sensitivity to disillusionment of the ideal for members of educated society. In 1876 he predicted the outcome of society's attempt to resolve the mystery of the peasant soul, anticipating astutely what types of images would replace the vague concept of the *narod,* when he said that educated society, if disappointed or disillusioned by the reality of the folk, would, "immediately renounce them without regret."[90]

As the Populists discovered and as Dostoevsky correctly sensed, the positive aura surrounding the concept of the *narod* resulted from its very lack of definition, by the absence of detailed, individual, powerful features which might yield an image of many peasant characters, rather than one characterless but moldable mass. As a simple, unenlightened, and homogeneous unit of humanity, the peasant *narod* were capable of receiving society's projected ideals. However much the image of the *narod* served these psychological needs of various groups of educated Russians, those groups also were beginning to recognize that it was not a very useful image or concept. It did not offer answers or guidance on those pressing needs of the moment in post-Emancipation Russia which demanded some solid knowledge of the peasant. Of those needs, one of the most insistent was the need to define the place of the peasant as a citizen in Russia's reformed legal system, a need which spawned an intense search for a definition of the peasant's attitudes toward law and justice. In that search, new images of the peasant would emerge and new approaches to the mysterious peasant soul would be defined.

3

The Peasant as Judge

Among the Russian *narod,* in addition to the recognition of the need for external law (*zakon*), there is precisely that for which many reproach them, but which many are prepared to view as a virtue: the inadequate feeling (*eina*) of legality or lawfulness (meaning external law). Among the *narod,* the demands of a higher moral justice are constantly alive.

I. S. AKSAKOV, "On the Judicial Reform"

Laws! With us there is one law—vodka. Whoever brings the most will be judged in the right. Whoever is related to the elder or judges—he gets the decision. That's what kind our judges are.

V. S. KROTKOV, "*Volost'* Courts"

These two assertions of the true nature of peasant attitudes toward the law illustrate the contested concepts of rural legality and images of the peasants as legal actors that commanded the attention of public opinion in post-Emancipation Russia. The first came from the pen of I. S. Aksakov, a prominent Slavophile, intellectual, editor, and publicist whose loyalty to the image of the *narod* led him to affirm their "higher moral justice." It was a statement that rested not so much on personal knowledge of the peasant or observation of the practice of rural justice as on Aksakov's own convictions about the nature of law and justice and on his idealized vision of the *narod.* The second statement was the declaration of a peasant whose opinion of the functioning of rural justice was reported by V. S. Krotkov, a lawyer who had lived and worked in the countryside. Two voices, two opinions, two images of the peasant as an agent of justice—one founded on ideals, the other on experience. They represented the two extremes of a spectrum of public image making on the peasant as an element in Russia's reformed judicial system. They represented equally the distance that was traveled in that image making from conclusions drawn from philosophical

54

principles stressing moral concerns to those drawn from empirical observation of the social and economic reality of the village.

The lack of definition of the peasant mass began to give way in a development that ran parallel to the search for the nation as *narod:* the study of rural institutions of justice and of the character of the individual peasant as judge. Although the urge for rapprochement and redemption was manifest in the image of the *narod,* the question of the relation of the peasant to the law occupied many members of educated society who were motivated by a faith in the power of law and legal consciousness to bind divided Russia together. Liberal jurists, Populist ethnographers, local officials in the judicial system, rural lawyers, publicists, and literati alike debated the actual and potential legal consciousness of the Russian peasant.

It is fair to say that for all of them, the goal was a unified nation; there were serious differences of opinion, however, on how to approach that goal through the agency of law. The universally acknowledged challenge was the existence of two legal cultures in Russia, that of customary law (*obychnoe pravo*) and that of the formal legal codes and statutes (*zakon*). Customary law was largely associated with the village, whereas formal law governed relations in educated society. The effort somehow to draw these two systems together prompted study of the peasant's concepts of justice as a means of charting the appropriate course in developing a truly national legal system and a nation ruled by law across all levels of society, from top to bottom.[1] In the search for the peasant soul or mentality, the study of the peasant as judge, as an executor of justice, yielded each of the five competing images of peasant behavior that would replace the nebulous image of the *narod.*

Two institutions of the Reform Era brought the peasant as judge into the public quest for a definition of the peasant soul: the *volost'* court and the jury system for criminal cases. The *volost'* court, included in the original Emancipation legislation in 1861, served as a separate court of peasant judges who were to try petty civil cases according to customary law. Trial by jury was introduced in Russia as part of the Judicial Reform of 1864, which made peasants eligible for jury duty on most criminal cases. In the debates surrounding the introduction of trial by jury, the predominant image of the potential peasant jurors was that of the *narod,* an image which enabled reformers to draw the peasants into that area of justice where morality played a significant role, an image which stressed community of beliefs and conscience among educated and uneducated Russians. The master image of the *narod* held through this debate. In the debates over the fate of the *volost'* court, which continued through the end of the century, the wholesale image of the *narod* broke up into distinct and competing images of peasant behavior. These in turn emphasized the distance between customary law and formal law, between the peasant soul and the legal consciousness of educated society. Peasant attitudes toward the law then became a subject of study distinct from national legal consciousness as students of peasant life recognized the tenacity of popular concepts of justice. Within the debate about peasants and the law, the shift from the inclusive image of the *narod* to images of the peasants as agents of popular justice underscored their "otherness" and contributed to the sense of frustration at failed rapprochement.

Peasants as Jurors: The Essentially Just *Narod*

The Judicial Reform, of which trial by jury was perhaps the most progressive feature, took shape within a special commission in the State Chancellery between 1861 and 1864. The first draft of the Reform was ready as early as 1862, when it went to the State Council, the Minister of Justice, and Tsar Alexander II for review. In September of that year, the *Basic Principles* of the forthcoming reform were published and public comment was solicited. The commission received some six volumes of comment. There was also lively discussion in the press.[2] Records of the commission's debates and commentary by the public reveal the extent to which the image of the *narod* prevailed in this early phase of the post-Emancipation period and was exploited by both advocates and opponents of trial by jury to defend their position. The key elements of benightedness, lack of sophistication, cultural homogeneity, distinction from educated society, and sympathy for suffering all appeared at some point in the design of the jury system and the debate over the wisdom of allowing peasants to serve as jurors.

The goal of the reformers was not simply reform of the judiciary but a major transformation of Russian society, a transformation that would develop conscious, engaged citizens who understood and respected the laws.[3] For the men who designed the Judicial Reform and the educated public who witnessed its birth, the new system of justice in Russia was to be a vehicle for furthering progress in Russian culture. The Judicial Reform was viewed not only as an end but, more important, as a means to bring the rule of law to Russia both by eradicating the corruption of law at the level of governance and by developing comprehension of and trust in the law among the population. Central to their effort was their recognition of the persistence of the two legal cultures of customary law and formal law. The reformers looked to the reform as a means of mediating, if not indeed closing the gap, between those two cultures.

Trial by jury was to further that goal by drawing the simple folk, the *narod,* the recently emancipated peasants of rural Russia, into an understanding of formal law, trust in the courts, and respect for the legal system of the Empire.[4] Such a combination of understanding, trust, and respect for the law was considered the sine qua non of true citizenship and would represent the culmination of emancipation to the status of free individuals set in motion by the Emancipation Edict of February 19, 1861.

The single greatest virtue of the jury system in the view of the reformers was its ability to engender trust in the court system. The principle of the jury as a court of society, as a voice of the conscience of society, served the aim of convincing the population that decisions on questions of criminal actions were to be made not by the state through its officials but by members of the society in which the accused lived. In arguing that the need for a judgment of peers was exceptionally acute in Russia because of the legacy of serfdom and the general bifurcation of Russian society, the reformers relied on the characteristic paradigm of divided Russia.

> The introduction of the jury in Russia is more necessary than anywhere else because nowhere, perhaps, has the historical life of the nation established such sharp differentiations between the various classes of society as here in Russia, with the result that there are greater differences between the concepts, customs and patterns of life of our judges who generally belong to the upper class and those accused from the lower classes.[5]

The jury system as a court of peers in Russia would thus be better able to protect the interests of society in a divided culture than a system of individual judges from the educated classes. It offered the additional advantage of replacing arbitrariness, *proizvol,* as manifested by either corrupt or inept members of the old judiciary or the person of the serf owner in his jurisdiction over his serfs, with a court of peers whose number and distance from officialdom would make them more trustworthy judges in the eyes of the *narod.* A prerequisite for the comprehension of law as the sole orderly, predictable, consistent means of defending the rights of the individual and society was the extirpation of the widely held and quite understandable popular perception that not law but the personal will of individuals in authority decided a man's fate in Russia.[6]

The composition of the jury would also contribute to popular trust in the institution. For this reason, the authors of the reform voted to include representatives of all levels of society except the clergy, military personnel, public school teachers, and personal servants. The most obvious issue that this decision raised was the suitability of Russia's uneducated simple folk, fresh from the bondage of serfdom, to serve as members of the judicial system with the power to decide innocence or guilt in criminal cases. By deciding to include the peasantry in the jury system, members of the reform commission rejected the criticism of the former chair of the State Council, V. P. Bludov, a firm opponent of the liberal principles that pervaded the reform itself and of this aspect in particular. His dismissal of the ability of the peasants to serve stressed the familiar features of the *narod* as benighted, immature, and sympathetic to the unfortunate—here presented in a negative light.[7]

> It would hardly be useful at this point to introduce the jury system in Russia. It is easy to imagine the activity of such a court when the majority of our simple folk lack not only legal education, but even the most basic education, when concepts about right, duties, and the law are so immature and unclear that the infringement of other people's rights, especially infringing on other people's private property, is viewed by many as the most ordinary affair, and other crimes as acts of daring, while the criminals are seen only as *unfortunates*. To allow such people to decide the important, sometimes extremely difficult question of the guilt or innocence of the accused will risk not only difficulties, but even outright lawlessness.[8]

The justifications that the reformers offered and which many comments from the public echoed to meet these objections highlight the capacity of these same features in the shared image of the *narod* rather to encourage faith in a common approach to serious wrongdoing in the community writ large.

The seriousness of the charge of ignorance was clear. The Russian folk were ignorant. This was the legacy of serfdom. Supporters of the jury responded, however, that this widespread ignorance both heightened the need for a jury system and made the *narod* particularly suitable to fill the role of jurors. Again, because of their lack of knowledge of the law, accused members of the uneducated mass of the population needed a court composed of jurors who understood them and identified with their reasoning, born of local conditions and customs.[9] The knowledge of the daily life and worldview of the accused that any juror from the same area would have would be far more important than education because "for the decision, according to conscience, of the question of guilt or innocence of the accused, there is no particular need either for special judicial education or for judicial experience: this question can be correctly decided by anyone, even by a man of little education, as long as he has common sense."[10] The combination of basic common sense and familiarity with local conditions would equip the jurors well for their duty. Furthermore, supporters of the jury system were quick to defend the simple Russian man and to point to his special qualities.

Leading the effort for the jury system within the reform commission, D. A. Rovinskii argued for correction on two counts of Bludov's view that the *narod* looked at criminals only as unfortunates and did not take criminal acts seriously. First, the harsh treatment of criminals by the peasant belied any notion that they were nonchalant about crime. The well-known practice of peasants' beating thieves to death on the spot should reassure any critic that the simple folk would be sufficiently severe with accused criminals.[11] Second, the Russian simple man's capacity for viewing convicts with pity was itself a sign of deep moral sentiment, a sympathy for suffering, a quality that was surely desirable in a juror.[12] Similarly, the reformers were confident that one could depend on the "incisiveness of the quick Russian mind."[13] Rovinskii's view of the peasants as adequately severe was affirmed by a prosecutor from Kovno who assured the commission in his comments, "Severity, with a hint of despotism, is a characteristic of our lower and middle classes."[14]

The defense of the particularly moral approach of the peasants in deciding questions of wrongdoing is especially important. On the simplest level, it was a reflection of the common notion that, as one member of the Senate reminded the commission, "it very often happens that a poor man is more honest and loyal than a rich man."[15] In his criticism of the jury system, I. S. Aksakov was more obviously concerned with this moral approach as a sign of superior Russian exceptionalism, as a sign of the dominance of the Russian spirit over the rational Western mind in its approach to the law. He questioned the opinion that the *narod*'s tendency to judge actions primarily from the moral standpoint and with little consideration of formal law was a weakness. In doing so, he questioned the prevalent view that the merger of morality and legality was a sign of cultural immaturity. On the contrary, he asserted, this was a cultural advantage, for it indicated that the moral urge was still active among the Russian common folk. The success of the judicial reform would rest on its ability to accommodate the activity of this moral urge by members of the *narod,* on the degree to which it allowed for the influence of conscience.[16] Morality was clearly the substitute for knowledge of the law and an acceptable alternative during the folk's schooling in the principles of formal legality through the reformed judicial system. Despite their concern over the persistence of two legal cultures in Russia, defenders of the jury system seemed to hold an image of the *narod*'s morality as a common cultural bond that they shared. At the very least, they were willing to employ this image as a response to Bludov's skepticism about the institution of trial by jury.

Cautionary statements about the reliability of Jewish jurors underscored the element of moral communion in the perception of *narod* as both peasantry and nation. In contrast to the support for the eligibility of uneducated members of the *narod* to serve as jurors despite their distance from official culture and law, there was serious suspicion of Jews. Some critics from the western provinces questioned the advisability of allowing Jews to serve as jurors. They recognized that it was probably impossible to exclude them altogether, given their large representation in the population of these areas. Even so, they warned the commissioners of the risks they saw in giving Jews such a position of responsibility. Jews could not be trusted to be dispassionate in their judgment of either Christians or their fellow believers, and the more orthodox the Jew, the less suitable he would be to sit on the jury.[17] A member of the civil court in Vil'na Province offered the most elaborate analysis of the problems involved in allowing Jews to serve as jurors, stressing the central role of conscience in the jury's decision and reminding the commissioners that conscience develops through religious teachings and beliefs. Thus, Jews would not share the collective conscience of the Christian population. Furthermore, the Christian had always been and continued to be an enemy in the eyes of the Jew, with the result that the Jews in Russia constituted a "nation within a nation" (*narod v narode*).[18] Reservations about Jewish jurors placed Jewish conscience and morality outside the Russian Orthodox morality assigned to the peasants. For these critics, Jewish morality was not an appropriate substitute for "legal consciousness" in the way that that of the Russian folk, of the *narod*, was. The prospect of having non-Orthodox Christians did not generate the same form of concern.

Faith in the native, peculiar qualities of the *narod* overcame discomfort over their distance from formal law in the establishment of the jury system in reformed Russia. The simple Russian man made up for his legal ignorance with common sense, knowledge of the daily life of his milieu, a deep moral sentiment, and an incisive mind. All of these qualities would make him a reliable juror, reliable both in the eyes of the state and in the eyes of the accused who looked to him for a fair judgment. Active participation in the justice system as jurors, furthermore, would bring the peasantry into the practice of formal law, would educate them and develop their "legal consciousness," and would contribute to the emergence of a truly national system of law in Russia.

Peasant Jurors as Literary Images

These expectations provided the motivation behind the most important literary treatment of peasants as jurors, Nikolai Nikolaevich Zlatovratskii's "Peasant Jurors." Written in 1874 and 1875, this piece established Zlatovratskii as a major figure on the literary scene and pointed to the position he would consistently occupy as a defender of the peasant as an essentially moral actor. In this short story, the main characters are eight worthy peasants who have been appointed to jury duty in the city. The tale recounts their journey to the city, their experiences there, and their trip home. The narrator introduces the peasant jurors as "more gullible artists than strict thinkers" who, after having slowly considered all of the evidence before them, will suddenly throw out all of that evidence and reach a decision.

Sometimes, he explains, the decision might be completely contrary to the evidence, but consistent with their moral state (*dushevnoe nastroenie*). Although they are highly impressionable, thus "gullible," they tend to decide things "according to their souls, and not by clever constructions."[19]

Zlatovratskii juxtaposes the peasant's ability to judge within the community of peasants en route to town with their inability to judge according to formal law in the city. Along the way to the city, the peasant jurors decide several cases in villages where they are asked to do so by the local residents. They decide each case according to the specific circumstances and according to their morals, again *po dushe*, by their soul. They take their role seriously, explaining, "In our work, friends, we are responsible to God and men!"[20] In the city, however, the jurors are at a loss; they continue to make judgments according to their conscience, but their decisions usually are contrary to the evidence before them. Jury duty turns out to be a distressing experience for the peasants, who find the court to be "completely alien."

> The general impression on the peasant jurors of the formal side of the court was very confused and unclear; it was just as if they were all walking in a fog and could not understand anything. It seemed to them that they were constantly being led somewhere, seated, told to stand up, being called and constantly being ordered, "Stand up, sit down, come here, go there. . . ."[21]

Failing to understand city justice, they ignore the evidence and reach their decisions as they have en route to jury duty. Zlatovratskii's message was not that the peasant failed as a judge, but that there was no conjunction between the peasant's natural law and the city's formal law. His description of peasant jurors largely conformed to the image of the *narod* that the designers of the jury system had used in stressing the value of the peasants' morality in judging criminal cases. Yet, his was a pessimistic rather than an optimistic portrait of peasant jurors as fledgling citizens, because it suggested that serving as jurors would not necessarily school peasants in formal law or draw the nation together.

Reviewers of the sketch seized on the moral aspects of the peasant characters and accepted them as appropriate images in the discourse on the question of peasants and the law. Zlatovratskii's peasant jurors exemplified the special strength of the Russian peasants, who "know human suffering better than anyone else; they see it before them, they do not need a book to acquaint them with it; . . . they also know what this suffering can lead a man to; they also know that it would be difficult even for them to stand strong against temptation."[22] The progressive literary critic Aleksandr Mikhailovich Skabichevskii proclaimed Zlatovratskii one of the great writers on peasant life of his generation on the basis of this sketch: "What a splendid sketch this is, how much simple, ingenuous truth there is in every line in it, what warm love for the peasant and what knowledge of his life!"[23] Even Skabichevskii found something not quite accurate, however, in the peasant figures. Another unnamed critic declared that however true the broad strokes in the story were, the language of the peasants was pure fantasy. He accused Zlatovratskii of attributing too much abstract philosophy to the peasants and thus departing from the reality of the peasant juror as he, the reviewer, knew him from his own jury duty.[24] These criticisms were an indication of the shift that had occurred in the reception of depictions of the peasant. The insistence on an accurate portrayal of the peasant juror based on personal knowledge and observation was a warning that idealizations would falter in the public arena.

Two years after the appearance of Zlatovratskii's "Peasant Jurors," Dostoevsky began work on his final novel, *The Brothers Karamazov*. There, too, peasant jurors would figure prominently in the decision of crime and punishment during Dmitrii Karamazov's trial. In that trial, the prosecutor and defense lawyer are equally eloquent and equally adept at playing off legal concepts in brilliant arguments. Dmitrii's fate is sealed, however, when, against the expectation of educated observers of the trial, the peasants convict him. As one voice in the crowd exclaimed, "Our peasants have stood firm."[25] Dostoevsky's implication is that they have stood firm against the reason and abstract legalism in favor of the solid morality of the *narod*. Like Zlatovratskii, then, he retained a paradigm of division in the concepts of justice among the peasants and educated Russians.

Peasants as *Volost'* Court Judges: Competing Images

By the time that Zlatovratskii's "Peasant Jurors" appeared in the winter of 1874–1875, educated society was also examining the question of peasants and the law through the institution of the *volost'* court, which had been brought to the forefront of public debate by the government's decision to undertake its reform. The *volost'* court was a court of peasant judges drawn from the villages in any given *volost'*, the smallest legal-administrative unit established by the Emancipation legislation in 1861.[26] It was a court of peers, made up of four to twelve judges elected by the *volost'* assembly, with jurisdiction over cases within the *volost'* up to a value of one hundred rubles. Decisions were to be made according to customary law, with the sole limitation that the civil code of the Empire not be flagrantly violated in these decisions. Personal insult and injury, family disputes, right of venue, damage to and theft of property, and failure to fulfill labor contracts were the most frequent cases taken before the peasant judges. According to law, sentences could include community work up to six days, a fine of up to three rubles, arrest and imprisonment of up to seven days, and a maximum of twenty lashes with birch switches. Many considered the inclusion of this institution in the Emancipation Edict to have been one of the most pragmatic and wise elements of the Reform.[27] These were clearly matters better decided by the peasants themselves, especially in light of the right of appeal which plaintiffs gained in 1866 through a law providing that anyone who believed the verdict of a case decided before the *volost'* court had been illegal could appeal to the local justice of the peace.

The *volost'* court as it was designed in 1861 was itself based on the system of justice established for state peasants through the Kiselev Reforms in 1837–1839. When members of the Editing Commissions turned to the question of rural justice, they had the model of Kiselev's program as an important precedent for rural administration and justice. N. M. Druzhinin has convincingly demonstrated that they followed Kiselev's lead in many areas, including the system of justice for state peasants.[28] The reformers took special care to make a sharp separation between the judicial and administrative spheres of government and set as their goal the "establishment in a peasant instance of a separate, independent court."[29] They viewed the *volost'* court as a temporary solution to the problem of rural justice: they hoped it would begin the process of educating the peasants in the principles of formal legality but recognized that a review would be necessary after five or ten years.[30]

It was against this backdrop that the government took up the question of reviewing and possibly reforming the *volost'* court in 1872. In the search for the peasant soul, the state-sponsored Commission on the Reform of the *Volost'* Courts of 1872 served as a catalyst by providing valuable material on village culture and provoking widespread debate on the larger question of the legal consciousness of the Russian peasant. The commission's method, as well as the specificity of its questions, contrasted sharply with the efforts of the 1860s and the hopeful, naïve approach of the Populists, and thus added an important dimension of objectivity to the discussion of the peasant question. The commission was made up of six men, chaired by Senator M. N. Liuboshchinskii, who investigated the position of the courts in fifteen provinces, interviewing the peasant judges, *volost'* clerks, and local administrators, as well as inhabitants of the *volost'*. They also examined court records and attended as many court sessions as possible.[31] In 1873, the seven volumes of data began to appear, thus making available thousands of pages of material fresh from the village to anyone interested in popular justice, the *volost'* court, and rural culture in general. The central question for the state was whether the *volost'* court was a viable institution, which implied the question of the peasant's ability to execute justice.

Members of society, observing the commission's work, were interested in the second question and devoted considerable attention to the peasant's concepts of legality, of property, of right and wrong, of innocence and guilt. Members of the legal profession, ethnographers, and contributors to major journals hotly debated this evidence on the peasant mentality. After the publication of the results of the commission's work in 1873 and 1874, a diverse body of material appeared on the subject, including journal articles, monographs, editorials, eyewitness accounts of peasant justice, and literary sketches. The Russian public was treated to various vignettes of the peasant judge, as well as to weighty analytical tomes which sought to present a clear view of how the peasant's legal reasoning functioned.

Questions revolved around the peasant as an agent of justice in his community. What was the level of development of the peasant's legal consciousness—indeed, did he have legal consciousness? Could one discern principles of legal behavior among the peasants? If so, what shaped the peasant's concepts of justice and how were they made manifest in his resolution of disputes? Finally, what relationship existed between formal law and customary law, and did the peasant comprehend and respect the principles of formal law?

The various responses to these questions offered images of the peasant that would replace the vague concept of the *narod*. Educated society began to feel confident of their newfound knowledge of the peasantry, based on the study of one aspect of rural culture. As sharper images came into view, there seemed to be no excuse for generalized, idealized concepts of the *narod*. Instead, alternative definitions of the peasant took shape, based on the various interpretations of the peasant's legal consciousness that raw data, analytical reviews, eyewitness accounts, and literary portrayal introduced to the reading public. Each image of the peasant as judge identified a critical aspect or relationship in the peasant's rural, agricultural existence. Contradictions within village culture, in turn, invited contradictory interpretations of the peasant's legal mentality. The result for the larger debate over the peasant soul was a set of highly contested images, each one resting on a claim of objective research and experience in the countryside.

The Peasant Judge as Rational Actor

When members of the reform commission asked peasant judges who served on the *volost'* court how they reached a verdict, the peasants rarely cited any code or system of law. Instead, they responded that they decided "according to the man," "according to conscience," "according to fairness," "according to the circumstances," or "so that no one will be insulted."[32] This pattern of responses prompted the conclusion that the peasant had no legal consciousness, no *pravosoznanie,* which for most observers meant understanding of and respect for formal law as a system of consistent legal norms. This definition of legal consciousness and the denial of its existence among the peasants had two implications. The first was that consciousness of the law implied law as the system that served and protected the social and political order of the state. Law was the codified law, not abstract law as justice. The second was that to say that peasants lacked consciousness in this arena meant that they lacked reason, that most basic of faculties signifying humanity and maturity. To state that the peasants lacked legal consciousness thus suggested that they stood both outside the state and outside mature humanity, or civilization.

Some observers and scholars refused to accept the view that the peasant had no legal consciousness and turned instead to analysis of published materials on the courts, determined to sort out the principles hidden there. Through a thorough reading of transcripts of the trials and of court records filed with the *volost'* administration, these authors were able to discern patterns of logic and verdicts which revealed that the peasant was, in fact, a rational judge. Whereas critics of the courts accepted the peasant's denial of legal principles, such scholars as S. V. Pakhman explained that the peasants clearly operated according to traditional principles but were unable consciously to separate the principles they followed in deciding legal disputes from the general principles of daily life.[33] The popular mentality in regard to issues of justice was thus tightly interwoven into the whole cloth of village culture. The inability to extract their approach to settling disputes from that fabric had prevented the peasants from understanding the question of the commissioners, Pakhman argued. He went so far as to say that he found many instances that indicated a "relatively high development of legal consciousness" among the peasants, while admitting there were also instances that reflected the absence of legal consciousness.[34] Whereas many St. Petersburg and Moscow experts evaluated the *volost'* judge according to his comprehension of formal law, defenders of the system rightly reminded their readers that the peasant court was designed to allow for justice according to peasant tradition, and that the divergence between peasant legal traditions and formal legal conditions did not render peasant law useless or nonsensical. In fact, peasant law made perfect sense for peasants and could do the same for the careful student of the evidence. They were issuing an important instruction on how to approach the study of the peasant. From their perspective, preconceived notions about the law, legality, and justice among educated observers were likely to obscure their vision of how the peasant viewed these issues. If the problem was the peasant and the law, then one should begin with the peasants as the critical factor, not the law.

P. P. Chubinskii voiced the conclusion of this group in his independent study of the *volost'* courts in the southwest. He argued, "The general characteristic of peasant customary law is that it serves as an expression not of formal, but of material law," being shaped by the economic structure and by moral and religious concepts.[35] Of these three factors, the economic order, or material circumstances, was most influential. To demonstrate that the peasant judge was a rational judge whose decisions followed identifiable principles and whose behavior in disputes was comprehensible to legal scholars as well, both Pakhman and Chubinskii organized their studies around categories familiar to the educated reader: civil and criminal law, contract law, personal injury, family law, inheritance law, and property law. They thus imposed the categories of formal law on their evidence in an effort to define the logic of customary law. By grouping related cases under these divisions, they were able to document patterns of consistent reasoning and behavior. When we look at their analysis of cases which they assigned to the categories of property and contracts, their approach as well as the strength of their conclusions becomes clear.

Educated observers interested in developing a truly national system of law concentrated on the issues of contracts and property in the peasant mentality for two reasons. The first was that these were the areas in which local gentry and peasants were most often in conflict, as landowners found themselves dependent on hired labor after the Emancipation and engaged in constant quarrels with the local peasants about poaching wood from forests assigned to the gentry as part of the Emancipation settlements.[36] The second was that respect for private property was the linchpin of the vision of legality held by liberals and reformers in general in their pursuit of a rule of law in Russia.[37] On both counts, there was widespread sentiment that the peasants were lawless and incapable of comprehending the law because they failed to respect laws that would have protected gentry interests. They were willful children, at best, and anarchists at worst. Even the liberal K. D. Kavelin, a voice of measured concern for seeking solutions to Russia's ills, exploded in a diatribe against the peasants on his estate in 1873, calling them terrible workers, lazy drunkards, careless and dishonest petty thieves.[38]

Pakhman addressed these concerns by saying that there was ample evidence in the *volost'* court records that the concept of private property was, in fact, "not alien" to the Russian peasant, who had a strong sense of "mine" and "yours."[39] He pointed to the numerous disputes over land and property brought before the court to support this claim. Concrete evidence of the peasant's perception that certain things were his private property took the form of brands and marks of ownership. Thus, a peasant would brand his livestock, mark his tools, and carve his sign on any trees that grew near the boundary between his plot of land and his neighbor's.[40] Chubinskii described several cases involving theft of honey, grain, or seed, in which the guilty peasant had to compensate the injured party fully for his loss and often had to pay a fine as well.[41] The weight of the materials presented by

Pakhman and Chubinskii supported the prevalence in the village of strong notions of property and established systems for its protection.[42]

Another common complaint of landowners about the peasantry was the failure to fulfill labor contracts, and by extension the lack of comprehension of contracts and legal obligations in general. Here too the rebuttal to this claim could be found in the records of the *volost'* courts, whose strict dealings and severe penalties for peasants who failed to fulfill their end of a deal indicated how seriously they viewed these obligations when they were taken on between peasants.[43] Pakhman argued that the general principle behind all bargains, deals, and contracts among the peasants was that every such agreement—properly made—obligated the parties involved to fulfill it.[44] From the testimony and evidence presented during *volost'* court sessions, he was able to determine the following limitations on deal making in the village. First, all contracting parties had to be of sound mind when the agreement was made for it to be considered valid.[45] This principle invalidated any bargains struck when one of the parties was drunk, overcome by grief, or in so much distress that he could justifiably claim that he had not been thinking clearly. Any element of force or deception also invalidated a bargain. Only adults could enter agreements involving loans or exchange of property.[46]

The penalties for failing to fulfill a contract were severe and consistent. Because labor disputes were the source of much gentry criticism of the peasant's attitude toward legal agreements, Pakhman's analysis of these was relevant and detailed. The peasants required strict adherence to the terms of the contract, with the broad limitation of "no substitutions allowed." A worker had to do the job defined by the agreement and no other.[47] Similarly, the peasant who made the agreement had to fulfill it himself. He could not send a brother or son to do the work for which he had contracted his time.[48] Should the worker cause any damage through negligence to the property of the person who hired him, he had to pay the full cost of any losses. If the peasant had agreed to a certain number of days' labor, he had to work the full number. Absence due to illness did not lessen the total obligation, which had to be met after his recovery. Finally, the *volost'* court heavily fined peasants who left one job before completing it to take on another one for higher pay.[49] By presenting these principles of peasant adjudication, Pakhman was declaring that the peasant did have a legal consciousness because he had a reasoned approach to disputes and that that approach served the interests and stability of the peasants who employed it.

One aspect of sentencing contributed to the view of the peasant as a fair and rational judge: concern for the household or communitywide repercussions of a penalty. Of the sentences available to the judges, fines and beating were the most popular, while imprisonment and community work

were the most rare. Because labor and labor time were the peasant's most
valuable commodity, *volost'* judges were reluctant to impose penalties
which would deprive a man of his time in the field and, thus, possibly ruin
an entire growing season. Imprisonment usually was demanded only for
drunkenness and lasted for the two or three days a peasant needed to dry
out. Similarly, the schedule for payment of losses or fines took into account
the peasant's ability to pay and was not so strict as to imperil a household's
economy to the point of collapse.

To many St. Petersburg and Moscow critics of the peasant judges, these
patterns of sentencing were evidence of the arbitrary, illegal, and primitive
nature of the peasant's approach to law. Of particular concern was the
frequency of corporal punishment as a sentence, especially when the guilty
party was a woman. The preference for flogging over fines and arrest pointed
to the peasant's bestiality, critics asserted, while their lax attitude toward the
fines imposed pointed to the ineffectual nature of peasant justice.

As Chubinskii had concluded, however, these sentences were neither
"absurd" nor "unscrupulous."[50] Instead they reflected the material conditions of the Russian peasant's life, which shaped his conception of legality
as much as they shaped other aspects of his daily existence. In an approach
that would prove typical of the discourse over the peasant soul, Pakhman
and Chubinskii sought explanations of the peasant mentality in the external
conditions of his existence. The peasant was a rational actor within his
specific environment. This was an important shift away from the focus on
the inherent nature of the peasant as a member of the *narod* and was
similar to the discovery that the Populist radicals had made in their experience in the village. The physical, economic, and social environment of the
village was what shaped the peasant soul or specifically the peasants' attitude toward disputes, crimes, and punishments, concluded Pakhman and
Chubinskii. Whereas in the codified laws of the Empire educated society
preferred confining transgressors or extracting payment from them to ensure the stability and security of the society, the peasants had their own
distinct concerns. For them, stability and security in the community depended more basically on agricultural production, on the ability of each
member of the community to provide for himself and his family. Rulings
and sentencing in the peasant courts would thus serve those aims. The
peasant's milieu had its own logic, its own rationale, these observers argued, and peasants understood that logic. Thus, they might not seem to be
lawful citizens to gentry observers, but they were rational actors within
their own environment.

Two things were happening here. First, in fashioning an image of the
peasant as a rational actor within his environment, these authors moved
away from moral or spiritual emphases in defining the peasant soul and
toward an analysis of the culture that shaped the peasant. Second, despite

Pakhman's efforts to frame this conclusion in the application of the principles in codified laws to customary practices, the effect of stressing the distinct environment and thus the distinct legal logic was to reaffirm the separateness of the worlds of peasant and educated society.

The Peasant Judge as Communal Actor

Other supporters of the *volost'* court were not so quick to ascribe the principles of formal to customary law. For these students of village justice, the first, crucial principle of discussion was the recognition of a basic distinction between formal or written law and peasant customary law. Whereas Pakhman and Chubinskii concentrated on concepts of formal law which were "not alien" to the peasant's legal consciousness, such scholars as I. G. Orshanskii emphasized elements which were "foreign to written law."[51] Thus, whereas the former had organized their studies according to categories of formal law, Orshanskii divided his into comparisons of customary and formal law on important issues. Drawing heavily on the report of the commission, he emphasized the disparities rather than the similarities in the principles of formal and customary legal consciousness which he detected in the records and transcripts of court proceedings.

Orshanskii argued that the central distinction between customary law and formal law was that in the latter the individual was the legal entity around which the legal system revolved, whereas in the former legal concepts subordinated the individual to either the family or the commune. He supported this view through analysis of the concept of property in the village. He argued that here private property meant family property, as could be seen in disputes over inheritance.[52] This principle was also evident in the area of contracts: frequently, he explained, a family would find that it was responsible for a debt that one member of the family made.[53] Finally, the formal code stated that a person above the age of eighteen was responsible for his actions and could not be represented at the court by his parents; in peasant practice, the custom was for the head of the household to be its representative in any dispute involving a family member.[54] Orshanskii concluded, "In rural life, every peasant looks at himself primarily and before all else as a member of the commune, and then as an independent person. . . ."[55]

In addition to emphasis on the group rather than the individual, the other noteworthy features of the peasant's legal consciousness in Orshanskii's analysis were his aversion to judging a case according to abstract principles and the seriousness with which he viewed breach of contract. On the first, Orshanskii found that the peasant judged cases less according to the evidence before him than according to his and the community's long-

standing acquaintance with the accused: "according to the man." The verdict depended more on the whole man as the commune knew him than on
the case as it had occurred.[56] This did not signify, however, that peasants
took wrongdoing lightly. On the contrary, Orshanskii asserted, it was striking to observe the honesty and responsibility of the "simple people"
(*prostoliudie*) in matters pertaining to contracts. Even when the terms of a
contract may have seemed onerous, if it had been properly made, the
volost' court called for full execution of its terms with the stated purpose of
serving as an example of the importance of fulfilling one's obligation.[57]

Orshanskii was winding his way to the conclusion that the realm of
peasant justice was that of a separate culture, a culture that revealed moral
strength in its insistence on community concerns and an approach to the
law that was not hampered by impersonal formalism. This notion was taken
up by other individuals who went a step further to argue that peasant legal
consciousness was a manifestation of a culture which not only differed from
that which shaped the formal code but also reflected a true Russian culture
that provided valuable principles, worthy of imitation in the formal code
because of their special moral virtues.

The most famous advocate of this viewpoint was Aleksandra Efimenko,
whose writings on peasant culture and legal consciousness throughout the
1870s and 1880s were so popular that one reviewer wrote in 1884, "We are
sure that there is no educated person in Russia who is interested in the fate
of the peasant who would not know the name of Mme. Efimenko."[58] From
the first page of her collected articles, *Research on the People's Life,*
Efimenko made her position clear by referring to customary law as natural
(*estestvennoe*) law and formal law as artificial (*iskusstvennoe*) law.[59] The
two were distinct phenomena, in her view, and the peasant's legal consciousness reflected his distance from the world of the educated, Westernized elements of society. She criticized Pakhman's approach directly, saying
that his effort to systematize customary law according to the tenets of
formal judicial theory was fruitless, given the complete separation of the
underlying concepts.[60] She argued that the "natural norms of the *narod,*
their customary legal perceptions, were the result of all social factors and
especially economic factors."[61] Because legal consciousness was so much a
product of the material conditions of the rural milieu, it was clear that any
analysis of the peasant judge had to be set in the context of his environment, not in the framework of formal legal theory.

As had Orshanskii, Efimenko pointed to the communal element in
peasant consciousness as the distinctive feature of customary law. She described the public rituals which peasants required for solemnization of
bargains and contracts: handshakes, public exchange of money and goods,
community observance of public statement of the terms of the agreement,
joint prayers and toasts.[62] She also emphasized the social, communal na-

ture of the wedding ceremony as a reflection of the peasant's view that recognition by the community of the marriage was more important than its recognition by the Church.[63]

Efimenko equally stressed the natural native aspect of peasant law, and the superior morality it represented. Although she agreed with Orshanskii's emphasis on collectivism as one feature that set the peasant legal mind apart from the educated legal mind, she found that the crucial distinction lay elsewhere. In terms reminiscent of the Slavophiles, especially Kireevskii, she identified natural Russian law as highly subjective in contrast to the abstract and objective Roman law adopted from Byzantium and Western Europe by the educated classes. The retention of "the pure form of legal subjectivism" distinguished the peasant's legal consciousness and made it a proper source of inspiration for legal reform.[64] The moral code of the community, expressed by members of that community, was preferable to any abstract alien code of law. Efimenko placed particular stress on the importance of labor in shaping the peasant's worldview and family and social structures. Collectivism and subjectivism both stemmed from the common ground of the labor principle which pervaded the peasant's daily life as a member of various laboring units, from the married pair through the extended family to the village to the commune itself. The peasant judge of Orshanskii's and Efimenko's analysis was thus a product of a separate, communal culture, the truly Russian culture which had retained the native principles of the *narod* as distinct from Westernized, formally educated society. In the context of the debate over the *volost'* court, these special qualities of peasant judges made them more suitable to decide local community disputes than representatives of the formal judicial system. Orshanskii and Efimenko diverged from those who employed the image of the *narod* in their emphasis on the peasant's environment. Although they both used the term *narod,* their methods and conclusions about the primacy of environment, specifically the environment of communal institutions in rural agricultural existence, distinguished their judge as a communal actor from the mass of the *narod.*

Victims and Strongmen at the *Volost'* court

In the chorus of voices proclaiming the peasant to be rational, communal, Russian, and just, there arose dissonant notes of extreme skepticism and brutal criticism of the peasant's ability to judge. To some extent these views had encouraged the state's review of the *volost'* court in the first place, but charges from the city found unexpected support in eyewitness accounts by observers in the village. The central theme of criticism was that the peasant judge was too frequently overwhelmed by evil influences, that he was vulnerable to the temptations of the bottle, the threats of the village strong-man, the machinations of a clever state clerk, or the momentary impressions of a given case. Critics infantilized the peasant and were thus able to call for the protection of the peasants from themselves by representatives of the educated classes in the form of the justice of the peace. When outsiders depicted the peasant judge as corrupted by wealthy and manipulative peasants in the village, they imposed a scheme which divided the rural community into victims and strongmen, exploiters and exploited, a scheme that spelled failure for any attempt to use a peasant-run court as a channel for raising the legal consciousness of peasantry. They also offered strong negative images of the two partners in that relationship: the peasant as exploiter and the peasant as victim.

The eyewitness accounts discussed here came from men who served in the village legal system either as *volost'* clerks, rural lawyers, or as justices of the peace. Their personal experience made them authoritative voices in the debate, which in turn meant that their forceful criticism made their descriptions of village justice that much more damning. Also, it is worth remembering that these figures, unlike Pakhman, Chubinskii, Orshanskii, or Efimenko, went to the village with some goal, some purpose related to the functioning of rural institutions of justice and the education of the peasantry in the practices of law. As frustrated reformers or enlighteners, they looked for culprits in their failed enterprise.

As early as 1872, the view of the peasant judge as an immature individual in need of protection from himself and his peers found expression in a series of articles by V. N. Nazar'ev, a justice of the peace in the Volga region, who wrote about his experiences for the liberal journal *Herald of Europe.* Between 1872 and 1880, he offered a dim vision of rural Russia and its inhabitants. He stated early on that the level of their comprehension was strikingly low: "I looked around, looked attentively, and I had no more doubt that I was surrounded not by adults, but children who did not understand anything. . . . On everyone's face I saw signs of childishness, all were children's faces, only with black, red, and even grey beards."[65] On the question of the peasant's views of property, he repeated this image: "The naïveté of our peasant knows no bounds."[66] During his tenure in the countryside, Nazar'ev was consistently impressed by the distance between his concepts of justice and those of the peasants he served. The longer he stayed in the village, the bleaker rural Russia seemed to him. He concluded that the few rays of light penetrating the backwoods could not compete with the weight of ignorance and intellectual and moral immaturity of peasants, which stymied the efforts of those who sought to enlighten them. By 1879, he characterized the experiment in peasant institutions after the Reform as having passed through its spring and summer, then deteriorated in the chill autumn when every day grew darker and darker. In 1880, he would write that to live in the rural backwoods was "pure death" for anyone who hoped to improve life there.[67]

Another exponent of the image of the weak peasant judge was V. S. Krotkov, who served as a rural lawyer and reported his impressions in *Notes of the Fatherland* in 1873. He found court sessions to be scenes of incredible confusion where peasants would scream and shout before the judges, while several arguments took place at the back of the room.[68] He asserted that law had no function in these courts, where the bribe and the bottle decided every dispute. During one session he reminded the judges that there were laws by which they had to abide and was met by the response of one peasant, who shouted in the statement chosen as one of the epigraphs for this chapter, "Laws! With us there is one law—vodka. Whoever brings the most will be judged in the right. Whoever is related to the elder or judges—he gets the decision. That's what kind our judges are."[69] Krotkov himself observed that the winning party always took the elder or the judges next door to the tavern after the proceedings. He also described a scene in which a peasant woman threw herself on her knees before the judges after she lost a case, crying that she had paid one of the judges ten rubles to be sure that she won.[70]

Contributors to *The Juridical Herald,* many of them jurists and jealous defenders of the formal judicial system, were especially vehement in decrying the abuses of the law at the *volost'* court. One such author in 1873 dismissed the value of the *volost'* courts as an "outstanding example of what illiterate and ignorant judges can make out of the court."[71] General criticism included the opinion that the courts "only exist nominally, that all of the peasants' cases are decided by drunken clerks or uneducated elders who have unlimited influence over the *volost'* judges. . . ."[72] In the report of the Liuboshchinskii Commission, statements from local government administrators usually opened with an assessment of the independence of the peasant judges and an explanation of their vulnerability to manipulation and bribery. The majority of respondents asserted that, indeed, peasant judges rarely were able to decide the cases before them without taking village politics into consideration or were unwilling to pass judgment without adequate lubrication of the wheels of customary justice.[73]

N. Astyrev, who served as a *volost'* clerk in the Voronezh region, reported similar conclusions in 1885. In his depiction of life in Kochetov, he identified the forces of obstruction with wealthy or simply powerful peasants in the village who were able to control politics and justice in the community by intimidating the peasants who depended on them in one way or another.[74] Astyrev thus made explicit what other critics implied: the critical question in the functioning of the *volost'* court and peasant justice in general was not whether the peasant judge was rational or communal in his thinking but whether he was a weak or powerful figure in the community, whether he was a victim or a strongman.

Women at the Court: An Early Glimpse of the *Baba*

The discussion of peasants as judges, as agents of justice in the village, necessarily focused on male peasants, because only they served on the *volost'* court and it was also they who largely controlled such other institutions of justice as the village assembly, the court of elders, and the court of neighbors.[75] In the debate over the legal consciousness of the Russian peasant, institutional and social reality encouraged the already gendered assumption that the question, Who is the Russian peasant?, really meant, Who is the Russian *male* peasant? Debates over the jury system and the *volost'* court did little to bring peasant women into the discourse. They were a part of the scene, however, as plaintiffs at the court. Their presence before the court did not capture the attention of most outsiders engaged in the definition of the peasant as judge, but the cases they brought introduced issues about peasant family life that would soon explode into a full-blown separate debate about the breakup of extended patriarchal households. These cases have been the subject of a separate study by Beatrice Brodsky Farnsworth.[76] The title of Farnsworth's article points to two of the crucial images of the Russian peasant woman in the post-Emancipation era, the victim or the shrew, who, in either form, was likely to come to the attention of outsiders as a disruptive influence in rural life. Farnsworth's article examines the position of daughters-in-law in the peasant family through a study of court decisions reported by the Liuboshchinskii Commission. She herself refers to the dual image of the daughter-in-law in folk wisdom and in observations of educated outsiders as the "dissatisfied troublemaker or invariable victim,"[77] a dualism that extended to all peasant women in the discourse on the peasant question. Her conclusion is that indeed "the daughter-in-law was the most litigious member of the family."[78] The complaints that brought her to the *volost'* court, after presumably exhausting the other informal courts at her disposal, predominantly involved property disputes with or abuse by her in-laws. In some cases, she was the defendant, brought to court by a father-in-law who complained of her insubordination. The picture of peasant family life available to educated Russia through the Liuboshchinskii Commission report was one of discord and tension whirling around the figure of the daughter-in-law. Investigations into the functioning of rural justice provided information about the peasant woman, but it was not put to great use within the debate about the peasant's legal consciousness. No images of the peasant woman took shape here. She was simply not a part of this agenda. Her images would be defined against a different backdrop, a different "crisis" in cultural definition, when outsiders confronted the reality of patriarchy in family structures in the village.

Conclusion

The debate about the *volost'* court thus altered the nature of discussion of the Russian peasantry, served as a catalyst for the study of village culture, and suggested the images of the peasant that would dominate public opinion for a generation. Whereas the image of the *narod* had held firm in the early debates over the peasants as jurors, the *volost'* court debate provided realistic empirical alternatives to the nebulous ideal. The Liuboshchinskii Commission established a precedent in its effort to examine a broad sample of regions in the Empire; to provide raw, unmediated data in the transcripts of court cases, interviews with peasants, and copies of court records; and to collect statistics on the economy of the districts visited. Expeditions such as Chubinskii's and studies such as Efimenko's added to the gathering store of knowledge of village culture based on study of peasant institutions. Vague opining from the city had no legitimacy in this debate nor would it henceforth in the general discussion of the "peasant question."

Anyone who wanted to discuss the peasant had to demonstrate study of the peasant and his world. Eyewitness accounts such as Nazar'ev's and Astyrev's soon filled the pages of Russia's serious journals, proclaiming the worth of their personal observations over a long period of time. And in literature, the insistence on demonstrable knowledge of reality as the source of literary inspiration would be a sine qua non until the late 1880s. In an atmosphere of fidelity to the principles of science, the *volost'* court debate satisfied the requirements of empiricism, objectivity, and realism. The images of the peasant it generated therefore held all the more force in a discussion where the *paysan* had been banned and the Russian peasant had been drawn onto center stage to be examined under the spotlight of determined, scientific inquiry. Finally, through the development of the competing images of the peasant as a legal actor, the importance of setting had been established. Whereas the *narod* had been a dark and silent mass defined by its separateness from educated society, the peasant images constructed to illustrate legal consciousness in the village depended on the environment. As they took fuller form over the next decade, these images would be ever more firmly placed in their environment with the effect of distancing them further from the educated society who had so eagerly sought rapprochement with them in a united nation.

4

The Peasant as Rational Man
of the Land

Thus, for the agriculturalist there is not a step, not a move, not a thought which does not belong to the land. He is completely harnessed to this bit of green grass. It is so impossible for him to tear himself away to go anywhere else to get out from under the yoke of this dominion that when he is asked, "What do you want, jail or the rod?", he always prefers to be flogged, he prefers to endure physical torture if only to be free immediately, because his master, the land, will not wait: he must mow—the livestock need hay, the lands needs the livestock. And it is in this constant dependency, in this mass of burdens under which the man cannot move an inch on his own, it is also here that the unusual *ease* of existence lies, thanks to which the peasant . . . can say, "Moist Mother Earth *loves* me."

G. I. USPENSKII, *The Power of the Earth*

At the same time that public debate over the nature of the peasants' legal consciousness was generating a shift in images and approaches, two authors were constructing a powerful image of the peasant as a rational actor in the physical setting of agricultural labor on the Russian soil in the Russian climate. Whereas the debate over the peasant's legal mentality had emerged in large part from educated society's concepts of the law and justice and from their ambitions regarding the role law could play in the countryside, the image of the peasant as rational agriculturalist took shape primarily within the context of the village itself through the personal experiences of Engelgardt and Uspenskii. It was an image which resulted more than any other from focus on the material culture of the peasants' existence; which was presented as the product of empirical, objective observation; which drew directly on the model of biological processes developed by Darwin; and

76

which incorporated answers to some of the most persistent questions about the future of agriculture and peasant farming in Russia. This combination of qualities inhering in the image, as well as the publication history of the writings which created it, ensured that the peasant as rational agriculturalist would be the new core or master image which displaced the image of the *narod*. It marked a major step toward exclusive concern with the economic aspects of rural life and an environmental, rather than essentialist, definition of the peasant. Even so, within this image as well, moral concerns intruded and moral judgments were made, reflecting the fact that this image issued from the search for the peasant soul.

The two major proponents of this definition of the Russian peasant were Aleksandr Nikolaevich Engelgardt and Gleb Ivanovich Uspenskii, the former a chemical agronomist turned farmer, the latter a writer turned amateur sociologist. In their description of the peasant, they set him firmly on the soil, exclusively in the context of agriculture and the constraints of living on the Russian land in the Russian climate. The Russian peasant, they declared, was a man constantly engaged in a contest with the land and nature, a contest for survival which in turn shaped all of his thoughts, actions, and values. To understand and approach the Russian peasant, therefore, one had to penetrate the primary relationship of man and earth in the rural world.

Engelgardt's and Uspenskii's writings represented the best and most influential of their respective genres: the eyewitness account and the sketch. Similarly, their approach to the village was both typical and normative for their generation. Profoundly different in background, status, personality, and fate, these two men largely determined the discourse on the Russian peasant soul for nearly two decades.[1] The noble chemist in exile and the tormented, poverty-stricken writer offered their vision of the countryside and the peasantry to an audience in the city which witnessed their discoveries with excitement and anticipation of more to come. After 1877, their works appeared together in *Notes of the Fatherland,* where the editor M. E. Saltykov-Shchedrin, operated under the assumption that "[t]he peasant is the hero of our time" and thus the most compelling subject for prospective readers and subscribers to the journal.[2]

Both Engelgardt and Uspenskii wrote on the basis of personal knowledge of village life. Both declared loyalty to the principles of objectivity, empiricism, and realism. Both recognized the necessity of immersion in rural life. Engelgardt wrote from the perspective of the gentry farmer engaged in interdependent economic relations with the peasants of his area. Uspenskii wrote as an observer of peasant culture. Each brought intellectual and emotional predilections to the task, and each responded to the shock of confrontation with the reality of rural life in post-Emancipation Russia. Their descriptions of the peasant converged on the same image, presented in strikingly similar terms of struggle, subsistence, labor, and the logic of the peasant economy. These masters of the eyewitness account and the sketch, then, did not contest each other's image making but reinforced each other's texts in a potent combination of energies.

Aleksandr Nikolaevich Engelgardt: Intellect and Personality

Aleksandr Nikolaevich Engelgardt's contribution to the search for the peasant soul was a series of twelve letters, "From the Countryside," which appeared annually in the journal *Notes of the Fatherland* from 1872 to 1884, with a follow-up letter in 1887 in the liberal journal *Herald of Europe.* He wrote from his family estate, Batishchevo, in Smolensk Province, where he lived in internal exile from 1871 until his death in 1893. Engelgardt was a member of the landed nobility who had been a prominent member of the scientific community in St. Petersburg before his exile to Batishchevo. Educated at the Mikhailovskii Artillery School, he served from 1853 until 1866 as a caster at the St. Petersburg Arsenal. During those years, he maintained an active life outside his position, joining in the vibrant intellectual exchange of the capital and continuing to develop his scientific interests. Chemistry was picking up momentum as a national science in Russia, and Engelgardt was very much a part of this development.[3] He was a co-founder of Russia's first journal of chemistry, he opened the first private chemical laboratory in St. Petersburg, and he was involved in the founding of the Chemical Society at St. Petersburg University. In 1864, he began teaching part-time at the St. Petersburg Agricultural Institute as the first professor of chemistry there. In 1866, he left military service to become a full-time member of the faculty and to direct the institute's chemistry laboratory.[4] Engelgardt also delivered public lectures on recent developments in science, as well as publishing numerous articles popularizing scientific theories and methods.[5] Of these, two were particularly important as an indication of what his outlook and interests would be. In 1863, he published a review article on a translation of the work of Justus Liebig in organic chemistry.[6] Of Liebig's various contributions, his demonstration that plants depleted the soil of major elements and his advocacy of the use of mineral fertilizers had the most obvious impact on Engelgardt, who would eventually become the pioneer of phosphate fertilizer use in Russia. In this article, he juxtaposed farmers who farmed according to "rational" methods with those who farmed according to old habits and suggested that those who hoped for continued economic dependency of the peasants on local landlords fell into the latter group.[7] This theme would be central in his concerns as a farmer himself and as author of the letters "From the Countryside."

In 1864, he wrote a series of three articles on Darwin's theory of evolution after the publication of the Russian edition of *The Origin of Species.*[8] Here Engelgardt presented a synopsis of Darwin's theory of natural selection and stated his own position in favor of evolutionary theory rather than creationism. Engelgardt's letters from Batishchevo reveal the strong imprint that Darwin left on his worldview. He examined peasant culture with an eye for competition and mutual aid and explicitly described social arrangements in terms of natural selection. One can argue that his entire construct of the image of the rational peasant was based on an appreciation of adaptive mechanisms in a contest between man and nature that had enabled the Russian peasant to survive in his harsh environment. Engelgardt was typical of his generation in his quick interest in Darwin but atypical in his use of the Darwinian metaphor. As Daniel Todes explained for biologists and Alexander Vucinich for social thinkers generally, educated Russian society strongly resisted the concept of the struggle for existence in their early reception of Darwin.[9] Engelgardt, however, incorporated this concept into his description of life near Batishchevo. As we shall see, he recognized the centrality of the struggle against natural conditions in rural life, while ruefully admitting that competition was more prevalent than cooperation in the relations among peasants.

Engelgardt's two salient features were his scientific bent and his energetic optimism. It is clear from contemporary sources that he was a charismatic figure who drew people to himself and his interests through the strength of his intellect and the force of his personality. He was described as devoting his entire life to "the struggle against ignorance and prejudice" and of imposing "sober views of the countryside and the role of the educated man there."[10] His colleague at the Agricultural Institute P. A. Lachinov wrote to him in Batishchevo in 1881, "I have always marveled at your organizational skills: to propose some kind of enterprise, to excite the sympathy of society for it, to attract appropriate people, to make your views popular—you have always been a great master at this."[11] Engelgardt was not unaware of his magnetism and explained it thus: "The secret of my influence lies in the fact that I believe in myself and never doubt what I say."[12]

Engelgardt Enters the Rural Context

This self-confident, prominent St. Petersburg chemist wound up in the rural backwoods because of an indiscretion as rector of the institute. He was named rector in 1870 and was responsible in that capacity for student affairs as well as for matters of administration and curriculum. During his brief tenure, students met weekly on Saturday evenings for socializing and discussion of matters of common interest. Engelgardt was arrested in December 1870 because of the supposedly revolutionary character of those meetings. There are various explanations of the story, ranging from one student's contention that it was all a setup by an agent provocateur[13] to support for the government's case against the radical students, who were inadequately supervised by their rector.[14] In any event, after a month-long investigation, the government found Engelgardt the individual most responsible for the disorders at the institute and sentenced him to exile from St. Petersburg and all university cities in the Empire. He was also denied the right to travel abroad. He was, however, granted the privilege of choosing his place of residence beyond these restrictions. He chose Batishchevo, a neglected family estate in the Dorogobuzhskii District of Smolensk Province, which he had last visited fifteen years earlier. On January 23, 1871, he was notified of his dismissal from his position at the institute by the Ministry of State Domains, under whose jurisdiction it fell.[15] Shortly thereafter, he found himself settling into his new life as a practicing agronomist in the non–Black Earth Region of Russia, facing the self-imposed challenge of making a profitable enterprise of his long-neglected, half-empty, marginally productive fields and wastelands.

Engelgardt immediately began the process of penetrating the relationship of rural man and his natural environment and himself underwent a transformation from a socially active St. Petersburg intellectual to an isolated, financially constrained gentry farmer in Smolensk. In an experience that set the norm for observers of the peasantry, he increasingly assumed the habits of his peasant neighbors, lived as they did, dressed as they did, ate as they did, and for more than ten years viewed the business of farming from their perspective. He challenged his readers to meet his reversal of habits and viewpoint in order to get at the truth, as it were, about the countryside and the peasant. The record of that transformation took the form of his letters "From the Countryside," which the astute editor of *Notes of the Fatherland* proposed he write. In a letter of March 31, 1871, Saltykov-Shchedrin suggested that Engelgardt use his free time to describe rural life and gentry-peasant relations in an enterprise which would both serve the interests of the journal by offering fresh material on the peasant question and provide Engelgardt with some much-needed income.[16] In May 1872, the first letter appeared, opening with the lines, "You want me to write you about our rural way of life. I am fulfilling your request, but I warn you that I decisively cannot think, speak, or write about anything else but farming. All of my interests, all of the interests of the people I see daily, are focussed on firewood, grain, livestock, manure. . . . Nothing else matters to us."[17] With these lines, Engelgardt forced his readers into the material culture of the village, right down to the manure, and declared that that was what really mattered. It was an indication of the conclusions that would follow. After this opening, he launched into a powerful description of a typical winter day, February 5, 1872, one year into his life in Batishchevo. He both drew his readers into his experience and introduced the major questions and themes that would run throughout the rest of the series.

He conveyed the atmosphere of rural life and the setting of the peasant's existence most effectively by describing his own daily routine, his dress, diet, interests, tasks, and social interaction. He lived an isolated life, shaped primarily by the climate and the demands of farming. The deepest impressions during his first year were cold, poverty, and the need to alter the system of farming on his estate in order to survive, much less to prosper. His adoption of peasant dress was one example of his vulnerability to the climate.

> Having had my daydream and my cigarette, I put on my felt boots and sheepskin coat. My house is rather poor: when you heat up the stoves, it is impossibly hot by evening, by morning it is cold, there is a draft from under the floor, a draft from the door, the windows have frosted over; it is just like being in a peasant hut. At first, I wore a German suit, but I quickly came to the conclusion that would not do and began to wear felt boots and a sheepskin coat. They are warm and comfortable.[18]

More evocative and convincing, however, was his description of the pleasure of sitting out in the sun on a February day after four months of nearly total darkness.

> On practically the first clear, sunny day, everything comes alive and tries to make use of the life-giving light of the sun. At noon, when it begins to drip from the roof in the warmth, the chickens, ducks and all living things spill out into the yard to warm in the sun, the sparrows rush up and down there between the large birds and twitter gaily. The cow, driven out for watering, stops in the sun, blinks and warms herself. In the stall, all of the cattle push against the window which faces the sunny side. The bulls, sensing the approach of spring, bellow, grow angry and tear the manure with their feet. You seat yourself on the porch in your sheepskin coat, turning your face to the warm sunlight, you smoke, you dream. It is fine.[19]

His daily routine, like that of the peasants who worked on his estate, followed the cycle of the sun. Farming was an all-consuming, demanding occupation which required total commitment of Engelgardt and peasants nearby to eke out an existence in the harsh, miserly environment in which they lived. He did not become a peasant and did not pretend to, but he did claim new sensitivity to their physical environment and used that sensitivity to place the peasant in his material setting for his urban readers.

Engelgardt's Vision of the Peasant as Subsistence Farmer

The challenge of this stuggle and the fragility of the system which the rural population had developed through generations of labor emerged as central elements of his eyewitness account. In the first letter we find the outline of Engelgardt's vision of the peasant economy as a subsistence economy that functioned according to an internal logic or rationale. He stressed here the fragile equilibrium of subsistence and the constant presence of the spectre of hunger. Following the Darwinian metaphor, Engelgardt offered a graphic description of the struggle with the physical conditions of existence which pressed against his urban consciousness with special force. He also offered evidence of systems of mutual aid. His lengthy discussion of the custom of begging for crusts of bread in the village served to illustrate both the tenuous nature of the peasants' lives and a system that had evolved to protect each member from starvation.

He first forcefully explained to his urban readers that the peasants of his area constantly lived on the margin: "In our province, even in good harvest years, rare is the peasant who has enough of his own grain to last until the next season: almost everyone must buy grain, and those who have nothing with which to buy grain send their children, old men and old women to beg for crusts of bread around the community." He continued by describing the failed harvest of 1871 and the consequences for the peasant community. Most visible of these was the appearance of large numbers of peasants begging in the area.

> Everyday at the end of December, as many as thirty pairs would go about begging for crusts of bread; they would walk and ride, children, *babas*, old men, even healthy children and young married peasant women. Hunger will drive a man to anything; if he has not eaten, he is ready to sell his soul. . . . There is nothing to eat at home—do you understand this? Today they ate up the last loaf, out of which yesterday they gave crusts to people who came by begging, they ate it and went out into the commune.[20]

When a peasant went begging in this way, he or she would go to a neighbor's house and stand quietly while the mistress of the household cut off a piece of bread. These pieces of bread were collected in a sack and dried out at home to serve as the staple of the diet for the remainder of the winter. Any household that still had bread was obligated to give to those begging; to do otherwise was considered a sin. Unlike an earlier observer, Skaldin (Elenev), Engelgardt neither glorified nor romanticized this custom; he scrupulously avoided the temptation to attribute a special or superior communal morality to the peasants.[21] Rather, he presented this custom as a pragmatic response to an ugly reality. Each peasant offered the starving man a crust from his store because he was aware that it might soon be his lot to seek similar assistance. Loyal to the rule of reason himself, Engelgardt discerned the logic of rural ways that other observers would summon to fend off the model of struggle and define as the fruits of an exceptional, native Russian morality. For Engelgardt, in the struggle for existence begging for crusts of bread was an adaptive mechanism of the rural organism.

This was equally true of another rural tradition, that of doing work "out of respect." Such work consisted of unpaid labor on some special task, such as mending a bridge or bringing in and processing the garden produce, either for a local gentry landowner or for a peasant in the community. It resembled collective assistance in the form of work parties, which, like bees and barn raisings in the British and American experience, involved everyone in the community in a large farming or building job. Engelgardt explained that unpaid labor in such circumstances was the product of the peasant's calculated self-interest in his subsistence economy.

> Of course, this all happens because, even now, the peasant is always dependent on the neighboring landowner. The peasant needs a little firewood and a little meadow, and pasture, and sometimes he needs to lay his hands on a little money. . . . How can you not show respect to the nobleman just in case! And in the village, well, it is the same thing: everyone goes "out of respect" to the rich peasant to a work party because it just may happen that they will have to turn to him for help for one thing or another.[22]

Engelgardt thus dismissed the argument that systems of mutual aid in the village stemmed from collectivist impulses and consistently reminded his readers of the environmental factors that made cooperation an imperative rather than a gesture of unspoiled generosity. By identifying these systems as the rational product of conscious, logical decisions involving memory of the recent past and anticipation of potential hardship in the future, Engelgardt took them out of the realm of moral instinct and placed them in that of reason. Perhaps the fundamental motivation was the instinct for survival, but Engelgardt's stress in the image of the peasant taking shape from his pen was on learned behavior and reasoned employment of it.

Engelgardt's Vision of the Peasant's Farming Expertise

The practical knowledge of the Russian peasant in all areas of agronomy and animal husbandry was another example of adaptation in the struggle for existence. In a broader discourse over the appropriate system of agriculture in post-Emancipation Russia, Engelgardt defended two approaches.

One was his own fifteen-field rotation of grasses, grains, and fallow, with the use of artificial fertilizer. The other was the rational farming of the Russian peasant. For our purposes, his defense of the latter is the more important, for it generated the image of the peasant as a rational actor. Over the course of his first decade in the countryside, Engelgardt shed not only his German suit but his German training, and his expertise as a chemical agronomist trained in the school of Liebig and other German experts. He came increasingly to rely on the expertise of his peasants and on several occasions excoriated urban agronomists for their total inability to meet the needs of Russian farming. Although it is true that he would return to a more scientific approach to farming in 1883, concentrating then and for the remaining ten years of his life on experiments with phosphate fertilizers, his first decade as a practicing farmer produced in him profound respect for the abilities of the Russian peasant. His portrait of the capable Russian peasant farmer remained a legacy of his years on Batishchevo.

Engelgardt's positive peasant portraits contributed to his reputation as a Populist, for he consistently juxtaposed the pragmatic, natural Russian peasant with the impotent, artificial educated man of the city. He praised the activity of the peasant household and the benefits for peasant children of living in a home which was, in fact, "a kindergarten where all the children work happily and hard at useful tasks," in contrast to St. Petersburg children, who spent their days occupied with "meaningless games and . . . boring, sentimental songs." The peasant child's immersion in the activities of life and labor around him ensured that he was more observant and capable in several ways than his St. Petersburg peers. Engelgardt emphasized the superior counting ability of peasant children and their knowledge or arithmetic in general because they applied this knowledge in their daily lives. He went so far as to say that when he saw a St. Petersburg child in the village, it was possible "to think that he has neither ears, nor eyes, nor legs, nor hands."[23]

He remarked further on the peasant's memory, which he found nearly incredible, and grew to respect the peasant's ability to remember the details of every transaction in terms of time, money, and goods—a skill necessary to his survival.[24] Not only did the peasant remember the details of any given transaction; he also faithfully fulfilled any obligation he undertook, as long as the agreement was clear and both parties were fair. Or so was Engelgardt's observation. To some extent he explained this in terms of the peasant's fear of reprisal from other peasants or from the courts, which they perceived to be arbitrary and inconsistent in dealings of this kind. On the other hand, he stated that he found the peasant to be a very honest man, "in no way worse than people of the educated class."[25] Statements such as these, as well as his fond accounts of the peasants most closely attached to his household—the housekeeper Avdotia, the steward Ivan, the confectioner turned handyman Savelich, the "Old Woman" who ran the dining hall—identified Engelgardt as an advocate of the peasantry.

St. Petersburg and other urban readers of *Notes of the Fatherland* found more than biographical sketches in Engelgardt's letters. Their value lay in his careful analysis of peasant actions and attitudes and in his use of specific examples to support and illustrate his position on a number of the issues included in the search for the peasant soul. On the value of book learning in the village, he was painfully clear. Two years into his stay at Batishchevo, Engelgardt wrote what must be one of the most colorful diatribes ever written by a frustrated scientist trying to apply his academic training to the demands of real life. In the third letter, he confessed, "When I was leaving Petersburg, I took a multitude of books on agronomy; it seems that I have everything that has been published in this field in Russian; I subscribe to three agricultural journals . . . and would you believe that every time I turn to a book, in the end, the business ends with me tossing it under the table."[26] He went on to say that for all the scholarly information in every article and book, there was nothing of any practical use. He found that too many, if indeed not all of them, were based on German scholarship and offered solutions based on German rather than Russian conditions. This led him to conclude, "[R]eally, all of these books have been written by eunuchs."[27] The complete absence of practical knowledge and therefore of any applicable advice turned Engelgardt against the field of agronomy itself. "The study of agronomy in books, just like the study of chemistry or anatomy in books is onanism for the mind. . . . Pity him who begins to farm with the aid of these books; it is no accident that the view has developed among us that whoever farms 'according to agronomy' will be ruined."[28]

What books failed to give him, the peasants on and near Batishchevo did. His day began and ended with a talk with his steward, Ivan. With his housekeeper, Avdotia, he learned about home economics and dairy produce. He described the "Old Woman" as superior to any trained veterinarian in her care of the animals. From members of diggers' cooperatives he discovered the basics of the relationship between nutrition and hard labor.

Throughout the text of Engelgardt's letters, the steward Ivan appears as an advisor and partner. In the daily journal that he kept from April 1871, the frequent appearance of the phrase "Ivan says" attests to the fact that landowner and steward worked in the closest possible consultation and that Ivan was the authority on many matters.[29] In the fourth letter in the series, Engelgardt describes his trip to visit an agricultural exhibition in his province, where one of his hired hands, Sidor, serves as his interpreter and guide, dubiously viewing the profitability of looking for expertise in what does indeed prove to be a most disappointing exercise. At the exhibition, the collection of livestock and produce is small, unimpressive, and uninformative. Here, as in his books on agronomy, Engelgardt is reminded again that the practicing farmer, namely the Russian peasant, has more to offer than any specialist or society of agriculturalists.[30]

In the seventh letter, Engelgardt devotes more than twenty pages to an analysis of the diet of the peasants and their conscious, rational selection of foods which varied according to the nature of the work they were doing. He took this lesson from a group of diggers who were working on his land and eating a monotonous diet of potatoes. When he asked them why they limited themselves in this way, they replied, "Well, there is no reason to eat any better when you are working by the day." If they were working by the job through piecework, on the other hand, they would eat cabbage soup with ham and buckwheat, "hearty, solid food." To Engelgardt's amazed request for an explanation, the foreman replied:

> It's not worth it for us to eat well now when we are working by the day because it's all the same how much we get done, the salary's the same, it's always the same forty-five kopeks a day. But if we were working by the job, if we were digging ditches, hauling dirt, that's a different matter: then it would be more profitable to do more, to earn seventy-five kopeks, a ruble a day, and this you can't earn on just potatoes. Then we would eat solid food—lard, kasha. Everyone knows that you'll work as well as you eat. If you eat potatoes, then you'll make potatoes, if you eat kasha, you'll make kasha.[31]

This revelation led Engelgardt to examine the peasant diet more closely, and as a chemist he could not resist an analysis of the scientific logic of the peasant's diet. He found that it ideally included vegetables, nitrogen substances, and something acidic or fermented at every meal. It rarely included meat, which, he observed, the peasants never ate during the heavy work of harvesting and always traded for vodka.[32] Here, as elsewhere, the peasant had adapted to the requirements of his labor; he had devised a system for survival.

In the care of animals, no one could compete with the "Old Woman" who oversaw the dining hall and the swine and poultry. In his first letter from Batishchevo, Engelgardt offered a long fond portrait of her ability to tend animals, to know their specific needs, to treat them appropriately when they fell ill, to maintain clean and orderly stalls, to fatten them up beyond reasonable expectations. She was a natural healer, eschewing medication in favor of poultices and caustics, fresh air and tenderness. In response to his herdsman's suggestion that the Old Woman had supernatural powers over the animals, Engelgardt replied, "The Old Woman simply 'understands animals', as the *muzhiks* say; she knows in detail their nature, she loves animals, she commands enormous experience, because she has lived among cows, sheep, swine, and hens for fifty years."[33] The key to the

Old Woman's skill was a life of practice, a life of intimate engagement in raising and healing farm animals.

In an era when specialists were calling for the practice of "rational agronomy" in Russia, when the term *rational farming* was applied almost exclusively to gentry farming, a use that Engelgardt had himself applied in 1863,[34] he took the term away from the gentry and gave it to the peasants, much as he advocated taking the land away from the gentry and giving it over to the peasants as well. Here was another reversal intended to shock and unsettle the complacent experts in St. Petersburg. In the public debate over rational agronomy in Russia, his chief opponent was Sergei Sharapov, the agricultural editor of I. S. Aksakov's Slavophile journal *Rus'* and, like Engelgardt, a St. Petersburg specialist who returned to his family estate in Smolensk to try to improve agriculture through the practice, in his case, of rational agronomy.[35] In the 1870s and 1880s, these two men engaged in a largely friendly debate in the press and in their private correspondence. On Engelgardt's death, Sharapov would deliver a most moving memorial eulogy in honor of his former intellectual sparring partner.[36]

During their tenures in the countryside, Sharapov and Engelgardt debated the respective roles of the gentry farmer and the peasant in the future of Russian agriculture. While Sharapov advocated improved gentry farming, Engelgardt consistently argued that there was no future for gentry farming, because it could succeed only if there were a stable force of unemployed, landless peasants to provide the hands to cultivate gentry lands. The final three letters in Engelgardt's series addressed this issue and declared that the land should go to those who worked it, the peasants. In a complex analysis of the mutual dependency of gentry and peasantry in post-Emancipation Russia, Engelgardt forcefully rejected the logic of gentry farming in its current system, described the peasants' ability to innovate when it served their self-interest, and finally returned to the topic of the need for artificial fertilizers in Russian farming. He explicitly stated that so-called rational gentry farming was rational only for the individual gentry farmer, but irrational for Russian agriculture overall as the backbone of the national economy.[37]

Engelgardt thus did not retreat from his belief in the abilities of the Russian peasant farmer. In 1878 he wrote to a student who had requested permission to study farming on Engelgardt's estate as part of a group of aspiring young Populists: "For practical study, the best book is the *muzhik*. Study with him, look at what he does, how he does it, try to learn what the *muzhik* knows. You will have to work very hard to learn what the *muzhik* knows, for he knows an awful lot."[38] Later, in 1882, he reiterated this faith in notes after conversations with Sharapov: "I believe in the *muzhik*, I believe in the fact that he is a real master, a real agronomist, capable of developing in farming matters."[39]

Engelgardt's Peasant as Master

In the same notes, Engelgardt returned to a theme that had resonated throughout the letters and would also dominate Gleb Uspenskii's image of the peasant: the contest between man and land, the relationship between the peasant and the soil, a relationship characterized both by the struggle for mastery and by intimate attachment. "It is essential that the land find her master. The land without a master is dead and infertile. . . . I say that it is desirable that the land go to the real master, to the *muzhik,* who will protect her, spare her, care for her as for his mother, wet-nurse, will love her, and the land will love her master."[40] In this fundamental aspect of the life of the peasant, the alternative to his mastery of the land was the land's mastery of him.[41] Not all peasants had what it took to survive in this struggle for existence.

For Engelgardt's peasant, "[t]o be a good farmer, it is necessary to love the land, to love farming, to love this manual, hard work," he wrote in the seventh letter of the series.[42] He observed that all peasants did not necessarily love either the land or the work and, in fact, found nothing interesting about it. Their roles in the village or household were usually as handymen; for this reason, it was they who suffered most by the division of the extended family into separate households. With neither affection for nor interest in farming, most of these peasants also lacked the ability to farm and lost the struggle with the land.[43] Never having absorbed the accumulated wisdom of the successful peasants, they fell behind in the effort to work their own land productively while paying off debts to others through labor elsewhere. "Finally, the land masters the *muzhik,* as the peasants say, and once the land becomes the master, it's all over."[44]

Engelgardt thus placed his peasants first and foremost in the setting of land and labor, in a struggle for existence against natural conditions. His urban sensitivities made him especially attuned to these conditions; his scientific worldview led him to examine causes, relationships, systems; his exposure to Darwin heightened his awareness of the questions of struggle and mutual aid. The peasant as rational agronomist was not Engelgardt's last word on the Russian peasant. On the contrary, his letters from Batishchevo would also contribute to the development of the image of the village strongman, the *kulak,* and the Russian peasant woman, the *baba.* The image of the peasant as man of the land represented Engelgardt's comprehension of the tenuous nature of rural life, of subsistence farming, and of the adaptive mechanisms that peasants had developed over centuries of living in the physical environment of Russia. This was his first, and perhaps his most profound, impression in his early years on Batishchevo. As he developed a more intimate acquaintance with village mores, he would increasingly apply the template of struggle to struggle between peasants, intraspecific struggle applied to the Russian village, and out of this struggle his images of the *kulak* and *baba* would emerge. In the discourse on the peasant soul, however, the image of the peasant as a rational actor was a major contribution to comprehension of the Russian village and the earliest image to emerge so thoroughly from a concentration on the material culture of the village. Engelgardt's careful, analytical construction of this image was reinforced by the forceful peasant portraits that appeared in the pages of *Notes of the Fatherland* in the form of rural sketches by Gleb Uspenskii.

Gleb Ivanovich Uspenskii: Intellect and Personality

Little known beyond Russia, Gleb Ivanovich Uspenskii was one of the central figures in Russian literary and journalistic activity of the 1870s and 1880s, admired from afar by provincial readers and beloved by most of his Moscow and St. Petersburg peers. The Jubilee Edition of his works was published in ten thousand copies in December 1888. Three thousand were sold in the first two weeks, the remaining seven thousand by August 1889.[45] As Uspenskii's reaction to the celebration of his twenty-fifth anniversary as a writer described in the opening pages of this book indicates, his was a completely different nature from Engelgardt's. Whereas Engelgardt was self-confident, energetic, and optimistic, Uspenskii was insecure, inconsistent, and prone to a pessimism so profound that it would eventually lead to a complete mental breakdown. Whereas Engelgardt wrote and spoke with the ascerbic wit of the privileged intellectual, Uspenskii was ever modest and dependent on the kindness of his friends and patrons. Although both men grew up in the provinces, moved to St. Petersburg for their higher education, and devoted a considerable portion of their lives to the study and description of the village, they were of different social classes and milieus. Combined, their writings formed the backbone of *Notes of the Fatherland* in the 1870s, yet their experiences as authors were diametrically opposed: Engelgardt's contributions were eagerly solicited while Uspenskii flooded the editorial offices with short pieces of writing in the effort to earn enough money to get by.[46] Despite Engelgardt's clear advantages, however, Uspenskii was his equal as an authoritative voice on the "peasant soul," and his writings on the village largely shaped the mood of public opinion on the peasant question for the decade 1875–1885.

Born in Tula into a family of civil servants, Uspenskii followed a predictable pattern for the son of a provincial bureaucrat. As a student in the gymnasium, he earned mediocre marks and spent most of his time reading current Russian authors. He was described by his family and peers as an overly sensitive but pleasant fellow. From gymnasium, he entered the university in St. Petersburg, where he registered in the departments of history and philology in 1861. His university career was to be short-lived, however, first, because of the closing of the university in December 1861, and, second, because of his loss of financial support at the unexpected death of his father in 1863.[47]

Unable to continue his studies, Uspenskii found work editing and typesetting a minor journal. A pattern began to emerge which would shape the rest of his life. Short on cash, he turned to friends for help. He began to write as a source of income; in 1863, his first piece, "Starevshchik," was published in *Reading Library.* Soon he developed the habit of requesting advances for planned works. By 1874, he owed the Populist poet and editor Nikolai Nekrasov, who was only one of many willing to help him, between three and four thousand rubles.[48] Uspenskii did not have a cavalier attitude toward these loans, however. In 1889, after the success of his Jubilee Edition, he apparently set to the task of clearing his debts. Thus, in the personal archive of A. N. Pypin, we find a letter accompanying twenty-five rubles as repayment for a loan dating to 1866. He urges Pypin not to think that he had accepted the loan lightly or ever forgotten it. He explains that he simply could not have repaid it any sooner and declares his gratitude for Pypin's early assistance of his efforts.[49]

During the 1860s, Uspenskii spent much of his time in the company of the *raznochintsy* writers, drawn into the group by his cousin, N. V. Uspenskii. Here he was introduced to the genre of the sketch and the subject of the peasant. He would eventually reject the hyperrealism, the naturalism, of the *raznochintsy* depictions of Russian society because he found that they lacked any clear views on "society, the *narod,* or the intelligentsia."[50] He did follow the example of the sketch as a genre by consciously developing a mixture of journalism, sociology, and fiction. He never produced a single great work to rival those of the leading lights of nineteenth-century Russian literature. The best-known and most complete of his efforts was *Vlast' zemli* (The Power of the Earth), to be analyzed in depth later. Otherwise, he produced a constant stream of short pieces on the basis of his observations of life around him. The sketch was both the quickest way for him to earn the money he always lacked and a reflection of his intellectual restlessness. He constantly sought new materials through life experience. This search took him as far away as Paris and London, to Bulgaria, and throughout the Russian Empire. So peripatetic was his existence that he never had his own desk but wrote on whatever table happened to be in the lodgings he rented. Clearly Uspenskii's intellectual and emotional restlessness and inability to settle down for the length of time needed to mature as a writer handicapped him and restricted the range of his works. Still, he left behind a series of short pieces which are precious in the immediacy with which they convey the world and interests of the author.[51]

Uspenskii's "peasant studies" were the product of his most creative years in the late seventies and early eighties. He moved to the countryside in 1877 after a disappointing trip to Paris. Like many Russian intellectuals of the nineteenth century, he was struck by the urban isolation of the individual in the West, which distressed him and provoked a crisis of insecurity. He returned to Russia and fled to the village with the hope that it would be an environment where the struggle for existence was carried out not in isolation but with the whole commune.[52] Thus he turned to the village with an expectation of some kind of moral superiority in its reputed collectivism and hoped to find his own "moral healing" there. This suggests that he was not initially inclined to focus on the material realities of rural life, but on the spiritual or moral mood of the village that would distinguish Russian culture from the excessively individualistic West. For the next five years, he would live in villages in Samara and Novgorod provinces and, like Engelgardt, penetrate the logic of the peasant economy as a first step in unraveling the mystery of the peasant soul. As an urban intellectual, Uspenskii would share Engelgardt's discovery of the physical challenges of rural life and the demands of labor on the land. Because of his personal experience of constantly living on the financial margin himself and of seeming always to be off balance, Uspenskii would also be especially sensitive to the restrictions of subsistence farming and the fragile equilibrium that characterized the peasant economy in its autarkic form.

Uspenskii's concept of the peasant as a man of the land took shape in the three major works of his peasant cycle, published between 1877 and 1883: *Iz derevenskogo dnevnika* (From a Village Diary), *Krest'ianin i krest'ianskii trud* (The Peasant and Peasant Labor), and *Vlast' zemli* (The Power of the Earth). In each of these works, the peasant as man of the land emerged full-blown in one central character who embodied all of the qualities and habits that Uspenskii attributed to the true Russian peasant as he understood him at that stage of his writing. Through his presentation of three Ivans—Ivan Afanas'ev, Ivan Ermolaevich, and Ivan Bosykh—he introduced the readers of *Notes of the Fatherland* to his Russian peasant.

Ivan Afanas'ev: Pure Man of the Land

Ivan Afanas'ev represented the authentic peasant of Uspenskii's early peasant writings in *From a Village Diary,* a series of nine sketches based on his experience in Novgorod Province between 1877 and 1880. He introduced this character as well as the major themes that would appear throughout his peasant cycle in the first sketch.

Ivan Afanas'ev is a rare example of "the peasant" (*krest'ianin*) in the full sense of the word, that is, a man who is irrevocably bound to the soil— mentally and spiritually. The land, in his understanding, is the real wet-nurse, the source of joy, sorrow, fortune and misfortune, of all his prayers and thanksgivings to God. Agricultural labor, agricultural concerns and joys could fill the entire internal world of Ivan Afanas'ev, not giving him the chance to think about exchanging agricultural labor for something else, for some other kind of more profitable work. Ivan Afanas'ev is not in love with the land, as it might appear to the reader . . . ; no, he is tied to the earth and to everything it goes through in the course of a year, tied like a man to his wife, in fact more closely, because they, really, live almost as one entity. But at the same time Ivan Afanas'ev is not "chained" to the land, no: agricultural land is good in that the relationship between the man and this land, this labor is not one of force, since the union grows pure from the pure, clearly visible good which the land gives the man, who is convinced without any force that for the good the land gives, it is necessary to please it, to care for it. It is on the basis of such pure, conscientious foundations that the entire practice of the true, unspoiled peasant family depends, and this family would be sincere and incomparably splendid if it could develop these foundations, that is, a free, natural union, based on the unwavering recognition that good begets good.[53]

Several elements enter into this definition of the peasant. A true peasant is bound to the earth in every aspect of his nature, not simply physically, through labor, but also through his intellect and his emotions. His bond to the land is, in fact, his primary relationship: more intimate than his bond to his wife and similar to that of a suckling babe to his mother. All joys and sorrows come from the land, which also dominates his spiritual world through his relationship with his Lord. Ivan Afanas'ev earns the title of *krest'ianin* "in the full sense of the word" because he has no other occupation beyond agriculture, which so consumes his physical, intellectual, and emotional energies that he does not have time even to think of "some other kind of more profitable work."

This bond to the land, however, does not result from affection or passion, but from the peasant's understanding of the logic of the relationship. Perceiving the land as his wet nurse, he recognizes that it provides him with his needs as long as he cares for it properly. Agricultural labor is not a labor of love, then, but a labor of reason. Finally, the peasant's primary relationship with the land defines, in turn, all other relationships, the "entire practice" of the peasant household. Uspenskii had rapidly come to Engelgardt's similar conclusion that material conditions of life were the primary determinants in the peasant's life.

This passage reveals two other themes that pervaded Uspenskii's image of the Russian peasant. The first is that the land itself becomes a protagonist. Here identified with the figure of a wet nurse, the land would take on other feminine qualities as Uspenskii developed the theme of man and land on the basis of his observations of life in the village. The second theme is that this relationship and the agricultural labor that embody it are pure, but only so long as the relationship remains natural and spontaneous. The purity of the peasant's bond with the earth was the crucial element for Uspenskii at this stage of his writing, for he was most interested in the corrupting influence of money as it invaded the village. Ivan Afanas'ev represents the true peasant because he is "unspoiled." This indicated that Uspenskii had not traveled the full distance away from moral concerns to an exclusively materialist or positivist perception of the peasant soul but continued to seek a moral anchor of some sort in the village.

Ivan Afanas'ev is a "rare" example because so many of the peasants whom Uspenskii has observed have been spoiled by corrupting influences from outside the village, most notably by money. The bulk of *From a Village Diary* treats the disintegration of peasants and village culture under the impact of "the accursed silver ruble."[54] The natural, authentic peasant somewhat avoided its touch, while others in the village fell prey to its charms and thereby lost their "peasantness." Uspenskii made this judgment through the stories of two men in the village, Mikhailo Petrov and Ivan Afanas'ev, thus continuing in the tradition of Turgenev of juxtaposing differing peasant types to illustrate the moral strength of the pure peasant.

Mikhailo Petrov was a local peasant who, having gone to St. Petersburg after the Emancipation and worked in a good position for several years, returned to the village. He married a young beauty but found that the life of the peasant no longer made sense to him. After the "easy work of the capital, the good peaceful sleep to his heart's content, the warmth, warm clothes, solid boots, he could no longer understand the pleasure of struggling like a fish on the ice in order to have none of the things he had known. . . ."[55] He and his wife were planning to return to St. Petersburg when their fortunes changed.

First a group of young students, census takers, and then a retired gentry officer fell under the spell of Agrafen'ia's physical charms. Husband and wife agreed to profit from these infatuations, and Mikhailo willingly played the role of the cuckold in order to receive sympathy payments from the young men and to unload an unwanted newborn on the gentry veteran. Despite these successes, Mikhailo and Agrafen'ia knew no satisfaction.

> [B]oth Agrafen'ia and Mikhailo Petrov became more and more insatiable for attainments every day in the desire for greater successes. "Not enough!" "More!" pressed over more firmly on their common mind (they were in fact one body and one soul), and they strained like hot horses, farther and farther, not knowing where their fast and still untiring legs would carry them.[56]

The key to the moral disintegration and material frustration of this couple lay in the fact that when Mikhailo returned to the village, he had lost the logic of the relationship of the peasant to the land and, therefore, could find no satisfaction in the labor it exacted from him. The pure and spontaneous bond had been tainted by his unnatural desire for money and city comforts. In essence, he had ceased to be a peasant.

In contrast to this corrupted couple stood Ivan Afanas'ev. When Ivan Afanas'ev was offered a job as caretaker on an estate 150 versts from his native Slepoe-Litvino, he refused. Although he had such a trying need for money that he could not buy the boots he had needed for more than two years, he could not leave the world he knew and trusted: "No amount of money could take him far away from his own."[57] Thus, of these two peasants of the same village, one became immoral under the influence of money, while the other was so bound up in his tradition that he could not change even for the honest pursuit of the rubles he so badly needed. Mikhailo Petrov saw his goals quite clearly and was willing to use his wife and play the cuckold to gain them, while Ivan Afanas'ev failed even to comprehend fully the possibilities which money might bring him and clung instead to the material misery of the world he knew. "Agricultural labor, agricultural concerns and joys" indeed filled "his entire internal world."

Ivan Ermolaevich: The Rational Farmer

Uspenskii explored the meaning of agricultural labor for the peasant in *The Peasant and Peasant Labor,* which appeared in the tenth through twelfth issues of *Notes of the Fatherland* in 1880. The experience on which he based the sketches in this series was his stay during 1879 and 1880 in a remote area of Novgorod Province near the estate of his friend A. V. Kamenskii. Disturbed by the conclusions of his observations in *From a Village Diary,* Uspenskii sought out this isolated spot to investigate more closely the workings of the peasant economy and the peasant mind. He concentrated on one individual, Leontii Osipovich Beliaev, who received the name Ivan Ermolaevich in the series.

He introduced this peasant of the backwoods as a curious, baffling creature whose worldview was quite distinct from his: "No matter how fixedly I looked into it, no matter how much I was horrified by its dimensions, I decidedly do not see that in the depths of this work and in its final result there lies a degree of thought and concern for man worthy of this unceasing labor.[58] Ivan Ermolaevich's concerns favored animals over men. As Uspenskii explained, "Let me repeat: there is concern, but it cannot equal the concern say, about the livestock." This relative lack of respect for the man rather than the beast Uspenskii observed when Ivan Ermolaevich's son fell ill. He and his wife used only home remedies to try to cure him, whereas when the mare was sick, they called in the veterinarian and paid him three rubles.[59] Ivan Ermolaevich's interest in the other people of his commune also seemed curiously limited. Although he knew their material circumstances precisely, he cared nothing about their internal, emotional lives. Neither he nor anyone else in the twenty-six households of the village, for example, could explain two recent suicides in their midst.[60]

Uspenskii was determined to decipher the peasant mentality by observing Ivan Ermolaevich, a true peasant living farther away from the city than Ivan Afanas'ev. He thus shifted from describing the corrupting influence of money on the traditions and equilibrium of the village to examining what those traditions were and what entered into the balanced equation of a "pure" peasant's culture.

Uspenskii's first revelation and answer to the question of why Ivan Ermolaevich struggled with so little reward were the result of two incidents in Ivan Ermolaevich's daily life. The first concerned a new calf who refused to eat and grew thinner and weaker by the day, to the peasant's total despair. Uspenskii wondered at his distress until he recognized that this distress was combined with disgust over the failure, the spoiling of something which should have been productive and beautiful. Suddenly he perceived in the peasant's concern about the calf the same care he had observed in Paris of an artist over his work. Ivan Ermolaevich was not distressed simply about the calf's loss of weight, but about this malfunction in his world, this disruption of the harmony of the peasant's agricultural existence.[61]

The second incident centered around one of Ivan Ermolaevich's ducks. For ten nights running Uspenskii observed the peasant perched on the fence of the poultry yard, intently watching the chickens and ducks. He was bemused by such a waste of time. After the tenth watch, Ivan Ermolaevich announced with delight that he had discovered the "secret."

> "Whose secret?"
> "Why, the duck's secret. Last night just before 12:00, I was sitting and I figured it out. Just look what a clever rascal she is! I even had to hide from her on the balcony. . . ." He said this happily, joyfully, and now, after the sad episode with the calf, I understood why it was that Ivan Ermolaevich had to sit for nights on end to hide behind the barn, on the balcony, and why the duck had received the name clever.[62]

Uspenskii went on to describe the duck's unique way of hiding her eggs, a mystery that Ivan Ermolaevich had spent so much time resolving. From these episodes and others, Uspenskii came to understand the wholeness, the integrity, of Ivan Ermolaevich's existence and the satisfactions which agricultural labor brought him. "Ivan Ermolaevich struggles not only because he needs to have his fill, to pay taxes, but also because agricultural labor with all its areas of activity, its adaptations, its happenstances absorbs also his thoughts, is the focus of almost all of his mental and even moral activity, and even almost provides him moral satisfaction."[63] He understood further that the creativity, diversity, and poetry of agricultural labor influenced, even determined, every aspect of the peasant's life and of his relations with others in his family and community. The struggle was not, therefore, without reward, although the rewards were not the material ones Uspenskii as outsider could understand. Instead, they were mental and moral, so that nowhere else could Ivan Ermolaevich, in his mind, be freer than with his plough, wagon, poultry, and livestock.

In fact, however, Ivan Ermolaevich was not free, for behind the harmony of his relationship to his labor lay a more compelling force—nature—and his utter union with her and submission to her dictates. The peasant was thus bound to the land but also had to respond to nature's bidding. It was in this relationship that Uspenskii discerned the factors defining not only the course of the peasant's labor but the shape of his human relations as well. Nature, it seemed, was an exacting teacher. First she taught Ivan Ermolaevich the meaning of power, that he must recognize her "uncontrolled, distinctive, capricious—whimsical, soulless and harsh power." Having recognized these characteristics of nature's power, the peasant also had to learn patience, the patience to wait unquestionably for the raincloud in the sky after waiting so long he could taste the rain.[64]

Through the peasant's submission to capricious nature, however, he also gained power.

> The immediate, constant union of Ivan Ermolaevich with nature, from which alone he can draw all of his knowledge and opinions, inculcates these two conditions into the very foundation of Ivan Ermolaevich's approach to life: that is, you will obey and you will command (you will *exploit*), to such a degree that . . . this union logically continues also in his family-communal life, so that there is decidedly neither the possibility of nor any sense in shaking off this whole well-balanced order in any way whatsoever.[65]

Echoing Engelgardt's emphasis on the importance of the peasant's mastery of the land, Uspenskii set this power within the context of nature's control over the peasant. He thus described the peasant as one element in a chain of command extending from nature through him to his household in a system designed for survival on the land. Because of the complexity of agricultural labor, one voice had to command all of the tasks which not he but nature defined: the collection of eggs, the shoveling of manure, the feeding of animals. Thus, "the rural man bases all of his decisions and human relations on the requirements of agricultural labor."[66] Uspenskii had found the key to understanding the patriarchy of the Russian family and village community in the peculiarly matriarchal relationship of the land and the peasant.

Ivan Bosykh: Minion of the Land

Uspenskii's consistent portrayal of the peasant as a man of his environment found its fullest expression in *The Power of the Earth*. Published in the first three issues of *Notes of the Fatherland* in 1882, this series was written during Uspenskii's stay in the village of Siabrintsa in Novgorod Province in 1881 and 1882. The third Ivan of the peasant cycle, Ivan Bosykh, appeared "a member of that unnecessary, incomprehensible class of people, shameful for our country, the rural proletariat."[67] Several aspects of village life received treatment in this third series; the main contribution was Uspenskii's theory of the power of the earth as it shaped the peasant's worldview.

Clearly, this represented a continuation and further development of his work in the previous two series on the role of agricultural labor and nature in defining the peasant's existence. The relationship between the peasant and the land, however, represented more than simple elaboration on previous conclusions. Two new elements entered the equation: first, the notion of the peasant's attachment to the land in a sense both magnetic and organic; second, the apocalyptic predictions of what would become of the peasants and Russia if that tie were broken or distorted. Whereas in *From a Village Diary*, Uspenskii had taken pains to emphasize that Ivan Afanas'ev was not "chained" to the land but joined with her in a recognition that "good begets good," in *The Power of the Earth*, the dominion of the earth was crucial.

Uspenskii gave this power a mixed appraisal. His initial comprehension of its effect followed his unsuccessful attempt to encourage Ivan Bosykh to join him in introducing communal ploughing and harvesting of grain. Having read about a landowner nearby who introduced communal ploughing at his own risk, with all of the peasants working in shifts with better yields and more free time, he discussed the possibility with Ivan Bosykh. He argued that this would ensure a better life for everyone in the village, especially those suffering handicaps of some sort. Ivan Bosykh was horrified at the idea of sharing his tools, animals, and labor with others. "What kind of master would I be?" he asked, if he were to allow another man to tend his land. Specifically, he went into a tirade about the various kinds and uses of manure, predicting that someone might put cow manure on his grain fields where he would have used horse manure. Generally he considered the suggestion nonsensical.

Uspenskii was mystified by this stubborn refusal to accept a suggestion based on proven success which could improve existence. In this he joined in the discourse with Tolstoy, Engelgardt, Sharapov, and others on peasant resistance to innovation. He concluded that the key to Ivan Bosykh's refusal was his sense that this system of farming would violate his relationship and responsibility to his land and would constitute his failure to obey her orders.

> And the secret is truly enormous and, I think, lies in the fact that the great majority of the mass of Russian people will be patient and powerful in misfortune; they will be spiritually young, both courageously strong and childishly meek—in a word, the people who on their shoulders carry everyone and everything, the people whom we love, to whom we go for the healing of spiritual torments, will preserve their powerful and mild type, so long as the power of the earth rules over them, so long as at the very core of their existence lies the impossibility of disobeying her commands, so long as those commands rule over their mind and conscience, so long as they fill all their existence.[68]

It was this bond with and subjugation to the demands of the land which defined the peasant and the peasantry as a whole. Any escape from these demands meant a loss of peasantness, a loss of self in the peasant's worldview.

> Tear a peasant away from the earth, from those cares that she imposes on him, away from those interests with which she worries the peasant; make him forget his "peasantness" [krest'ianstvo], and there will be nothing of this narod, no popular outlook, nothing of the warmth that comes from the people. There will remain the empty machine of an empty human organism. There will settle in a spiritual void, "complete freedom," that is, an unknown empty distance, an empty expanse without boundaries, a terrifying "go wherever you want."[69]

The Power of the Earth presented images not so much of the authentic peasant as of the uprooted peasant, the man who had escaped the dominion of the earth but had no other framework or anchor. A peasant of the land possessed a special, concrete faith, for example. The Bible took on meaning within the context of the earth. Among the peasants, the meaning of the Apocalypse was clear, namely, that a Tsar would come who would give the land freely. Furthermore, the meaning was that each peasant would receive fifteen desiatinas of land.[70] Because of this faith in their bright future, the peasants were able to submit to the power of the earth and to accomplish their voluntary obedience to each other in agricultural, "sinless" labor.[71] Thus the dictates of the land over the peasant explained not only his patriarchalism but also his collectivism in Uspenskii's construction.

Pure agricultural labor was sinless because it depended entirely on the labor of the peasant and the beneficence of the earth. If one peasant did better than the others in the village, according to this view, it must have been because of either harder work or greater beneficence of the earth, the "wet nurse." Sin entered the relationship when one man profited from another man's labor on the soil. Some examples of this exploitation appeared in the sketch "Greed," in which one peasant bought another peasant's cow at the village rate then sold it to the *zemstvo* for twice that amount; peasants stole the grain of other peasants to sell in the market, all as a result of the "pulling away from moist Mother Earth toward the purse."[72]

The consequences for the uprooted peasant were grim and boded ill for Russian culture. A peasant who crossed this boundary invariably became either a victim or an exploiter, in Uspenskii's view. These images will receive full treatment in later chapters. The peasant type, however, could be understood, according to Uspenskii, as a man born like all others but shaped by the reality of his narrow existence.

> I in no way mean to say . . . that the life of the common people and peasant life appeared to me in the form of something unique from the rest of mankind, that "the peasantry" is a caste, having nothing in common with the rest of humanity. Not at all. The peasant is the same as all men, but all of his needs and desires are satisfied in a special way, in his own pattern—they are satisfied from a certain source, they have a certain complexion, appearance and form, and all of this thanks to the one most important quality lying at the foundation of his existence, namely, agricultural labor.[73]

This passage demonstrates the extent to which Uspenskii was grappling with the problem of the origin of this particular species. Like Engelgardt, he was quite sensitive to the struggle for existence against the natural conditions of Russian rural life. Like Engelgardt, he stressed the issues of struggle and mastery, which led him to a comprehension of the peasant's methods of adaptation and to the forces which "shaped" the peasant's world.

Conclusion

These authors thus avoided ascribing to the Russian peasant any inherent qualities which made him different from the educated Russian. Instead, they pointed to his physical environment in land and nature and to his life of labor as an agriculturalist engaged in a struggle for existence within that setting. Land, labor, and struggle for existence: these were the primary factors shaping the image of the peasant as a rational actor. He was an adaptive creature who had developed all of the necessary qualities to succeed in his agricultural labor, a man of the land from which he had sprung and to which he would inevitably return.

Because the specific setting of subsistence agriculture in the Russian village was the defining feature of the peasant as a rational actor, this image reinforced the distinction between peasant culture and the culture of educated society. Whereas the image of the *narod* had rested on a perception of cultural distinction in the folk's ignorance and simplicity, the image of the rational peasant did so in the peasant's well-established rational consciousness, developed through generations of struggle for mastery over land and nature and, therefore, tenaciously resistant to intrusion or change. The image of the rational peasant posed a new challenge to would-be reformers or radicals, to anyone hoping to penetrate the village or to engage the peasant in a national enterprise: to understand a mentality and a culture that had its own history, logic, purposes, and defenses. This image thus both emerged in an intellectual climate of infatuation with science and its methods and encouraged a further development of an approach to the peasant question which would focus exclusively on material culture as the key to rural society.

Even in this image, which so heavily stressed the external environment as a factor in shaping the peasant mentality and focused on logic rather than sentiment, a moral judgment was clear. Uspenskii used the term *sinless* to emphasize the absence of exploitation. He contrasted "moist Mother Earth" with the "accursed silver ruble." Engelgardt also took care to describe the male peasant's aversion to dealings with money and his preference for informal personal arrangements made out of respect or as part of collective assistance. This attribute was one element of Engelgardt's positive portrait of the true peasant as agriculturalist intimately bound to the land. When he later turned to an examination of individualism in the village, to the lust for money in the peasant woman, and to the figure of the *kulak,* his own moral judgment, his own unease over profit and commerce, would find full expression.

In the spectrum of peasant images taking shape before the Russian reading public, the *krest'ianin,* the man of the land, held a positive position, not only because of the force of the logic that ruled his economic and social existence but, equally important, because of the moral purity of his bond with the land. His nature, his peasant soul, was shaped by the struggle for existence against natural conditions, but not by the struggle for existence against his fellow man. This aversion to the application of the concept of struggle between men, of intraspecific struggle, would be even more apparent in the most positive moral image of the peasant, the communal peasant.

5

The Communal Peasant

The Russian peasant commune is the most important manifestation of the Russian collective spirit, the cornerstone of its historical life, the promise of the originality and progress of the Russian people.

K. F. ODARCHENKO, "The Russian Peasant Commune and National Character"

Whereas the image of the peasant as a rational actor asserted the primacy of land and labor in shaping the peasant soul, the image of the peasant as a communal actor placed him first and foremost in the social and moral context of the commune. Mutual aid, reconciliation, and submersion of the individual spirit in the collective of the community identified rural man as a supremely moral being who approached life in all of its aspects from the perspective of the well-being of the group. Like the image of the rational peasant, this image also depended on setting for its definition, not on the material aspects of the culture, but the social institution of the commune. It was thus true to the search for the key to the peasant soul through the peasant's environment, but it focused on features of the culture that did not lend themselves easily to "scientific" explanations. Yet it was employed within the discourse on the applicability of the Darwinian model of struggle to Russian rural society, for it represented the peasant as a moral actor for whom not the survival of the fittest but the survival of the community and its cultural heritage was the central motivation.

The institution of the commune—the *sel'skoe obshchestvo* as the administrative unit incorporated into the Emancipation legislation and the *obshchina* as the economic system of land repartition—was at the center of political and economic debate throughout the post-Reform era.[1] For publicists, economists, agronomists, and statisticians engaged in the questions of Russia's development, the commune was the central feature of Russian agriculture to be examined, appraised, and advocated or rejected. In the debate over the peasant soul, however, where the peasant's mentality and morality were the key, the commune came into focus because of its moral aspects and because of the peasant's sense of communion and collectivism within it. The commune entered the discourse over the peasant soul less as a system of land repartition or mutual economic obligations than as the social unit denoted by the term *mir*.[2] Although emphasis on the role of the commune in shaping the peasant's worldview invited investigation of attitudes related to the economic role of the community and to property, the chief proponent of this image, N. N. Zlatovratskii, and others largely limited their vision to systems of mutual aid, to characters who represented the communal morality, and to the struggle between communal traditions and the intrusion of new manners and mores that placed the institution at risk.

The Slavophile Legacy

Although Zlatovratskii and other proponents of this image of the peasant based their conclusions on firsthand observation of the village, it is clear that this concept had its intellectual roots in the image making of the Slavophiles. Their emphasis on the commune and the principle of *sobornost'* (reconciliation and unity within the group) embraced many of the elements that entered into the figure of the communal peasant as he appeared in the writings of the 1870s and 1880s.

The major features of the Slavophile view of the commune bear repeating as a background to the composition of the concept of the communal peasant. For this purpose, the passage by Konstantin Aksakov selected by Marc Raeff to exemplify the Slavophile definition of the commune cannot be improved upon:

> A commune is a union of the people who have renounced their egoism, their individuality, and who express their common accord; this is an act of love, a noble Christian act which expresses itself more or less clearly in its various other manifestations. A commune represents a moral choir. In a choir a voice is not lost, but follows the general pattern and is heard in the harmony of all voices. In the same way in the commune the individual is not lost; but he renounces his exclusiveness in favor of general accord. And thus arises the noble phenomenon of harmonious joint existence of rational beings, there arises a brotherhood, a commune, a triumph of the human spirit.[3]

So defined, this basic unit of the Russian social order was moral, Christian, noble, conciliatory, founded on the renunciation of the individual in favor of a brotherhood whose ultimate aim was the common good. The first three concepts, forming the spiritual content of the commune, were fundamentally grounded in Orthodox Christianity. Just as Slavophilism was permeated by Orthodoxy, so its definition of the commune contained the conviction that the Russian man also carried faith into his noble and moral actions as a social being. These actions were characterized, above all else, by renunciation of the individual spirit and by service to one's brothers in a harmonious social order. The modus vivendi, *sobornost'*, was reconciliation of the individual with the community. The companion term, *obshchinnost'*, conveyed the ideals of love, justice, and equality.[4]

In the national self-definition of the pre-Reform era, the Slavophiles also emphasized the national distinctiveness of the commune in comparison to Western social institutions. This theme was echoed by non-Slavophiles as well, most notably Alexander Herzen. Haxthausen's conclusion, "The sense of unity in the nation, in the commune, and in the family is the foundation of Russian society," was embraced by most Russian intellectuals at midcentury and would continue to inform judgments on the village after 1861.[5]

The history of intellectual notions of the commune in the post-Emancipation era reveals a shift from the sphere of morality to political and economic debate. The urbanite's idea of *obshchina* or *mir* changed in this period from a religious, idealized concept of Russian national character to a conception of a real institution whose viability in a developing system became the focus of discussion. Positive and negative portrayals of the commune as an economic or social entity came to reflect political ideologies and visions for Russia's future.[6] Raeff noted this shift among such "second-generation Slavophiles" as Prince Vladimir Cherkasski and Alexander Koshelev, who, after lengthy exposure to the commune through encounters with the peasants on their estates, deemphasized its religious and spiritual importance in favor of a more practical political and economic assessment.[7]

Even as this shift occurred within the debate over the commune, however, key participants in the analysis of the peasant soul retained essential elements of the Slavophiles' view of the commune as the social and spiritual environment which molded the character of the Russian peasant. While the element of Orthodox faith faded dramatically, the concepts of fairness, morality, generosity, conciliation, and communality persisted in the image of the peasant as a communal person.

As the principal author of this image, Zlatovratskii was both conscious of his intellectual ties with the Slavophiles and eager to set his work apart from theirs. His exposition of the nature of Populism as a social, political, and literary movement in 1881 identified the scientific intent and methods of the Populists, their realism and empiricism, as the hallmark of their departure from Slavophilism. In the first article of the series of four "Sketches of the Rural Mood," he admitted that there were some continuities between the love of the people of the Slavophiles and that of the Populists in the 1870s, in that both were concerned primarily with the peasants. He asserted, however, that the new Populism of the seventies had a more realistic view and goal for the people. Whereas the Slavophiles had loved the peasants because of their formulations and idealizations of what they thought peasant life was and represented, the new Populists did not hesitate to study the existence of the peasants closely "to reveal their depressing ulcers in order to cure them more quickly and truly." To do this, he explained, the new Populists were willing to engage in "merciless analysis" to get at the truth.[8]

N. N. Zlatovratskii's Path to the Village

Zlatovratskii took up the task of merciless analysis through residence in the countryside in 1872 after an unsuccessful effort to live in the capitals. Born in 1845 into a family of civil servants, one generation removed from the rural clergy in Vladimir, Zlatovratskii grew up in a household exposed to the bureaucracy and nobility through his father's work and to the peasantry through his mother's religious views and reputation of welcome for pilgrims and other rural folk seeking shelter.[9] Visits to his grandfather in the village where he served as a deacon also introduced the young Nikolai Nikolaevich to the rural world. During the summer before his final year at the gymnasium, he also worked as a land adjuster helping to execute the Emancipation reform and gathered material that would appear in his peasant writings. On graduation from gymnasium, he went to Moscow, where he was an auditor at the university for a year before moving to St. Petersburg, where he matriculated at the Technological Institute. He soon had to abandon his education because of financial difficulties and turned to work as a proofreader for income. In the mid-sixties, he published several small stories; none brought him any fame, but they did set him in his career as a writer. Poverty's toll broke Zlatovratskii, and he was forced to return to Vladimir to recoup his physical and spiritual strength. He found himself back in the provinces in close proximity to the village just as the peasant question was coming into its own in the urban press.

Like Uspenskii, then, Zlatovratskii went to the country with a bad taste of the city in his mouth and hope for renewal in his heart. Wortman's study of these two searches provides a rich account of anticipation and disillusionment. His psychoanalysis of the two figures follows the general scheme of their contemporaries who juxtaposed them as Russia's Rousseau and Voltaire.[10] Where Uspenskii would identify decline, Zlatovratskii would look for potential growth; where Uspenskii would describe the apocalypse of the peasant milieu once spoiled, Zlatovratskii would try to predict resurrection of the best of rural mores. Where Uspenskii imposed the template of struggle, Zlatovratskii insisted on altruism.

Despite these inviting polarities, the very coupling of these two writers should alert us to the similarities of their condition, their approach, and, in the end, their message. Both were chronically poor and for that reason had to rely on the form of the literary-journalistic sketch as a genre.[11] Both took up residence in the countryside and insisted on the need for firsthand experience for anyone who hoped to write of the country and the peasant. Neither was a good writer, yet both gained tremendous authority in their time and their images of the peasant in the 1870s and 1880s held force through the end of the century. When Zlatovratskii was made an honorary member of the Academy of Sciences in 1910, it was not on the basis of the excellence of his prose, but of his moral purpose, the accuracy of his depiction of the peasantry, the consistency of his commitment to the *narod*, and his concern to describe the "psychology and morals of the peasant."[12]

Zlatovratskii's purpose was indeed more explicitly moral than that of his peers; his focus on the commune as a moral agent and his effort to contrast moral collective spirits with immoral individualists or profiteers made his own position on these matters perfectly clear. In this he was not exceptional, however, for every peasant image would carry a moral judgment. The image of the communal peasant simply was more easily identified as a normative figure and as a corrective for troubling evidence of new currents in the Russian countryside.

"The Peasant Jurors" (1875–1876) established Zlatovratskii's reputation as a writer on peasant themes and revealed his sympathies for the simple nature of the just *muzhik* over the logic of the sophisticated lawyer. Whereas in this sketch old rural ways and new urban concepts clashed in the city, Zlatovratskii's image of the communal peasant emerged from writings set in the context of the village itself, drawn from the example of the villages of Vladimir which he visited or in which he lived during his exploration of rural culture. His three major works were "Sketches of the Rural Mood" (1881); *Rural Daily Life* (1881), a series of journalistic reports; and *Foundations* (1878–1883), a novel of peasant culture. Several short stories completed his peasant cycle. With this cycle, Zlatovratskii joined Uspenskii and Engelgardt as one of the three most important authors of publicistic writing on the peasant soul. Zlatovratskii's image of the communal peasant injected an element of dialogism into the discourse on the pages of *Notes of the Fatherland*, but both his writing and his message were so much weaker than his fellow seekers' that the image of the communal peasant was ultimately a weak contender in the contest for public opinion.

Zlatovratskii's Communal Peasant in the Struggle for Existence

The penetration of Darwinism into Zlatovratskii's approach to the village was most apparent in a story that appeared in 1879, "Avraam." The central character, Zlatovratskii's rural Abraham, represented a true communal peasant in the same way that each of Uspenskii's three Ivans represented his vision of the man of the land. As the head of a household in an isolated village, Avraam was one of the "elders in this Aeropagus of the peasant *mir*," a protector of the old ways who stood before "the younger generation of the village as that ideal of peaceful and hardworking peasant life which he had realized in his own life."[13] In the contemporary village, however, Zlatovratskii explained,

> This is a type which is already dying out, like the heavy, immobile, contemplative kangaroo of the Australian forests which is being destroyed in the struggle for existence against the light, pushing plunderers of the newest stage of development. This type is already rare in the villages near the cities, but you will meet him in the interior with all of his inviolability. The more you get to know him, the greater the gentle sentiment you will begin to feel towards him, but, along with this, a vexing sadness will gather in your soul. Is it not so that the severe law of the struggle for existence rules all-powerful also among humanity?[14]

The struggle for existence in Avraam's tale revolved around conflict between him, representative of the old order and communal existence, and one of his sons, as representative of the urbanized peasant engaged in commerce, indifferent to the standards of patriarchy. Avraam triumphed in a Pyrrhic victory: he died shortly after banishing his son from his household, overwhelmed by grief over the disintegration of his family.

The theme of the struggle for existence ran throughout Zlatovratskii's peasant cycle. Whereas the image of the rational peasant as man of the land emerged from the theme of the struggle for existence with the material conditions of land and labor in Russia, the image of the communal peasant took shape against the background of the struggle between new social forms and old. Zlatovratskii set up the dichotomy of the old village he had observed as a land adjuster just after the Emancipation and the new village he found on his return to Vladimir a decade later. In a statement that declared his mission while criticizing the approach of such observers as the Liuboshchinskii Commission on the *volost'* court, he described his approach to the village.

> Finally, the significance of the village in the eyes of society has become so serious that everyone for whom the interests of the people are dear has hurried to go into this "new village" in order to bring out a series of honourable, sincere, conscientious observations. . . . To make a significant contribution in this common, rich undertaking—such was the motive leading me to the investigation of the "new village." . . . Before all else, unlike many of our official and unofficial investigators, who consider it more convenient to do their research, fluttering from village to village, from

district to district, from province to province, collecting drops of honey in a summer, I decided it would be better to spend all my time in one locality, entering as much as possible into the daily life of its inhabitants.[15]

The site he chose was the village of Iama, isolated in a distant region of Vladimir Province. He set as his goal the discovery of long-term developments rather than the striking novelties that had captured other observers' attention, in his view. He recognized that the village he observed was a social entity under stress, describing his time as "a critical epoch, an epoch of struggle," with a chaotic blending of old and new. The challenge for anyone studying this epoch was to discover the enduring, rather than the ephemeral, trends.[16] The struggle was manifest in chaos in the village, the decline of patriarchal tradition, the crumbling of the foundations of custom, economic differentiation, and conflict between the individual and the *mir*. These were the basic concerns of Zlatovratskii throughout his work on the peasants; through a prism of these concerns he observed peasant culture and presented his conclusions to the readers of Russia.

His articles on the mood in the countryside emphasized these threats to rural stability through vignettes of peasant life. Thus, for example, he described the decline of patriarchal authority through a scene between an old peasant, head of his household, and a young peasant woman who was his neighbor. In front of the entire village, the young woman abused the old man and accused him of taking advantage of all the young women in the household.[17] Similarly, the fissures in the *mir* were the subject of a conversation between two old men of the village which he reported. They debated the rights of the individual against those of the commune and decided that confusion and dissolution resulted from the fact that the *mir* no longer spoke with one voice but had instead broken into competing groups. The notion of mutual aid had disappeared, one said; the rich helped the rich, the middle peasants helped the middle peasants, and "the drunken—the drunken."[18]

Zlatovratskii argued, however, that these were the ephemeral trends that duped most observers of the village, who did not discern the essential relationship between peasant and commune. "But where, indeed, show me, where among all these figures, is that common trait of them all, which indicates that they are all people of the *obshchina* and *mir,* that all of them are born, live and die in the unique conditions of communal daily life?"[19] The central thesis of *Rural Daily Life* was that the commune was a vital element that would endure, that it had shaped the peasant's character and would rescue him from the forces of disintegration. He asserted that this communal character was made manifest in all his daily habits and relations to other men. It affected his economic decisions and the way he worked. Thus the commune was to Zlatovratskii's peasant what the power of the land was to Uspenskii's and Engelgardt's rational peasant.

To be ruled by the customs of the commune meant that one judged all questions in terms of fairness and equality and of justness: *po ravneniiu, po spravedlivosti.*[20] The *mir* assured the peasant that these standards would rule his life: he would never be allowed to sink into poverty, nor to attain great prosperity. It was according to these principles that land was divided and labor in the fields allocated. So important were they that for one half-hour's communal work in the field, the entire village would gather and spend at least twice that amount of time dividing the labor among the peasants, "so that it will be fair among us."[21] When offered the option of buying a new piece of land as a commune or as individual households, the peasants debated the two at length and in the end chose to purchase communally. Zlatovratskii explained that they preferred to give more to the *mir*, because of the long-term guarantees it offered against the ups and downs of agriculture.[22]

These guarantees took the form of mutual aid, of which Zlatovratskii described twelve forms. He described patterns of mutual aid which he had himself observed, including communal assistance in the event of fire, support of orphans and the elderly, aid to widows, help in such major tasks as building a house and hauling manure. Zlatovratskii was telling the reading public nothing new; throughout his letters "From the Countryside" Engelgardt had also described these patterns of collective labor. There was no dispute over the existence of such mechanisms in the village; the distinction lay in the motives each observer attributed to them. For Zlatovratskii, these were testimony to the peculiar, and superior, morality of the commune. Where Engelgardt saw calculated self-interest, Zlatovratskii saw selflessness and service to the commune as the goal in and of itself.

Zlatovratskii argued that the crucial ingredient of "peasantness" was the sense of affiliation with the commune and responsibility to it. He reported that peasants held this view and thus considered those who took up work other than agriculture but maintained ties to the commune to be peasants. He discovered this when he shifted from the isolated village of Iama to the more economically diverse villages of Upper and Lower Lopukhin, which were larger and more frequently touched by the civilization of the outside world. There he met wealthy merchants whom he asked why they had not moved to Moscow to join the merchant class. They replied, "Why should we? . . . We are peasants. . . . Our *obchestvo* [*sic*] is here."[23] This tie was not one with the land, Zlatovratskii was quick to point out, as the merchants said of land and agricultural labor, "Land, that's a dirty, lazy job, woman's work. . . ."[24]

This phenomenon of peasants' living in the commune without being involved in agricultural labor was, according to Zlatovratskii, the great compromise of the era. Peasants were learning to manage their affairs in a businesslike fashion, *khoziaistvovat'*. This quality connoted profit and cleverness, ability to manage, but did not necessarily imply exploitation and therefore did not mean that a peasant who possessed it was a *kulak*. By defining the peasant in terms of the *mir*, rather than the land, Zlatovratskii was able to consider such an individual a peasant. The peasant merchants would thus be considered peasants because of their profession of obligation to the *mir*: "We are obligated to hold communal land, to keep the peasant commune in order, so that there will be no call for accounting from the government."[25]

When *Rural Daily Life* appeared as a bound collection in 1882, Zlatovratskii felt compelled to defend himself against the criticisms leveled against him since its appearance in the previous year. "I am being accused of changing my attitudes toward the *narod*, that I am falsifying and idealizing them. Not so. My faith in the firmness of the peasants' foundations—the land and the *mir*—grows. . . ."[26] The charges that Zlatovratskii had both falsified and idealized the peasants in *Rural Daily Life* reflected the public's perception that the author was wavering in his own understanding of peasant life. Whereas he had been able to depict communal types such as Avraam on the basis of his observations of the post-Reform village as a land adjuster, the peasants of Iama and Upper and Lower Lopukhin were at the center of the transitions occurring in the countryside as the penetration of the outside world became more prevalent. Faced with the phenomena of peasants who were proud of their ability to manage business, the increasing numbers of village men who left the village for seasonal labor elsewhere, and the breakdown of patriarchal rule in the family and *mir*, Zlatovratskii had to develop a view which would allow for the persistence of the commune in peasant life. He did this by asserting that the commune was quite elastic, capable of adapting to new trends while retaining the affiliation of the peasants. It was important to him that merchant peasants could still see themselves as members of the commune and that older traditional peasants held firmly to their notions of equality and fairness in the commune, operating through various forms of mutual aid to ensure that those standards prevailed. These aspects of village life constituted the foundations on which the current peasant culture existed and on which Zlatovratskii hoped, the commune of the future would be built.

The Communal Peasant Falters

Zlatovratskii's best-known work, *Foundations*, developed the theme of the communal peasant's faltering as a full-length novel describing the clash between the old ways and the habits of the outside world which invaded a traditional, almost utopian peasant community. In *Foundations*, Zlatovratskii presented a veritable hagiography of peasant saints who embodied all that was pure and good in his image of the communal peasant. In this work, the early threads of his image making came together in a confusion of tangled strands reflecting his ultimate uncertainty about the myth he had made. The novel centered around a small settlement dominated by one peasant family, the Volks. In the first half of the work, Zlatovratskii set up a confrontation between the matriarch of the settlement, Ul'iana Mosevna Volk, and her nephew, Petr Vonifatich. Ul'iana Mosevna represented the old peasant communal way of life. Throughout the novel, she stood firmly on the principles of communal ways as she understood them. The most important function of the commune, in her view, was to look out for all its members, protecting the vulnerable; supporting the orphaned, aged, or poor; and providing land to those peasants who desired to live and work in the village. Unmarried with no children of her own, Ul'iana Mosevna raised the children of her brother, Vonifatii, as well as other motherless children of the village. She was always the first to visit a home where tragedy had struck, to respond to a neighbor's call for help, to defend the interests of the weakest members of the commune.

Petr Vonifatich, on the other hand, was a young man who had gradually extricated himself from the commune and its mores by going to Moscow as a member of a workers' cooperative from the village, only to leave the *artel'* to live in a room rented from a noble family. There he became the center of attention for the two adolescent daughters who fancied themselves Populists and were infatuated with Petr as a "son of the people." Under their tutelage and through study with a philosopher and psychologist, Petr went through a process of self-realization. "And never in his life had Petr felt himself to be 'fully a man', free and independent, conscious of his human worth, as in this stormy period of his youth. . . ."[27] His bubble burst, however, when he found himself barred from the family's drawing room when a suitor appeared for the older daughter. Unable to fit in with either the men in his old *artel'* or the society of the educated, Petr decided to return to the village but to do so with plans of living well.

Central to Petr's plans was rational farming. He wrote to warn his family to hold all their land intact, then returned to set himself up in a profitable farming enterprise. The villagers in his community declared that he had lost his communal way of thinking, his *mirskoi razum*. In this they were correct. The foundations of communal existence, which, according to Zlatovratskii, were the essence of peasantness, required sublimation of the individual interest to that of the *mir*. This Petr Vonifatich Volk would not accept. Shunning the habits of the peasants, feeling himself to be "fully a man, free and independent," he was no longer a peasant, and his return to the village spelled disaster for the Volk settlement.

The village man is accustomed to living openly. The greatest part of his life passes "in the *mir*", on the street, under the eyes of everyone. He does not know how to hide even the most intimate moments of his life from the street . . . all of this is known to the *mir*, to the street, down to the smallest detail. . . . The inhabitants of the Volk settlement were communal people, they lived by communal instincts, as did the people of Dergacha who lived nearby. It is understandable that the appearance among them of Petr with such a sharp statement of greater and greater striving to keep to himself apart from communal life could not but arouse in them some kind of unconscious dissatisfaction, and consequently, also an indeterminate fear before some kind of calamity.[28]

Petr's repudiation of identification with the *mir* and his insensitivity to its customs enabled him to take over one third of the family land, displace his family from their original settlement, and set himself up in a former lord's house. For these actions, he earned the epithets not only of egoist, but also hater of the *mir*, and drinker of his own family's blood.

These events occurred in the first sections of *Foundations*. Thereafter, the plot line weakened considerably as Zlatovratskii concentrated more on depicting peasant types and responses to disruption and confusion in their world. In this cast of communal characters, all were old and all broke down before the onslaught of such phenomena as individualism and drunkenness among the younger men of the community. The foundations of communal life dissolved into chaos, as did Zlatovratskii's writing at the end of the book. Although the first two sections of *Foundations* constituted a clear, if somewhat unsophisticated, presentation of characters, plot, and theme, the second half of the novel reflected the author's confusion and the result was virtually incoherent fiction.

Despite the poverty in the style of *Foundations* in particular and his other works in general, Zlatovratskii's writings on the peasant were at the forefront of debate on the true nature of the peasant soul. A polemic over the peasant question in literature brewed between the critics of *Week* and *Notes of the Fatherland,* the focus of which was Uspenskii and Zlatovratskii. In a letter to Zlatovratskii in 1890, the writer A. I. Ertel' aptly described the reception of his works: "I want to say that these writings have acquired the character of classics in the eyes of society—if not always because of their craftsmanship, then in the sense of the trend they represent. . . . You have both admirers and the kind of readers who know that they may not love you, but that they cannot not read your work."[29] To understand the discourse on the peasant soul, one simply had to know the works of Zlatovratskii.

Beyond the function that his image of the communal peasant served as an antidote to the images which focused on other factors in explaining the peasant, Zlatovratskii's moral message struck a responsive chord. His black and white division between the individualism of Petr Volk and the selfless communalism of the Volk settlement was consistent with the implicit judgments of other observers and other images. Uspenskii and Engelgardt were equally averse to the intrusion of money and profit into the rural idyll; both also decried individualism in the village. This rejection of the peasant as individual would become the central element in the images of the *kulak* and the *baba*. The image of the communal peasant was a comforting alternative to the stark images of the new peasant in the new village, and that in itself contributed to Zlatovratskii's authority as a voice in the discourse.

Alternative Versions of the Communal Peasant

Zlatovratskii's image making was reinforced by other contributors to the major journals. Petr Petrovich Chervinskii, a frequent contributor to *Week* during these years, maintained a positive view of the peasantry and tied that perception to the commune. Chervinskii spoke as an eyewitness from the Chernigov region, where he spent the 1870s and 1880s engaged in *zemstvo* statistical investigations. In light of his quantitative approach to the study of the village, his highly qualitative approach to discussions of peasant behavior was somewhat surprising and suggested again the pervasiveness of moral concerns for all observers of the post-Emancipation peasantry. The central theme of all of his articles on the peasants was their moral superiority: "Yes, the simple people have moral gifts and instincts which are healthier and purer!"[30] He attributed this moral superiority to the native environment of the commune, which shaped the peasant's character. The result of living in this environment was that "the peasant's body, heart, and soul are permeated with the sense of moral obligation to submerge the 'egotistical I' to something larger and higher."[31]

The Populist radical S. M. Kravchinskii also emphasized the commune as the breeding ground for the admirable qualities of the Russian people. In a discussion of the *mir* as the basic unit of rural life, he explained:

> Everybody must make concessions for the general good and the peace and welfare of the community. The majority are too generous to take advantage of their numerical strength. The *mir* is not a master, but a loving parent, equally compassionate to all of its children. It is this quality . . . that explains the high sense of humanity which forms so marked a feature of our rural customs—the mutual help in field labor, the aid given to the poor, the fatherless, and the afflicted. . . .[32]

Figure 1.   V. G. Perov, "Easter Procession in the Country" (1861) (Tretyakov Gallery).

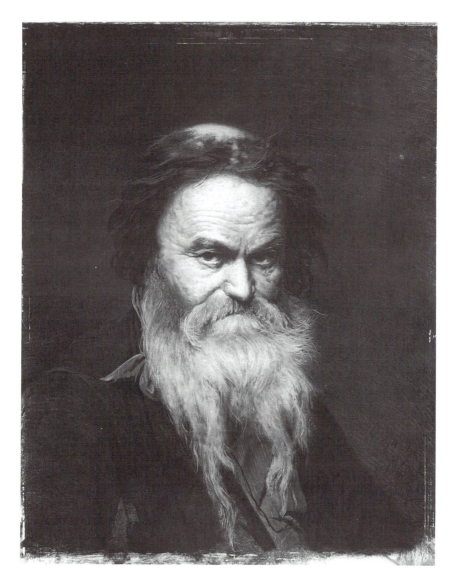

Figure 2. V. G. Perov, "Fomushka-the Owl" (1868) (Tretyakov Gallery).

Figure 3.   V. G. Perov, "The Wanderer" (1870) (Tretyakov Gallery).

Figure 4.   I. N. Kramskoi, "Peasant, A Life Study" (1871) (Kiev Museum of Russian Art).

Figure 5. I. N. Kramskoi, "Study of an Old Peasant. Muzhik with a Walking Stick" (1872) (State Art Museum of Estonia).

Figure 6.   I. N. Kramskoi, "The Peasant Ignatii Pirogov" (1874) (Kiev Museum of Russian Art).

Figure 7.   I. N. Kramskoi, "The Woodsman" (1874) (Tretyakov Gallery).

Figure 8. G. G. Miasoedov, "The *Zemstvo* Dines" (1872) (Tretyakov Gallery).

Figure 9. I. E. Repin, "The Drunken Husband" (1888) (The Russian Museum).

Figure 10. G. G. Miasoedov, "Mowers" (1887) (The Russian Museum).

Figure 11. I. I. Levitan, "March" (1895) (Tretyakov Gallery).

Figure 12.   V. A. Serov, "October in Domotkanovo" (1895) (Tretyakov Gallery).

Figure 13.   A. E. Arkhipov, "The Return Trip" (1896) (Tretyakov Gallery).

Figure 14.   V. A. Serov, "Peasant Woman in a Cart" (1896) (The Russian Museum).

Figure 15.   A. E. Arkhipov, "Day Laborers" (1896) (Tretyakov Gallery).

Figure 16. A. E. Arkhipov, "Washerwomen" (1901) (Tretyakov Gallery).

Still other writers echoed Zlatovratskii's emphasis on fairness and egalitarianism as the elements of natural law which formed "the basic characteristic of communal life."[33]

In 1881, the series "Letters on the Russian Peasantry" began to appear in Ivan Aksakov's Slavophile publication, *Rus'*. The author, Dmitrii Kishenskii, was offering a Slavophile perspective on the village to counter Engelgardt's powerful series in *Notes of the Fatherland,* as well as the works of Uspenskii and Zlatovratskii, "pseudo-Populist writers" characterized by "the absence of talent, inadequate creative force, along with superficiality of observation and the inability to understand the soul of the *narod.*"[34] He declared his goal of reminding readers of positive features of the peasantry in contrast to the consistent negativism of the "pseudo-realists." Beginning with the second letter in his series, Kishenskii focused on the commune as the definitive institution of rural life, and as the most important moral agency acting to mitigate the corrosive effects of the intrusion of money and economic differentiation into the village.

What began as a defense of the commune and an affirmation of its positive force in shaping the morality of the peasant concluded as a recognition that this force was rapidly failing. Like Zlatovratskii, Kishenskii set up the model of the communal peasant only to admit that he was becoming a figure of Russia's past. He presented the communal peasant in his fullest form in the figures of elders in the village, for whom "[t]he Tsar and the commune are the beloved authorities of the Russian people, authorities from whom the people have known no injustices of any kind and in whose divine origins they believed blindly."[35] Like other observers, however, he could not present young communal peasants' further testimony to the fact that "[t]he *mir,* the *obshchina,* and unanimity are the strength and pride of the Russian people . . . and with sadness the honest Russian citizen recognizes that this force-power of the Russian people is being eaten into and is decomposing with each passing day."[36] The sources of decay lay without and within, in Kishenskii's view. External factors included the inadequate allotments of land, the right to leave the commune, and the imposition of competing institutions of justice, primarily the *volost'* court. The internal factors he identified all fell under the concept of individualism, primarily the emergence of the exploitative figure of the *kulak* and the decline of the patriarchal principle. He restricted the term *kulak* to peasants who lived outside the communal principle, outside its moral authority, while the decline in the patriarchal family resulted from loss of respect for "God, the Tsar, the commune, and the Holy Scriptures."[37] Kishenskii's attempt to prop up the image of the communal peasant thus ended as a lament for the loss of all the moral authorities of traditional pre-Reform Russia, and as an apocalyptic vision of deterioration equal to that of "pseudo-realists" whose observations he had set out to diminish.[38]

Even the liberal camp, where advocacy of the strong individual could be expected to counter the positive image of the communal peasant, fell prey to this image's peculiar moral charms. Throughout an article in 1877 on the pros and cons of communal landholding, the liberal historian K. D. Kavelin emphasized the peasant's sense of community, his voluntary submission to the will of the whole, his recognition that his daily efforts contributed to the well-being of the community. The result was that the Russian peasant possessed a special gift, the ability to live with others in harmony.[39] This was, in fact, the definitive national characteristic of the Russian people, as the Great Russian peasantry was "a communal people, with all the qualities and inadequacies that emerge from this special, dominant trait of the national character."[40] The Russian peasant was thus, first and foremost, communal, Kavelin agreed, with the result that all the mores of the commune flowed into the Russian national spirit.

Conclusion

This blending of the national and moral attributes of the peasant as a communal being underscored the extent to which the search for the peasant soul was an exercise in national self-definition and the legitimate heir to the debates between Slavophiles and Westerners in the pre-Reform era. The image of the communal peasant was peculiar to the post-Reform era, however, in the challenges it was designed to meet. This image was a response to the concepts of individualism and competition, concepts which grew out of the reality of the changing village and of the metaphors that Darwinism offered to explain them. The principal author of the image, Zlatovratskii, declared himself an empiricist, an objective observer who hewed to the requirements of scientific inquiry. This forced him, despite the fact that his preferred image was the communal peasant, to admit other figures on stage who he may have hoped would exit shortly, but who he realized were indeed forceful elements in Russia's developing drama. The scene he depicted did not differ greatly from those of less sanguine observers, which one contemporary critic considered logical, for they "observe one and the same subject—peasant village life; it is understandable that they should see the same phenomena. . . ."[41] The image of the communal peasant, however, required that he stand alone in the light of moral approbation, while the other characters sank away into the dark realm of the unclean.

These other characters, as the remaining three images to be discussed will illustrate, somehow violated the concept of peasantness and all of the worthiness that this notion assumed in the images of the *narod,* the *krest'ianin,* and the communal peasant. The power of the appeal of the communal peasant in his self-abnegation, his respect for tradition, and his loyalty to patriarchal structures raises important questions about the capacity of members of educated society to embrace any fully independent peasant figure and, by extension, the elements of individualism and competition in their own cultural self-image. These questions become all the more insistent in the figures of the gray or unadorned peasant, the *kulak,* and the *baba.*

In the end, the image of the communal peasant was a failed image. For several reasons, it did not effectively contest the image of the rational peasant or preclude the more negative images of the peasant that were taking shape. First, it failed because of the weakness of Zlatovratskii's writing. This was critical because he was the recognized chief defender of the image. Second, it failed because it did not focus on material aspects of the peasants' environment and thus was roundly criticized for being idealized or romanticized and insufficiently realistic. Third, it failed because more compelling evidence of competition and exploitation within peasant culture was coming to the attention of the reading public. There was a growing sentiment that the real peasant could not bear any halo or be set within any kind of aura. Rather, he had to appear in his unadorned authenticity revealed by stark, photographic realism.

6

The Gray Peasant:
Unadorned and Besieged

Obviously, the elements for the development of these forces lie in the gray peasant himself, in the economic, moral, and mental conditions of his life. What do these elements consist of? How can their influence be weakened or put to use? The resolution of these questions is equally essential, equally important for those who wish to use them to cause harm and for those who wish to use them to serve the interests of the people. But in order to know how to use them, it is necessary first of all to understand them. Our society is beginning to understand this—that is why it has so actively begun to take an interest now in the "gray peasant" in his daily life and his internal world. That is why people have been heading recently from all directions to the peasants with scholarly goals, goals of moral enlightenment, and purely aesthetic goals.

P. NIKITIN [TKACHEV], "*Muzhiks* in Contemporary Literary Circles"

The competing images of the communal peasant and the rational agriculturalist depended primarily on setting and environment for their definition. A peasant in either form was what his economic reality or social and moral community made him. Both images reflected their makers' confrontation with the world of the village, their personal predilections, and their response to Darwinian social theory as a model of inquiry applied to rural life. Both of these images held full force, however, only as long as the setting itself remained insular and undisturbed, or as long as the solution which had produced the rational or communal peasant was stable. The peasant was a rational agriculturalist within an autarkic system of subsistence farming. The communal peasant was imbued with and operated according to a collectivist morality within a society dominated by the commune.

By the mid-1870s, however, it was becoming apparent that the economy of the Russian village was no longer autarkic and that dissident voices and forces were threatening the authority of the commune. Although urban observers of the village like Uspenskii, Engelgardt, and Zlatovrataskii had been impressed initially by the static *systems* that distinguished rural culture and their taxonomic approach led them to begin by shaping peasant types within those systems, they rapidly became attuned to *processes* and change. The processes that captured their attention involved the intrusion of external economic forces, the exchange of social mores through out-migration of peasants as seasonal laborers, and the disintegration of such social structures as the extended patriarchal household.[1]

These processes and changes suggested that a definition of the peasant which rested on an assumption of stable economic or social settings could not hold and that the peasant soul would have to be identified more essentially. At the same time, the urge toward realism in literary and artistic treatments of the village was approaching its zenith. This would culminate in a nearly photographic method of depicting the peasant. These developments converged to produce a new image of the Russian peasant, deprived of the systems that had shaped the rational and communal peasant images.

As early as 1878, the peasant for whom the commune was not adequate protection against the onslaught of new trends and pressures was known to the Russian reading public as the *seryi muzhik*. The direct translation of this term is "gray peasant," gray in the sense of being neither pure and untainted white nor wholly evil and thus dark or black. In this sense, it also connoted the essential peasant. One can also translate this as the drab or dreary peasant, a choice which conveys both the absence of adornment and the oppressiveness of the image. A review in 1878 of recent works by G. I. Uspenskii in *The Week*, "The Liberal on the *Seryi Muzhik*," opened with the recognition that the intelligentsia had been laboring for some time over the question, What is our Russian *seryi muzhik?*[2] At this point in the public controversy over the peasant soul, the peasant had gained a new label which carried with it several implications.

The concept of being gray as being unadorned was a product of the insistence on realistic, objective observation. When writers, critics, and village observers spoke of the gray or dreary peasant, they implied that they were talking about the real peasant, Russia's peasant as he lived and breathed, not the peasant in noble dress, or the Russian peasant forced into the idealized sentimental image of the *paysan*. This was the real thing. The frequent coupling of the term *seryi* with the word *muzhik* emphasized the specifically Russian nature of the subject, for *muzhik* was a word that exclusively denoted the Russian peasant as opposed to the generic peasant type, and certainly the Western peasant most frequently referred to as the *paysan*. P. Nitikin (P. N. Tkachev) observed in his capacity as literary critic, "There began to appear, one after another, *muzhiks* who in no way resem-

bled either the fools or the idyllic *paysans,* or the sentimental slaves. . . .
The salon filled with them. . . ."[3] Tkachev captured the sense of invasion
that was taking place in educated society as peasant images which reversed
the image making of the pre-Emancipation era began to dominate intellectual life. He suggested that somehow the authors who offered the gray
peasant to the public were not in control of the images they had created,
but rather that the *muzhiks* themselves were forcing their troubling features into the consciousness of educated society.

As the image took shape, this figure was a weak human being who
lacked either the moral or the intellectual strengths to survive with integrity
in his changing world. Dependent on the assimilated traditions of the old
village, he collapsed in one way or another under the pressures of the new.
He had a distorted worldview in which the pursuit of money in a confused,
sometimes desperate search for survival permeated his perception of the
society which surrounded him. Although the gray *muzhik* was intended to
be an objective, realistic image of the Russian peasant, it was fundamentally negative in its assessment of his human qualities or potential.

With this image and that of the *kulak,* the concept of the struggle for
existence expanded to include not only the struggle for existence against
natural conditions but also the struggle against new social and economic
conditions and against fellow peasants. If, indeed, such struggles existed in
rural Russia, and if there too the survival of the fittest was a rule in force,
then the *seryi muzhik* represented the unfit, those who were lacking the
adaptive mechanisms to ensure survival in transforming Russia. The attribution of passivity central to the positive image of the *narod* was apparent in
the image of the dreary peasant, whose passivity here made him a certain
victim in the new village. The *seryi muzhik* had a double visage. Under
assault, he was likely to collapse as the passive victim. The alternative was a
transformation from man to beast, a loss of all qualities of humanity as he
reverted to the most primitive of instincts. In either guise, he lost his
consciousness, his peasantness, his humanity, and therefore his potential as
a positive element in Russia's cultural progress.

In literary accounts, this image was a product of the increasingly psychological, realistic approach which characterized Uspenskii's and Zlatovratskii's writings. In more strictly publicistic writing, the image made its
way into reports on various signs of deterioration in the economy, society,
and general health of the countryside. In painting, the gray peasant was
one of the prime subjects of the most important school of Russian painting
in the post-Emancipation era, the Itinerants. These genres played off and
reinforced each other in constructing an image which both contested the
images of the rational and communal peasants and served as the necessary
partner in the paradigm of rural exploitation outsiders designed through
the figure of the village strongman, the *kulak.*

Early Exposition of the Image in the
F. M. Reshetnikov's "Podlipovtsy"

Contemporaries and later scholars alike considered F. M. Reshetnikov to be one of the first exponents of the image of the *seryi muzhik*. Reshetnikov was the consummate nongentry, classless, uprooted *raznochinets*. His father was a former deacon who had become a petty official in the postal service, leaving the clergy and entering the ranks of the lowest levels of the faceless bureaucracy. He was also a drunkard who delivered his son at ten months to be cared for by equally poor relatives after his wife's death. Reshetnikov was thus without any firm social or familial grounding, displaced in infancy and always conscious that he was an unwelcome burden. He grew up in poverty and dependency, exhibiting the worst traits of the resentful orphan. The only consistent pleasure of the first twenty years of his life in Perm Province was walking along the banks of the Kama River, where he began to know displaced peasants and barge haulers, figures with whom he felt a natural empathy and who would provide the material for his most important writing.[4] He moved to St. Petersburg in 1863 and began publishing in such progressive journals as *The Contemporary, Notes of the Fatherland, The Russian Word, The Cause,* and *The Week.* On his death in 1871, a volume of his collected works appeared, while separate editions of individual works were published as late as 1890.

Reshetnikov became a prominent figure in 1864 when *The Contemporary* published his grim account of contemporary peasant life, "Podlipovtsy: An Ethnographic Sketch." This piece was one of the most complete examples of the early form of the sketch as the genre for village prose and of the conflation of ethnography and literature in the immediate post-Emancipation search for material on the peasant. Stylistically and thematically, it was a forerunner of the literary-journalistic sketches of the 1870s and 1880s. Its most important function in the discourse was that it introduced the image of the gray peasant which subsequently dominated Uspenskii's writing and found its consummate expression in Chekhov's "Muzhiki" some thirty years later.

As the title of the piece indicates, Reshetnikov intended for his readers to consider "Podlipovtsy" a realistic account of the people he had known during his years in the countryside. *Podlipovtsy,* which means the real, the authentic, the genuine, was the name he gave the peasants of the village of Podlinnoe. This was an ethnographic, read scientific, sketch of real or genuine peasants. It had a clumsy and redundant title, to be sure, but one which made the point inescapable for any reader. Reshetnikov declared the authenticity of the account in a letter to Nikolai Nekrasov, then editor of *The Contemporary,* stating that he had known many peasants who lived along the Kama River in conditions just as he described them in the sketch.[5]

The focus and heart of the work was the life of barge haulers who had left the village seeking a living away from the land, but the history of the peasants before their departure from the village offered an image of the peasant that took hold in the popular imagination. In this early formulation of the concept of the gray peasant, two elements emerged. First, the conditions of peasant existence did much to explain his behavior. Second, as a victim of his circumstances, the peasant was a pale, colorless figure with no strong definition. Reshetnikov's Podlipovtsy, however, settled into the darker range of gray as he stripped them not only of the qualities of the idealized *narod*, but also of virtually all human qualities, presenting them as little more than unconscious animals.

The importance of environment was made clear through the structure of the sketch, which contained several smaller sections, each of which opened with a description of the setting. The demystification, even dehumanization, of the peasant emerged through narrative commentary as well as characterization through dialogue. Both themes appeared in the opening lines, which described the village as a miserable little settlement of six houses, dominated by hunger, filth, and poverty. The very origin of the village flew in the face of any idealized version of the communal peasant, as Reshetnikov explained that the settlement had been founded by a peasant who had quarreled with his village and wanted to live separately. There was no sign of health or happiness in the village, where the only people to be seen in the street were wailing children.

As for the adult peasants, "They love no one. No one loves them." They understood nothing and called every natural phenomenon God. Reshetnikov stressed their ignorance and lack of understanding or control over their lives. "They live, they marry, they bear children, they die— unconsciously—because that's the way it is."[6] As for any reverence for the land, "They know that they get food from it and bury their dead in it— nothing more."[7] In this early formulation, then, the peasant was set in a colorless world of dreariness, while he was denied any manifestation of consciousness or affiliation. This was a construction which predated the emergence of the peasant as a rational actor by almost a decade and by all rights should have been usurped by it. Instead, Reshetnikov's "genuine" peasants remained as a source to be tapped when the discourse swerved back to the unsettled peasant.

As Reshetnikov narrowed his focus from the wide-angle to the close-range view of the peasants of Podlinnoe, two peasants came into view. The story of the Podlipovtsy became their tale as Reshetnikov engaged in the exercise of exploring the psychology of the peasant. Pila, the older of the two, had a daughter who had borne a child by the second character, Sysoika. Sysoika was unable to move in with Pila's family because his blind and crazy mother and his four-year-old brother and two-year-old sister depended on him. Sysoika's hope and aim were that they should starve or freeze to death. "Fear somehow kept him from murder."[8] Not only Sysoika but everyone in Pila's household also "waited, watching, hoping for these three deaths."[9]

Death came to the children as they huddled in the stove seeking warmth. In a scene of grotesque horror, Pila visited the household and found the children dead. The girl was lying in a pool of blood, her head completely crushed by the weight of a stone which had fallen from inside the stove. The boy had frozen to death. Pila announced that they were dead, to which Sysoika replied that he could now move out. " 'But what about your mother?' Pila asked. He replied 'She'll die.' "[10]

Whereas these human sufferings did not move Pila, he lost his mind over the loss of his cow, which the village priest demanded as payment for burying the children and as a bribe to prevent him from reporting the deaths to the local constable. He left the village to work as a barge hauler, soon to return and take the remaining Podlipovtsy with him on the grinding search for a living in the brutal and tenuous world of the barge haulers. The remainder of the sketch described their experiences as uprooted peasants who lost track of each other in their search for a scrap of bread. They chose their course according to their physical wants and needs, with little control and no understanding of their lives.[11]

Even this short synopsis should make clear that the inclusion of *Ethnographic* in the title could not mask the intention of shocking the reading public by "telling all" about the Russian village. Reshetnikov's work and that of his fellow *raznochintsy* writers attacked the concept of the *narod* and left in its place peasants who were distinguished by their impassive response to life and death. The dreary peasant of Reshetnikov's description was an unconscious victim of his surroundings, who acted according to the most primitive of instincts: the search for warmth and food. The peasant's world contained no abstractions. Neither did human relationships mitigate the misery of his existence. Any step he made, any choice was at the bidding of his stomach, as he loved neither God, nor land, nor family, nor community. He was without any attachments or anchors. He was naked in the fullest sense of the word. As Reshetnikov fashioned it, this image was a brutal one, devoid of all elements of romanticization or humanization. One contemporary critic described the essence of Reshetnikov's idea and intention in this sketch as being "to present the life of the Russian simple folk in an unimaginably beastly condition, and the peasants themselves on a level of development where man is hardly different from animal."[12]

Reshetnikov's gray peasant was distinctive because of the qualities he lacked, not because of any positive action or mentality. He lacked belief in God; he lacked a sense of communion with the land; he lacked true membership in any social grouping; he lacked the ability to reason. He was the embodiment of the anomie of post-Emancipation rural Russia incarnate as the peasant cut loose from everything which previously or potentially bound him. Later contributors to this image were more subtle and more analytical in their effort to describe the peasant as a product of external forces of disruption, rather than the absence of the qualities of humanity or peasantness as they were understood in the early 1860s.

G. I. Uspenskii's Contribution to the Image

In the 1870s, the image of the gray peasant was to be most closely associated with the writings of Uspenskii. He shared both Reshetnikov's literary-journalistic style and his fundamentally pessimistic view of the future of village culture. Yet there is a certain irony in the fact that he would build on the foundation of the writings of the *raznochintsy* of the 1860s, and specifically on Reshetnikov's image of the gray peasant. For Uspenskii had rejected their vision of the *narod* as too imprecise and uninformed when he set off to begin a career independent of their influence. Uspenskii's image of the *seryi muzhik* differed from theirs and gained greater authority in the search for the peasant soul because of its juxtaposition with the image of the rational peasant in his natural environment. When the gray peasant appeared in Uspenskii's works in the 1870s, it became part of the contest between images in the discourse and between conceptions within Uspenskii's dialectic. The public controversy over the true nature of the Russian peasant provided the necessary energy to propel the image first formulated ten years earlier into the forefront of public opinion.

In Uspenskii's construction, the rational peasant was transformed into the *seryi muzhik* by the disruption of the autarky and harmony of his culture by the outside world, primarily in the form of money. Because the emphasis here was on disruption, on the intrusion of external forces, the image of the gray peasant offered the most explicit statement on such trends as the rise of a money economy, the elements of modernization, the destruction of the rural idyll and its effect on the inhabitants of the garden. Deprived of the system of nature, land, and labor as a meaningful whole, the peasant disintegrated into a misshapen fragment of his natural self. From Eden, Uspenskii traveled directly to the Apocalypse, and many lesser authors followed closely behind him.

We have already encountered some of Uspenskii's spoiled peasants through their juxtaposition with the rational peasant. The characters Mikhailo and Agrafen'ia Petrov in *From a Village Diary* fell prey to the seduction of the silver ruble and disintegrated morally as soon as they "could no longer understand the pleasure of struggling like a fish on the ice" in farming. The gray peasant had also appeared in an earlier incarnation in the sketch "Evil Tidings" (1875). In this piece, money appeared again as the endangering intruder, introduced to an isolated village by two symbols of modernization, the steamboat and the railroad.

From the first lines of the sketch, it was clear that this intrusion would be a mixed blessing at best. Uspenskii described the reaction of the peasants as they stood on the banks of the river, beholding the wonder of the steamboat upon its first appearance. "Not understanding what this creation was, these simple people experienced at the same time the sensation of something amazingly terrifying and amazingly gay."[13] These sensations disturbed the village, leaving the peasants in "a nervous, almost hysterical condition," which was only a prelude to the more permanent disruption that the steamboat and railroad would create.[14]

Uspenskii explored the breakdown of the rural milieu through the character of one peasant, Petrov, who landed a job with the railroad waking up the other workers in the morning and getting them out to the tracks. Uspenskii focused on the freedom that the money Petrov earned gave him, the independence from compulsion. That freedom, in Uspenskii's hands, was a dangerous thing, leading to Petrov's progressive dehumanization, drunkenness, and brutality. When the narrator posed the question of what such freedom had given to the villagers, the answer was that there were no benefits, only two major influences of moral disintegration. These were first, money, and more important, the freedom from his routine of unbroken labor that money gave the peasant. For freedom from labor gave the peasant his most dangerous enemy, thought, "the evil guest of dark places."[15] Having never had the time to think about himself or to make any personal choices in a world ruled by the need to fill his stomach, the peasant was lost when he began to think. The result was the moral chaos reflected in the deterioration of the peasant Petrov, a moral chaos that was "unimaginably terrible."[16] Released from the constraints of the agricultural cycle of nature, land, and labor, the peasant became not more human, but less so. Uspenskii's Petrov followed Reshetnikov's Podlipovtsy in becoming more brutish as he proved incapable of productive thought and instead was poisoned by thought itself.

In *The Power of the Earth,* Uspenskii developed this image through the central character, Ivan Bosykh, who explained that his deterioration was a result of freedom, *izza voli,* here meaning both the Emancipation and the freedom it granted.[17] He made money through occasional work at the railroad station, then promptly spent it on drink at the tavern. Because he was able to make quick and easy cash and answered to neither man nor the commands of the earth, he was terribly free to go wherever he wished and to do whatever he wanted. The gray peasant, liberated from the conditions which had bound him for centuries, could only weaken and fall prey to evil influences and instincts.

In his "From Conversations with Acquaintances on the Theme of *The Power of the Earth,*" Uspenskii explained this propensity for disintegration in the village to be a result of the absence of creative forces. However harmonious the traditional design of rural culture appeared, it lacked vitality. He declared that even where traditions persisted, the potential for disaster was ever-present.

> It is possible . . . to admire both this stability of the village patterns of life and their beauty and expanse, but it is not possible to explain their endurance and breadth by an abundance of creative consciousness. . . . There is no creative foundation in these beautiful forms of life—there cannot be, or there would not be those naive horrors, which, I repeat, immediately begin as soon as you turn aside from this . . . form (of human existence) either toward decline or toward well-being.[18]

Uspenskii stated here explicitly the implicit message in the figure of the *seryi muzhik:* neither rural man nor the environment from which he sprang had any inherent potential or strength. We see here the same basic type of contradiction that Dostoevsky had employed in his treatment of the *narod.* Whereas Dostoevsky's *narod* emerged as brilliant and shining examples of truth from the slime of centuries, however, Uspenskii's dialectic led to a different synthesis: the deflated peasant; the peasant who lacked consciousness, who had lost the reason so central to the image of the peasant as rational agriculturalist; the peasant who was the very opposite of national vitality or an expression of cultural promise. This was a sad indictment indeed of the countryside and the people from whom Uspenskii and his generation sought signposts for a vibrant future.

Zlatovratskii's Contribution to the Image

For all of his fame as the Rousseau of Russian village prose, Zlatovratskii contributed to this image of the peasant as well. However much he attempted to present the *muzhik* as communal and noble, he admitted features into the image of the peasant which invited his reception as potentially savage. This interpretation came through most clearly in the second half of *Foundations* and those articles on the mood in the countryside that he wrote at the same time he was completing the novel. In *Foundations*, the character of Petr Volk demonstrated what the loss of peasantness in the form of communal reasoning would bring, while the drunken rampage of the peasants in the village, and Ul'iana Mosevna's inability to comprehend it, served as further evidence of breakdown. Zlatovratskii thus presented two opposing tendencies springing from the same family origins which each concluded with the collapse of the communal peasant into the gray peasant, one beast, the other victim. Where Uspenskii identified the perils of money and the freedom it brought, Zlatovratskii focused on the urge for profit and dangers of alcohol. For both, freedom and consciousness acted as corrosive agents on their positive images of the rational and the communal peasants.

In his strictly journalistic series "The Popular Mood," Zlatovratskii moved away from assigning peasants inborn, permanent virtues that stood outside time and circumstance toward a recognition that the external environment and changing conditions of existence could and did shape the peasants. In the 1884 article of the series, he contrasted two visits to the same commune, the first during the mid-seventies, the second six years later. During the first visit, he had been impressed by the positive mood among the peasants, whose belief in equality held firm, as did their faith in the future. "No matter what their tribulations," he reported, "the peasants are always capable of finding within themselves the strength of renewal of rightful justice."[19] It goes without saying that these were the very qualities the intelligentsia, from Tolstoy to Uspenskii, were seeking as redemption and resurrection. After his second visit to the commune, Zlatovratskii returned with a darker view. He found that the prevalent mood was unrest and vague distress. Mutual aid had given way to universal mistrust and division, chronic complaints about decisions of the village assembly, and accusations against the constable.[20] He concluded that the concept of personal property was eating away at the communal ideal as the number of the very poor peasants increased and land was increasingly concentrated in the hands of a few.[21] In place of the confident claims about forthcoming "truth and beneficence," code words for a new, wholesale redistribution of the land to the peasants that he had heard before, Zlatovratskii met the question, How will we live now?[22] His reports thus indicated that the mood in the countryside had shifted from healthy confidence grounded in shared values of collectivism and justice to bewilderment and paralysis in the face of individualism and its by-product, economic differentiation. In his journalistic reports and his literary treatment of the village, Zlatovratskii had wound his way willy-nilly to an image of the gray peasant that reinforced Uspenskii's.

Further Reinforcement of the Image

A particularly ugly portrayal of these processes had appeared in the same journal, *Russian Thought,* in 1881 in a work by the pseudonymous Svetlin, "The Communal Soul, Sketches from Peasant Life." It rapidly became apparent to readers of this sketch that the author was employing the word *communal* as a trope, for the piece depicted tendencies in village culture which were the antithesis of the morality usually associated with the term. In this sketch of a village assembly and its deliberations, there are no positive peasant figures, only a cast of self-interested *muzhiks* gathered to decide the fate of an enfeebled, victimized old woman in the village. True to the form of the sketch, the author set up the tale with a statistical description of the economic condition of the community, one of unmitigated deterioration. He then described the wrangling of the men in the community about who would take on the care of the old woman, Abramukha, who had spent her life as a live-in servant in various households until her strength failed her. Each of the three most likely candidates to take her in fought bitterly to avoid having to provide for her in a stormy debate full of accusations and insults. The message that this scene conveyed was that if one scratched a communal peasant, one was likely to find a *seryi muzhik* who hardly represented the principles of conciliation and egalitarianism, much less nobility of spirit.[23] This sketch also reinforced the pattern in the demotion of village culture in public opinion where the expression of self-interest by the peasants was here, as elsewhere, coupled with exploitation and disrespect for others.

Engelgardt was less damning in his reporting on the peasants of Batishchevo. He did not proclaim the peasant under stress a potential animal who lost all human sympathy or conscious control of his life. He did, however, remain true to his definition of peasantness in terms of the requirements of land and labor. He asserted that once the land mastered the peasant, he was likely to abandon it, usually to become a lackey for a local member of the gentry. Usually such a peasant would look down on the physical labor of the peasant of the land, would strive to take his family out of the village and dress in German clothes, and his wife would take on airs. Once such a peasant made that move, there was no love lost between him and former villagers who could relate to him only as a fellow man of the land. Engelgardt followed the general view of the drab peasant when he stated that those peasants who left the land lost their substance; no other qualities remained to fill the void once the tie with the land was broken.[24] Although he was by no means as apocalyptic in his vision of the peasant without the land as was Uspenskii, he did contribute to the gathering sentiment that peasants were so much a product of their environment that they could not survive major changes to that environment.

Reshetnikov, Uspenskii, Zlatovratskii, and Engelgardt were actively engaged in the search for the peasant soul and thus framed their observations in terms of peasantness and the vitality of the peasant in his struggle for existence. Other observers went to the village to gather information or to serve without this particular goal. Even so, their reports contributed to the image of the failing peasant through graphic accounts of ill health and lethal addictions. As the network of *zemstvo* statisticians and doctors began to develop, the high morbidity of the Russian village came into view through the publication of data and personal experiences. Famine, cholera, high rates of infant mortality, and even the plague undercut any romantic image of rustic vigor and strength.[25] Ill health was largely attributed to poverty, filth, and ignorance.[26] Countering any popular notion of the cozy hearth in the peasant home, one eyewitness enjoined the reader, "Go to the country and you will see what misery is in the peasant izba that can hardly be called human habitation. . . . It is not a living space but a tomb."[27]

Drunkenness in the village also increasingly made its way into urban conceptions of rural life. All of the major publicists addressed the problem in their works, recognizing alcohol's pernicious effect on the health of the village, while many other eyewitnesses offered evidence on the phenomenon from their experiences.[28] As early as 1872, A. Aksakov explored the causes for the rise of drunkenness in the post-Emancipation village in a lengthy article in *The Russian Herald*. He concluded that for the Russian peasant, the social, political, and economic environment presented an irresistible temptation to drink.[29] In 1873, a major study sponsored by the Imperial Free Economic Society appeared. Although the author's focus was on alcoholism in the city, he also concluded that there had been a tremendous increase in the consumption in the village since the Emancipation, implying that freed peasants were likely to become drunken peasants.[30] The emphasis on the newness of the phenomenon, on the *rise* in alcoholism after the Emancipation, revealed the extent to which observers were nervous about the process of social and economic transformation they were living through. Similar alarms were being rung about the breakup of the extended patriarchal household in the village, about the incidence of mob justice, about poaching of wood and failure of peasants to respect contracts. In an atmosphere where anxiety about the true nature of the peasant, and about the newly freed peasant especially, was ubiquitous, reports of disease and drunkenness contributed to the perception that peasants were devoid of the requisite physical and spiritual strength to survive, much less prosper in reformed Russia.

The Gray Peasant as a Subject of the Itinerants

This image of the Russian peasant as the gray peasant, as a dreary and discouraging figure, found graphic representation and affirmation in the paintings of the Association of Traveling Exhibitions which began to cross Russia in 1871. It was to the concept of the gray peasant more than any other that the Itinerants contributed through their portraits of peasants and depictions of scenes from rural life. Self-consciously realistic in their style

and insistent on art's mandate to demystify the *narod,* these painters introduced a wide audience to powerful portrayals of rural Russian man. The
origin and aims of the Association of Travelling Exhibitions and the artists
who made up its membership are well known.[31] For the purposes of this
study, only a summary of their perception of the role of art and the artist as
observer bears review. My focus will be instead on placing the Itinerants
within the public debate over the peasant soul and analyzing the peasant
images they produced during the post-Emancipation period.

The peasant portraits and rural genre paintings of the Itinerant school
were the most obviously iconographic contribution to the search for the
peasant soul and revealed in a very direct way the traditions of icon painting in the history of Russian art. In the case of Ivan Nikolaevich Kramskoi,
who was the premier portraitist of the Russian peasant in the school, the
canon of icon painting was familiar from his work as an understudy to an
icon painter during his adolescence.[32] With the peasant portrait in particular, and paintings on rural themes in general, members of the Itinerant
school created plastic counterparts to the verbal constructs of the eyewitness account and the literary-journalist sketch. In the discourse over the
peasant soul these nineteenth-century realist painters were repeating the
relationship of the icon to Scripture as partners in the revelation of the
Orthodox Church. Lossky described the latter:

> [I]conography sets forth in colours what the word announces in written
> letters. Dogmas are addressed to the intelligence, they are intelligible
> expressions of the reality which surpasses our mode of understanding.
> Icons impinge on our consciousness by means of the outer senses, present-
> ing to us the same suprasensible reality in "aesthetic" expressions. . . .[33]

The inflection of religious art into this area of Russian realist painting
highlighted once again the peculiar combination of insistent objectivity and
loyalty to the principles of science with a concern for moral appraisals that
characterized the search for the peasant soul.

If the icons of the fourteenth through seventeenth centuries were designed to draw the viewer into the spiritual experience of the subject's
godliness, the peasant icons of the 1870s and 1880s were intended to draw
the viewer into the mundane experience of the subject. These paintings
often included the same poses, laconic expression, and absence of background detail characteristic of the classical icons. Although the limited
palette and the laconic nature of the works were the conscious result of the
artists' fealty to realism, their peasant portraits were formulaic in the tradition of icon painting. They resonated with the meaning of sacred symbols in
an era of scientific and critical realism. Saltykov-Shchedrin had called the
peasant the "hero of our time." These portraits suggested they might

equally be saints and martyrs, but the patina of heroism was denied them. Instead, they largely became images of vacuity and passivity, and thus devoid of the power to inspire. Just as the countryside was not the rural idyll or metaphorical Eden, so its inhabitants were not saints.

The Itinerants identified three major criteria for their art: that it be Russian, that it be contemporary, and that it be democratic or accessible to the Russian population beyond the capitals. Their view that art should treat themes which were both national and contemporary drew them, at the end of the 1860s, into conflict with the Imperial Academy of Art, where most of them received their training and at whose expense many of them had studied in the art capitals of Europe. While the Academy continued to emphasize painting that was classical in both theme and style, the young artists who broke free in the 1860s to form the Petersburg Artel' and the Association of Travelling Exhibitions rejected Scandinavian or Greek myths, historical epics, or Biblical tales as the only suitable subjects for Russian painting.

They preferred subjects which were closer to home, their four major genres being landscape painting, portraiture of major Russian cultural figures, topics from Russian history, and scenes from rural life—both landscapes or village scenes and peasant portraits. During the fifteen years or so of their existence as an association, the Itinerants produced works which were both realistic and critical; these were the years of innovation and aggressive autonomy, even opposition within the world of Russian culture.[34] The leading figures of this period were G. G. Miasoedov, V. M. Maksimov, I. N. Kramskoi, and I. E. Repin.

There is general agreement among Soviet and Western scholars that this school of painting, which set itself in opposition to the official art of the Imperial Academy as the free art of creative and independent painters, quickly came to dominate the Russian art scene of the post-Emancipation period. To quote only one of many similar appraisals, "The Society of the Peredvizhniki (Itinerants) gathered together or profoundly influenced for at least thirty years all that counts in Russian painting."[35] Much of their appeal to contemporaries and relevance for later generations resulted from their selection of subject matter. As Valkenier observed,

> Essentially they narrated the story of what Russia was living through during the thirty years of their ascendancy, times that were marked by rapid social, economic, and cultural change. Their pictures gave the contemporary public a commentary on current happenings and to succeeding generations a pictorial documentation of the past.[36]

Through this narration, Besançon concluded, "The Peredvizhniki performed the pictorial education of Russia."[37]

The notion of pictorial education was central in the aims of the members of the association and in their motivation in carrying art out of the capitals to such provincial centers as Kiev, Kharkov, Tula, Tambov, Poltava, Saratov, and Kazan.[38] Through these exhibitions, the Itinerants reached a wide audience and shaped the perceptions of tens of thousands of viewers about the land and culture of the Empire. We gain some sense of the extent of their impact from a report prepared by Miasoedov on the occasion of the twenty-fifth anniversary of the association's activities. For the five major cities of St. Petersburg, Moscow, Kharkov, Kiev, and Odessa, Miasoedov cited numbers of viewers at the first thirteen exhibitions. For Petersburg, these ranged from a low of 6,332 to a high of 28,666; for Moscow, 7,605 to 27,599; Kharkov, 1,998 to 9,780; Kiev, 2,831 to 11,105; and Odessa, 2,056 to 9,705.[39] Like the serious literary-political journals of the day, these exhibitions provided a forum for public opinion and a force of mediation among various levels of the culture.

The pattern of the treatment of the peasant in painting in the post-Reform era conformed to that in publicistic writing and literature, moving from relentlessly dreary pieces reminiscent of *raznochintsy* prose in the 1860s to more "objective," empirical studies of the peasant and his milieu in the 1870s and 1880s, and then to a retreat from realism in the 1890s. The shift to rural themes in Russia followed similar developments in European and American painting, particularly in the works of the French realists Millet, Courbet, and Breton and, of William Sidney Mount.[40] Although neither the artists themselves nor their Russian and Soviet biographers attribute much influence to the French realist tradition that emerged in the mid-1850s, many of the Itinerants studied in Paris in the 1860s and were certainly aware of the Salon movement. The aims of the association as incorporated in its charter in 1869 shared the general traits of European realism: "the requirements that art reach a broad, general public by using images that could be easily understood," as "an art form that examined the commonplaces of everyday life and meticulously rendered their details in order to record the world as each artist saw it."[41] The Itinerants' treatment of the peasantry, however, diverged from the French, especially that of Millet, and reflected the different intentions and purposes of the Russian artists.

On both the level of theory and the personal level, the Itinerants identified themselves and their work with the peasantry. V. V. Stasov, Russia's most powerful art and music critic of the era, was the self-appointed conscience of the movement. He shared the role of ideologue only with Kramskoi, who died in 1887. Stasov placed art squarely with the *narod:* "Art that does not originate from the core of the people's life, if it is not always useless and insignificant, is at least already untrue and always weak."[42] Four principles emerge here: art should originate with the people;

it should be purposeful; it should be true; and it should be forceful. Itinerant art originated with the people in that most of the major figures were either from the milieu of lower elements in towns or former state peasants who had grown up in the provinces, and knew rural life well. To maintain that familiarity, they frequently spent summers in the countryside, working in makeshift studios in abandoned storehouses or barns.[43] In this way, they gained authority in the debate over the peasant soul through empirical observation and personal experience. They also shared the moral and aesthetic requirements of literature of the period. This was evident in Miasoedov's description of the critical criteria of membership in the group: "The Association . . . united everyone who knew how to or just wanted to be sincere and true, according to one's strength and talent."[44] The Itinerants thus joined the larger discourse on the same terms as authors of literary treatments and publicistic writing. Through the conscious motivation of a sincere search for the truth, through investigation of rural life via personal experience in the countryside, and through sharing of their knowledge in a realistic medium, the Itinerants entered this public forum as full and legitimate members.

The peasant had begun to gain a position as an acceptable subject in Russian realist painting in the 1860s. Some of the most important works were those by V. G. Perov and early pieces by Miasoedov, Maksimov, and Kramskoi. Contemporaries and later critics agree in characterizing these early works as being less studies of the Russian peasant than depictions of the evils of Russian society reflected in vignettes from the life of the suffering *narod*. These peasant figures were cast as victims of serfdom and its legacies in Russia's social and economic order. Perov's *Easter Procession in the Country* (1861) is typical in its dual message of clerical drunkenness and peasant faith. Here we find an early emphasis on physiognomy which would be the hallmark of Itinerant peasant paintings in the following decade. The central points of this work are the faces of the peasant woman who carries the icon, the drunken priest who is holding himself up by grasping the porch post, and the old man who had fallen to the porch floor, spilling incense down the steps. In these three visages, Perov offered three examples of inebriation: one woman by ritual and faith and two men by liquor. All three illustrated the absence of consciousness characteristic of the gray peasant. If we recall Saltykov-Shchedrin's caveat against imagining a rural Eden in Russia in 1863, Perov's use of the procession of the faithful as a device to represent the dissolution of the peasantry holds particular force.

As the Itinerant school matured, they combined realism, portraiture, and psychological treatment of the peasant subject. Paintings which depicted the life and personality of the Russian peasant truthfully, they recognized, would strip him of much of the romantic haze that appealed to outsiders. Kramskoi expressed this realization in terms of the spectrum of colors he used in his peasant portraits, saying that in these works, "the closer to the truth, to nature, the more inconspicuous the colors."[45] Here we see conscious adherence to principles of realism being played out against a less obvious and perhaps unconscious loyalty to the canon of iconography. For in the icon, as well, it was essential to reduce detail to a minimum in the effort to produce a "maximum of expressiveness. . . ."[46] Similarly, the subjects of icons typically were "represented with their faces turned toward the congregation" in an effort to force communion.[47] In the canon of icons, if "the profile breaks communion, it is already the beginning of absence."[48] In the peasant portraits of the Itinerant school, the emphasis on the psychology of the subject and its various manifestations revealed much the same technique and message. Representations of the peasant in the 1870s and 1880s would follow this scheme of forcing communion with laconic peasants or depicting their alienation by turning their gaze away from the viewer.

Two further principles of the painting of peasants among the Itinerants may seem contradictory. On the one hand, they insisted that their peasant images introduce the public to peasant types and often so identified them, thus exhibiting the taxonomic approach so typical of the era.[49] On the other hand, they demanded that their portraits reveal the psychology of the individual subject. As Kramskoi wrote to Stasov in 1876, "For us, before all else (ideally at least) is character, personality, placed by necessity in a position through which all of the internal aspects come to the surface most clearly."[50]

It was this psychological aspect that both united the Itinerants with Russian educated society's search for the peasant soul and distinguished their realist art from that of the European school. More than other realist painters, the Itinerants painted detailed psychological portraits of peasants which they almost always labeled "studies," or *etiudy.*[51] In this sense the study in painting was what the sketch was to publicism. Whereas Millet and Courbet concentrated on the peasant at work in the field or in the farmyard as a figure with minimal facial definition surrounded by the physical elements which defined him, Maksimov, Miasoedov, Kramskoi, and Repin devoted considerable attention to the physiognomy and expression of their peasant subjects. French realists may have made psychological portraits, but they were of "anonymous peasants" defined more by the symbols of their occupation than by their expression or facial features. European realists produced images that matched the definition of the peasant as man of land and labor, while the Itinerants aimed for the essential peasant without his setting. In the end, the peasants of French realist construction would have more dignity than the Russian version, largely because of the positive value evident in the treatments of strength and vigor within the agricultural setting.[52] Viewers at the Traveling Exhibitions in Russia found themselves face to face with full-blown psychological portraits of peasant figures who were frequently set against a background of insignificant detail, with no elements within the frame to compete with the forceful elaboration of personality and its expression. Even in paintings which were essentially narrative, the characterization of the peasant figures set the tone of the work. In the education of the Russian public about village culture, these genres contributed fully to the evolution of concepts about the Russian peasants. The following analysis of several examples of peasant portraiture and genre paintings will explore how these works complemented literary and journalistic images of the gray peasant, while forcefully contesting the images of the *narod,* the rational, and the communal peasant.

In Perov's two portraits, *Fomushka–The Owl* (1868) and *The Wanderer* (1870), we see the convergence of realism, iconographic elements, portraiture, and psychological treatment of the peasant subject. These represent two distinct peasant personalities. With *Fomushka–The Owl,* the viewer encounters a sour, bitter, stubborn old man whose relentless glare and firmly compressed mouth make him a most unappealing figure. No background detail detracts from the portrait's focus: a peasant character whose wildness Perov illustrates with unkempt hair, knit eyebrows, and suggestive wrinkles around the eyes and over the forehead. In *The Wanderer,* on the other hand, Perov introduces a sympathetic figure whose posture, facial expression, and possessions combine to convey a more gentle, although equally realistic image of the Russian peasant. The details of his crossed hands on the walking stick, reminiscent of the staff held by saintly figures in icons; his bast shoes; his mild gaze; even the tin mug at his hip convey the essential humility identified with the figure of the holy wanderer in Russian culture. In these two treatments of the Russian peasant type, the dialogism of the larger debate is apparent. Just as with Turgenev's *Huntsman's Sketches* earlier, and in the work of many of the authors, observers, and painters of Perov's generation, the audience was faced with the question, Which is the real peasant? In his method here as in the other two works, Perov has used light and shadow to draw the viewer's attention to the peasant's face, to his physiognomy and psychology, which constitute the central focus of the work, adding to the urgency of that question. In the work of Perov, we thus see the two major tendencies of Russian realist treatment of the peasant theme: genre painting in the form of scenes from rural life and individual peasant portraits which aimed to convey the psychology of the subject, while drawing on the iconographic tradition in Russian painting.

When we move into the 1870s and 1880s, we find these qualities in full flower with an added emphasis on photographic realism. Portraiture, realism, and emphasis on psychology found their fullest expression in the work of Ivan Nikolaevich Kramskoi. Kramskoi was a talented and successful portraitist who supported himself and his family by painting for the social and cultural elite. His subjects included such individuals as Saltykov-Shchedrin, Tolstoy, Mendeleev, and Tret'yakov. When he painted his favored subjects, Russian peasants, Kramskoi also selected portraiture as his genre. He contributed not only the skills of a portraitist to his effort to paint peasant psychological types but also his experience with photography. As a young man, he had worked as the retoucher at a St. Petersburg photography studio, there mastering the technique of realistic representation in the medium of the photographic portrait of such figures as the Tsar and his family. From the loftiest subject to the lowliest, Kramskoi insisted on the realism of the photographer's eye.

His debut as an Itinerant painter in 1871 included peasant studies which were true to his dicta of realism, a limited palette, and a national subject. In *Peasant, A Life Study,* and *Head of an Old Ukrainian* we have two fine examples of the contribution the Itinerants made to the broad search for the real, true peasant. These figures are unalloyed *muzhiks,* with nothing of the idealized or romanticized *paysan.* Both works focus exclusively on the physiognomy of the peasant type, with all detail reserved for the rendering of the worn faces, the weary eyes, the chapped and wrinkled skin. Kramskoi turned his subjects' gaze away from the viewer, in both cases in a downcast gaze which adds to the general tone of dreariness and evasion often attributed to the peasants in written texts. This mood of dreariness became one of near-dehumanization in two portraits from 1872 and 1874, *Study of an Old Peasant. Muzhik with a Walking Stick* and *Head of an Old Peasant. Study of a Muzhik.* Again, the focus was on the face of these figures, with the light falling directly on the left side in both paintings. Here we find less distinction between the subjects and their backgrounds; their hair, beards, and clothing are disheveled. In each, the peasant's mouth hangs open as the head leans heavily forward and the troubled, empty gaze shifts downward.

Just as in the Reshetnikov's *Podlipovtsy,* these portraits convey as much through what they lack as through what they contain. They contain no sunlit setting of land and sky, no field and flower, no symbol of agricultural bounty, no fat cattle or full stalks of grain. In the peasants themselves, they contain not a single trait of health or hardiness, of pleasure, or of virtue. It is very difficult to identify any positive features of humanity. This starkness is all the more striking when compared with similar subjects in other cultures. In the United States, William Sidney Mount idealized the American farmer and his labor through setting and physical detail. As Elizabeth Johns has explained, his "farmers are not dirty, their clothes are neither soiled nor wrinkled . . . their cheeks are pink and their skin without blemish." Their effect was to "radiate good cheer and even amusement."[53] In France, Millet's peasants exhibited the effects of labor in their dress and features, their "figures echo the dignity of Michelangelo" and "displayed a domestic life that reasserted its humanity. . . ."[54] One need only to recall Millet's scenes of peasants gleaning, shearing, spinning, and praying to recognize the exceptional deflation of Kramskoi's peasant images.

Two further portraits from 1874 extended Kramskoi's presentation of these images, *The Peasant Ignatii Pirogov* and *The Woodsman*. *The Peasant Ignatii Pirogov* depicts a beaten man in ragged dress whose expression has been turned away from the viewer both through the use of the profile and by the obscured closed eyes. These make him the prime example of peasants Kramskoi described as "closed in on themselves." It was an image that took the evasion of gaze in the earlier portraits further and underscored the distance between the educated audience and the peasant subject.[55] *The Woodsman* similarly reinforced the concept of the peasant as other, as the peasant here greets the viewer with the wide-eyed glance of a startled animal. The colors in this portrait are limited to that of the forest, gold-browns and gray-greens. The peasant's animallike wariness is enhanced by the whiskerish quality of his mustache and beard, as well as by the lines of his hair as it sweeps back behind his ear. This peasant is a separate creature whose actions, Kramskoi suggests, follow a distinct pattern of logic. Of this character he wrote, "They act on their own. . . . He's an unsympathetic type, I know, but I also know that there are many such. I've seen them."[56] The two faces of the gray peasant being constructed simultaneously in the written texts of Uspenskii and others thus found visual representation in Kramskoi's alternative images of the peasant as dreary, passive, and defeated or as animallike and potentially disruptive or even destructive.

Grigorii Grigor'evich Miasoedov painted some of the most popular examples of pictorial narrative of scenes from rural life. His *The* Zemstvo *Dines* made a great splash at the second exhibition. In contrast to the monochromatic, empty background of peasant portraiture, this painting relies heavily on the setting to deliver its message. While the peasants occupy the foreground of the canvas, the title itself instructs the viewer to look beyond them through the open window of the *zemstvo* building. There is an element of irony in both the title and the theme of the painting. *The* Zemstvo *Dines* is set inside a cool building, with a meal accompanied by several wines from crystal decanters, while the peasants dine outside in the heat and dust on nondescript fare which they share, hunched against the wall of the building in the cool draft through the open door. Although the message that the peasants gain nothing from the *zemstvo* is only too clear, there is no idealization of the peasant himself. Each figure contributes to the mood of lethargy and resignation. One might imagine a simliar scene made up of animated peasants engaged in the camaraderie of an afternoon's respite, generously exchanging their hearty lunches as they discuss some issue or amusing incident. Instead, with the exception of the peasant who offers salt to his companion, each of these figures sits, stands, or lies wrapped up in his solitary world, separate from the others, smoking, sleeping or methodically working his way through a lunch of spring onions and salt. Loose limbs, bowed heads, dangling coats, disheveled hair, and blank faces deny the viewer the opportunity to make of these peasants anything other than listless, expressionless figures. Elements of the passivity and vacuity of the gray peasant fill the canvas.

The Itinerants complemented written images of peasants most directly when they illustrated works concerning the *muzhik.* Repin's illustrations for works by Tolstoy and Chekhov in the 1880s and 1890s confirmed the demystification that had dominated Itinerant art on the peasants since 1870. His sketches of drunken peasants for Tolstoy's brochures against alcoholism, his *The First Distiller* and *The Power of Darkness* and Chekhov's *Muzhiki* depict the dissolution of rural man under the impact of liquor. *The Drunken Husband* effectively portrays in minimal presentation the disarray and fear the drunken peasant creates in his household as he staggers through the door, board in hand. *Heads of Drunken Muzhiks* focuses on a trio of disturbed, besotted faces—one gay, one confused, one potentially violent— thus representing three ways alcohol can distort the man. Violence and the bottle go hand in hand in the village as depicted in Repin's sketch *On the Village Street,* where one drunken *muzhik* flails at peasant women while another waves the bottle, offering a shot to all comers.

These didactic sketches focused on alcohol as a temptation which the peasant must resist, yet the images they offered of drunken *muzhiks* conformed to the negative and discouraging figure of the gray peasant to be found in Itinerant peasant portraiture. As observers and investigators, writers and painters continued to concentrate on the village and to insist on realistic reporting and representation, fewer and fewer positive images of the peasant remained, and the peasant soul increasingly became a cause for lamentation rather than celebration. As the fate of the communal peasant suggested and the descriptions of the gray peasant confirmed, the good peasant was the weak peasant, the moral peasant was the endangered species, the peasant without the compulsion of labor or the traditions of the commune was ill-equipped to survive in his struggle for existence.

"Grandfather Sofron"

These conclusions came together in a short, but important literary sketch from 1885, "Grandfather Sofron," published in the Populist journal *Russian Wealth.*[57] Repin's illustration for the piece offers a graphic complement to the written message conveyed by the author, V. Savikhin. Savikhin populated his tale with the stock peasant figures of the previous fifteen years' development, set them in the familiar frame of the struggle for existence, but stressed not the struggle for existence against natural conditions or against extraspecific enemies. Here, the struggle is intraspecific as the consummate communal peasant who has become a gray peasant falls prey to the force of the village strongman, the *kulak*. In short, the gray peasant, Grandfather Sofron himself, is forced off his one-soul allotment of land at age eighty, despite the fact that he continues to work it to support his daughter-in-law and her three children. The *kulak* is able to secure this decision at the village assembly by buying drink for all the men who have gathered to vote. In Repin's illustration, everything about the figure of Grandfather Sofron speaks of helplessness and confusion, while the kulak at his side beams in the confidence of his position and his power. Grandfather Sofron has no recourse in the village or beyond; he can only stand in plaintive supplication as his hands dangle uselessly by his side. His plea spoke for all such gray peasants and voiced the fear of the educated members of society who had created his image.

> [W]hat am I without peasantness [krest'ianstvo]? Where am I to go? But here, I'm completely in charge! I've been used to the land, to Mother Earth since I was a baby, sixty years I have worked over her; I have torn my muscles and suffered heartache for her! She has become like a second daughter to me: you don't eat your fill, you don't get a full night's sleep, you're always thinking about your little strip of land. . . . And now . . . you would take it away. . . . Fellows, it's really my soul you're taking away![58]

Here Savikhin made explicit what the image of the gray peasant implied. As one of the leading liberal critics of the day recognized, the message in Uspenskii's *The Power of the Earth* and other crucibles of this figure's development was clear: "Tear the peasant away from his constant, all-consuming labor with the land and nothing of the peasant remains."[59] In the search for the peasant soul, the image of the drab, dreary gray *muzhik* offered the conclusion that there was no such thing as a specifically peasant soul, that there was no such thing as a peasant as a unique human type, born into this world with peculiar traits, proclivities, or talents. Instead, the peasant was a tabula rasa like all others, shaped and defined by his environment. Whatever peasantness represented, it was a product solely of the conditions of agricultural labor and the restraints of the commune. Once those conditions shifted or disappeared, so too would peasantness.

Whereas the concept of the tabula rasa usually connotes potential and promise, in this context it provoked pessimism. Critics understood that if the construct of the peasant psyche was such a fragile design that any disruption of the system spelled inevitable collapse, then all efforts to amend or strengthen the structure were doomed to fail. As one objecter queried, "And what will the authorities think of this *muzhik* of Ivanov's [Uspenskii's] who becomes a base creature once he is exposed to the world beyond his izba? How can they not believe that teaching this *muzhik* will lead to the 'destruction of society'?"[60] The problem was that the *seryi muzhik* was not really a blank slate. He was a dark slate, alternatively impassive or bestial, devoid of positive potential or inherent strength. He was capable of positive peasantness under the influence of land, labor, and the commune. Other influences in the shape of money, profit, and alcohol caused inward collapse. He represented the crisis of self-doubt in the search for cultural self-definition in a transforming world in its fullest expression. Poised on the threshold between paternalism and agrarianism and the urge for profit and industrialism, educated Russians found that they could not look back to the village as a taproot of Russia's future. They denied nostalgia for an agrarian traditionalism not only because of the heritage of serfdom, but also, the image of the gray peasant declared, because the peasants who had stood outside Russia's national development before the Emancipation did not have the requisite human qualities to participate in her national development afterward. Not all peasants collapsed in the transforming village, however. Not every peasant fell victim to change. There was a strong peasant image, a peasant survivor, a peasant strongman. He took the form of the even darker image, the *kulak*.

7

Kulak:
The Village Strongman

Under serfdom, the *kulak* and the exploiter did not exist, there was only the tavern-keeper, but the tavern-keeper then was minor and modest. This was still the embryo for whose development there was not a favorable environment, the appropriate opportunity had not arrived. But as soon as a favorable environment appeared, the embryo grew.

N. V. SHELGUNOV, "Ocherki russkoi zhizni. XXII"

The final image of the male peasant to emerge in the search for the peasant soul in the post-Reform period was that of the *kulak,* the village strongman, the local bigwig, the agent of manipulation and exploitation within the peasant community. With this image, the Darwinian model of intraspecific struggle was applied to Russian rural culture as educated outsiders grappled with the disconcerting evidence of competition, economic differentiation, and political and social structures that belied the vitality of mutual aid and the natural economy. This figure was also a product of the tendency of investigators of village culture to focus on economic structures and relations as evidence of the fundamental systems of village life that shaped all social relations. Observers of the village increasingly transferred their mental construct of exploitation from the familiar paradigm of gentry exploitation of the peasant, of *obshchestvo* exploitation of the *narod,* to peasant exploitation of fellow peasant, to *kulak* exploitation of the hapless communal or gray *muzhik.* In this aspect, the *kulak* became the embodiment of evil, of the desecration of the natural harmony and morality of the idealized village, and by extension an expression of the features of a money economy which alarmed many members of *obshchestvo.* His presence in the village also served as evidence of the average *muzhik's* inability to protect himself and as justification for the educated outsider to reassert his protective, paternalistic role of tutelage, *opeka.*

139

The *kulak* was equally, although less obviously, the symbol of individualism in the village, the symbol of a fully developed peasant personality who exhibited not only a distinct logic but also a distinct morality, and who enjoyed an appeal in the eyes of his fellow peasants who granted him the power to manipulate them. Whereas the *kulak* as exploiter was the object of universal condemnation, the *kulak* as stong individual received a mixed review. Populists, neo-Slavophiles, and that body of writers who could loosely be called progressive-radical and who wrote for *Notes of the Fatherland* and its successor, *The Northern Herald,* had nothing good to say about the *kulak*. Contributors to *Russian Herald,* on the other hand, wrote positive portraits of the *kulak* and implicitly approved of the individualism and force of personality he represented.

The primary meaning of the word *kulak* is fist, a physical gesture whose dual messages of strength and miserliness entered the morphology of the term as it was applied to peasants. A *kulak* was both powerful in village politics and infamous for his tightfisted control of money. The companion term for *kulak* was *miroed,* which literally means commune eater and thus expresses the full extent of exploitation and living off one's own kind. For outsiders, power and exploitation constituted the central characteristics of the peasant strongman. Engelgardt included these in his concise definition of the *kulak*'s basic motives: "individualism, egotism, and the striving for exploitation."[1]

For the post-Emancipation generation of writers, journalists, ethnographers, justices of the peace, and *zemstvo* activists, the *kulak* and his activity, *kulachestvo,* were a puzzle and a challenge. As Shelgunov's statement at the head of this chapter suggests, one of the central questions for *obshchestvo* was where this phenomenon originated. In addition to discerning where the *kulak* came from, outsiders were also eager to define his psychology and describe his role in the village. In contrast to later figures, notably Lenin and Stalin, members of the first generation of students of the *kulak* were cautious in their examination of this figure in peasant culture and self-consciously objective in introducing him to the reading public outside his rural setting. Their efforts to define the workings of the peasant soul led them into dark corners and obscure relationships which suggested that the peasant as *kulak* had his own internal logic and function in village life, a logic and function that made him and the peasants he controlled inaccessible to outsiders and their institutions.

Definition of the Origins of the *Kulak*

There was broad agreement on the origin of the *kulak* and his activities. The urge for profit and power was a latent peasant trait, the majority of observers concluded, which had blossomed in the environment of the post-Emancipation village. The *kulak* or *miroed* was a native product of the village, familiar to the community of peasants who recognized him as their kin. Just as he appears in Repin's sketch for Savikhin's "Grandfather Sofron," the *kulak* emerged from the background of village culture to assume a central and confident position. Engelgardt offered one of the fullest expositions of this conclusion.

> Every peasant possesses a certain dose of *kulachestvo*, with the exception of half-wits, and especially good-natured people and the "Russian carp" in general. . . . I have more than once indicated that among the peasants individualism, egotism and the striving for exploitation are very highly developed. Envy, mistrust of each other, intrigue against each other, the humiliation of the weak before the strong, forceful arrogance, worship of wealth,—all of this is highly developed in peasant culture. *Kulak* ideas reign there; everyone is proud of being a pike and strives to devour the carp. Every peasant, if the conditions are favorable, will be the most excellent example of an exploiter of anyone else, be he lord or peasant, to squeeze the juices out of him to exploit his needs.[2]

In Engelgardt's description, then, every peasant hoped to be a *kulak*, as long as he had the mental capacity to do so. In the catalogue of desirable qualities, the peasant included personal wealth, individual strength, the ability to manipulate others and to profit from anyone who was unfortunate enough to be vulnerable to exploitation. In this view, *kulak* qualities not only characterized the strongmen of the village but shaped the aspirations of the average Russian peasant. Engelgardt's reference to the pike and the carp drew on an established relationship in Russian folklore in which the pike inevitably outwitted or overwhelmed then consumed the carp and which thus made these two fish cultural images of strength and weakness.[3] His juxtaposition of the weak and the strong also conformed to the model of contest and struggle and thus resonated with the concept of the survival of the more adaptable species.

In his eyewitness account of his tenure as a *volost'* clerk, Astyrev also stressed the indigenous nature of the *kulak* in the village. He argued that *kulaks*

> could not be considered an inflicted or accidental phenomenon: they are an economic category, they are a product, inevitably produced by every commune of sufficient size, in which differentiation and individualism find enough ground for development. (The *kulak*) is an intellectual force, it is completely unnecessary that he be rich, but it is essential that the possibility of feeding himself around the commune be present . . . I repeat, (the *kulak*) is so necessary to the current peasant commune that in the event of

his accidental absence, the commune must produce another out of its
midst. . . .[4]

Although Astyrev's analysis was somewhat more conditional than Engelgardt's, he also placed the *kulak*'s roots in the peasant community. His
definition of the appropriate environment for full growth of the phenomenon as being "differentiation and individualism" suggested that the traditional commune of economic homogeneity and collectivism had to be giving way before the *kulak* could thrive. Yet, his assertion of the inevitability
of the figure in the contemporary commune accepted as a given that this
process was well under way.

The radical Populist and journalist N. V. Shelgunov placed equal stress
on the decline of the commune and communal principles in his exploration
of the pathology of *kulachestvo*. He identified the phenomenon as being a
novelty of the post-Emancipation era and a product of the new principle of
existence defined by the Emancipation: the free individual, "upon which
were set all hopes for resurrection and renewal."[5] Shelgunov quickly defended the principle of the free individual as progressive and full of potential for the development of Russia. Writing in 1888, he concluded with
regret, however, that the introduction of this principle in Russia had borne
only evil fruit. Whereas it was possible that the manifestation of this principle in the peasant's desire for his own plot of land, his own nuclear household, his own unrestrained will could have led to the emergence of a
vigorous and virtuous peasantry, quite the opposite had happened in fact.
"Unfortunately, it turned out differently and the village man with a sense of
individuality not only did not exhibit any kind of virtue, but, on the contrary, established for himself only the glory of the extortioner and the
thief."[6]

Why had this been the case? Why was it that the *kulak* seemed to be a
peculiarly Russian phenomenon, with no counterpart in America, for example? Shelgunov argued that it was not because the *kulak* was born a *kulak*,
not because God had made him that way. No, the *kulak* took shape and
thrived in the peculiarly Russian environment of weakness and impotence.
The pervasive feebleness of Russian society provided fertile ground for
exploitation and manipulation. Like Astyrev, Shelgunov went on to say
that as long as these conditions persisted, the *kulak* would be an inevitable
feature of Russian culture. "*Kulachestvo* is a phenomenon created by certain circumstances and as long as these circumstances exist, *kulachestvo*
will flourish. . . ."[7] Shelgunov thus followed Uspenskii rather closely in his
vision of an exclusively negative metamorphosis of the true peasant, the
pre-Emancipation peasant, into an individual spirit who could exercise his
free will only in a destructive or exploitative manner. His emphasis on the

weak as the determining agents of that metamorphosis also suggested that the concept of intraspecific struggle informed his diagnosis of *kulachestvo.* By arguing that the phenomenon of the *kulak* was unique to Russian culture because of the absence of vitality, of what Uspenskii had earlier termed "creative consciousness," Shelgunov also reversed the usual elements in the self-definition of Russia's national exceptionalism. This was a concept that had usually been linked with the image of the *narod,* and with the homogeneity, uniformity, and submission of the individual to the group that it connoted. Shelgunov's argument that the individualistic urge for profit through the exploitation of weak members of the community was to be found only in Russia illustrated the extent to which the public debate over the peasant soul had undermined and redefined cultural self-images by the end of the 1880s.

Although there was general agreement on the strictly peasant origins of the *kulak,* on the phenomenon of *kulachestvo* as the blossoming of an existing element in the peasant psyche and village culture, there was equal consensus on the fact that peasants who became *kulaks* somehow stepped outside the framework of peasantness, however defined. Thus, although Engelgardt believed that "every *muzhik,* at times, is a *kulak,*" he argued that he became one only when he broke free of the preoccupation of labor. Similarly, Uspenskii explained, "[A]ll their life is governed by nature and their will is totally subjected to it. If their circumstances are eased in any way that frees them from the laws of nature, then they discover human will with all its dangers. . . ."[8] Zlatovratskii's *Khoziaistvennyi muzhik,* or enterprising peasant, who sat on a narrow fence between retaining membership in the commune and becoming a *kulak,* had freed himself from subsistence peasant farming and managed his own life according to terms he himself established. Zlatovratskii was alarmed by the independence and individualism which they lauded. "Many clever *muzhiks* live here among us. We know how to run things,"[9] these enterprising peasants boasted, contesting an image of conciliatory governance of the commune by worthy elders. The paradox of the insistence that the *kulak* was both a product of the village and inherently potential in every peasant, yet that to become a *kulak,* the peasant stepped out of peasantness, revealed the resistance among educated outsiders to accepting the phenomenon as a native element, indeed as a defining element in transforming Russian culture. If we accept the search for the peasant soul as a search for the Russian soul, for the true nature of Russian culture, the degree of distress that *kulachestvo* elicited in members of educated society becomes more comprehensible. If the true peasant was capable solely of negative metamorphosis, then the future did not bode well for Russian culture writ large.

The *Kulak*-Individualist

There was no small amount of disapproval, even resentment, among outsiders who encountered village strongmen. Although they may have framed their criticisms of this willfulness in the context of the solidarity and collectivism they expected to find in the village, their rejection of *kulak* individualism suggests equally that they were uncomfortable when they discovered strong, fully developed personalities among the unenlightened and simple *narod*. The *kulak* of their description defied their concept of the peasant as child or tabula rasa. Remnants of their view of the *narod* as benighted, childlike, and victimized, however, persisted even in their appraisal of the *kulak*-egotist, whose second major trait was his exploitation of his fellow peasants whose vulnerability or naïveté was an essential foil to the *kulak*'s "maturity."

Given this discomfort among most Populist writers over the individualism manifested in the *kulak,* it is interesting to note the appearance of some positive portraits of enterprising, powerful, and rich peasants in the *Russian Herald,* an increasingly conservative journal in the late 1860s. As early as 1867, the eminent folklorist V. I. Dal' published a series of ethnographic sketches of the peasantry in which the *kulak* appeared as an admirable figure. Under the title "Samorodok" (The self-made man), Dal' described a character who incorporated all of the features which would enter the morphology of the *kulak* image in the 1870s and 1880s. His Merkula Artamonovich was an "efficient and intelligent *muzhik*" who was respected in trade, whose word was trusted, and who did not hide his profits but displayed them openly. He earned the respect of his fellow peasants through his evident strength and power, particularly his self-confidence in dealings with the gentry as a peasant delegate to the *zemstvo*. Although respectful, his fellow peasants were also wary of Merkula Artamonovich, because of his reputation for slyness and inflexibility in demanding fulfillment of the terms of any bargain he struck. "Watch out with him, take care: he'll take your hide afterwards, no matter what you do!" Finally, Merkula Artamonovich had a lot of money in circulation; Dal' thus suggested that he was thick in the practice of moneylending. For otherwise a "simple *muzhik,* without means, would not have forged so much wealth for himself with his fist (*kulakom*)."[10] Efficient, enterprising, powerful, sly, unforgiving when it came to demanding his due, and a moneylender—these were the features of the *kulak* which would soon become familiar to educated Russia.

Andrei Pecherskii introduced a similar character in a story rich in ethnographic detail one year later. In this rather lengthy tale, Pecherskii focused on the family drama of a powerful *muzhik*, Patap Maksimych Chapurin. In the opening lines of the first installment, Pecherskii took pains to stress the essential Russianness of the community and individuals in the drama, set in a village beyond the Volga. "There is old Rus', primordial Rus', old-fashioned Rus'. From the time that the Russian land was conceived, there have been no foreign inhabitants beyond the Volga. There old Rus' remains pure—she remains to this day as she was in the time of our ancestors."[11] Given the untouched nature of the region, the phenomenon of the powerful, prosperous *muzhik* there confirmed the notion of his native origins and alerted readers to the author's intention that this story be read as a parable of contemporary, true Russian culture.

In this area, such peasants were known as *tysiachniki,* as thousanders, because they had thousands of rubles stashed away. Unlike *kulak* and *miroed,* the term *thousander* did not have an explicit connotation of either the power of the fist or the bloodsucking of the commune-eater. Pecherskii described them as enterprising, self-reliant, hardworking peasants who, despite the challenges of the climate and the forest, "eat their fill, are well-dressed, have good shoes, and owe no taxes."[12] In the second installment of the story of Patap's family, Pecherskii explored the economic power that Patap and other thousanders had. As the owner of a pottery, Patap was typical of his type.

> All local industry is in their hands, and all the ordinary peasants are completely dependent on them and under no circumstance whatsoever can they escape their will. A thousander like Patap Maksimych, for whom several surrounding villages work, lives like a true lord in his area. His will is law, any kindness from him is counted as charity, and his anger as a calamity because he is a powerful man: if he wanted to, he could utterly destroy anyone he desired.[13]

In Pecherskii's tale, the powerful peasant Patap Maksimych did not destroy anyone through his economic power; quite the contrary, he was consistently a good-hearted man, however patriarchal. Pecherskii's morality tale revolved not so much around Patap's power over his fellow peasants as an employer as that over his daughter as a patriarch. She resisted his choice of a husband and in her protest voiced a strong defense of the principle of individualism, of her right to exercise her free will, however it may have opposed that of her father. Thus, although this tale contributed to the image of the *kulak* as a strongman, most of whose power devolved from his economic control of the peasants in his community, the author defended the principle of individualism and was able to conceive of a peasant both powerful and positive.

The *Kulak*-Exploiter

For most other observers, however, power and profit could only result from exploitation, an unacceptable manifestation of evil greed and of the presence of competition and economic differentiation in the village. The element of exploitation in the *kulak's* makeup is the most familiar aspect of the image for students of Russian history, who often use the term synonymously with the term *village usurer*. It was this element which gained Lenin's full attention in his study of capitalism in Russia, and on which the Soviet regime hoped to play in seeking support from the so-called poor peasants and *batraki*, victims of that exploitation.[14] Our usage of the term has largely followed Lenin's emphasis on exploitation as the characteristic feature of the *kulak* who lent money at high interest rates, rented land at exorbitant prices, and hired fellow peasants for low wages. Kingston-Mann, for example, defines the *kulak* as "(lit. fist) rich peasant; pejorative term commonly used to refer to peasants who lent money at high interest or otherwise exploited their neighbors."[15] To return to Astyrev's phrase, exploitation in the *kulak* image meant feeding himself at the expense of his community. The minor Populist writer N. Naumov also used this concept in 1873 when he divided peasants into two groups, "[t]hose who have profited well and those who are making their profit."[16]

Some of the richest sources on such activity were reports and memoirs of *volost'* clerks whose responsibilities included recording all contracts between peasants, observing *volost'* court sessions, filing complaints with the justice of the peace on behalf of disgruntled peasants, and keeping a file of all settlements of their disputes. The *volost'* clerk was thus privy to much of the wheeling and dealing in the village. His was the office not only of records but often also of appeal. He reported to the regional authorities on matters related to tax collection and arrears, a responsibility that required familiarity with the financial position of the various households under his jurisdiction. An honest and effective *volost'* clerk (a relatively rare phenomenon, it seems) familiarized himself with the economy of his area and frequently sent his impressions back to readers in the capitals. These reports provided material out of which the image of the exploitative peasant could be formed.

The Populist radical Ivanchin-Pisarev served as a *volost'* clerk in Iaroslavl' Province in 1877. He found himself in a settlement where, the elder warned him, the *kulaks* ruled.[17] Ivanchin-Pisarev found the warning well founded within days of his arrival in the *volost.'* The issue which brought the *kulaks* to the fore was *zemstvo* payment of insurance premiums to peasants who had recently lost homes in a fire. He was responsible for distributing the cash to the peasants who had made legitimate claims. Word soon spread throughout the *volost'* that this distribution was imminent, and several peasants appeared at the *volost'* administration office to demand the cash. Ivanchin-Pisarev discovered that these were not the peasants who had filed claims but their creditors, including the village priest. The priest's claim was against the peasant Petr Shchukin, to whom he had sold a horse worth forty rubles, which he charged with twenty rubles interest. The priest produced a signed agreement in which Shchukin had guaranteed his purchase with his possessions, including his house. The agreement included a clause that stated that the priest would receive any insurance if the house burned.[18]

This priest and other creditors insisted that the money should go directly to them to pay off debts owed them; they fully expected the *volost'* clerk to accede to their demands. The legitimate recipients equally anticipated that such would be the course of events, judging from past experience. The petty drama concluded with a village assembly which Ivanchin-Pisarev called and at which he read and explained the law stating that such premiums were to go exclusively for the rebuilding of lost homes. The *kulaks* were turned away.[19] Vignettes such as these introduced the reading public to the types of contracts *kulaks* were able to arrange, to the levels of interest they demanded, and to their recognition of the power of the written agreement in a rural society where illiteracy was the rule.

Astyrev reported that in his region the terms of the Emancipation had been a boon for enterprising peasants. As he explained, land was considered cheap in the early years after the Reform, so much so that peasants frequently traded a desiatina (2.7 acres) for a bottle of vodka. Many peasants were not interested in working their land and had given it to the commune to rent for income to cover communal expenses. The commune had 300 desiatin of such land at its disposal, all of which was rented out to "*kulaks* and *miroeds*" for half the going rate. They, in turn, chose either to work it themselves or, as land became more valuable, to rent it at the going rate to other peasants of the community. In either case, their profit was considerable, as was their power over anyone in the village who hoped to extend the land he cultivated.

Engelgardt also devoted considerable space in his letters "From the Country" to the phenomenon of the peasant landlord or employer and his willingness to exploit his fellow peasants. His definition of the *kulak* quoted previously arose from this discussion, which appeared primarily in the tenth letter, published in 1881. After the passage cited, Engelgardt continued in his description of the generic peasant, "if there is a chance to extort from someone, he will extort." He described a village of peasants who began to prosper by renting abandoned gentry lands, first exhausting nearby lands, then, "having exhausted the closest lands, began to take land in distant localities where the peasants are poor, simple, and in great need, they—and not just one, furthermore, but all of them—immediately began to exploit the need of the peasants there, they began to give grain and money to them in exchange for labor."[20]

Engelgardt insisted that such behavior in and of itself did not a *kulak* make. He drew a distinction between the motivation and the manner of the peasant's activities. "Of course, he makes use of another man's need, he makes him work for him, but he does not build his well-being on the need of others, but builds on his own labor." Most important, such a peasant exploiter was not a *kulak* because his goal was not money. "He expands his farm not with the goal of profit alone; he works to the point of exhaustion, he does not get full, he does not eat his fill. Such a peasant of the land never has a big gut, the way a real *kulak* does."[21] In contrast to such a true peasant of the land, Engelgardt offered a portrait of a true *kulak*. "This one does not love the land, or farming, or labor; this one loves only money. . . . This one prides himself on his fat gut, he prides himself on the fact that he himself does little work. . . . His idol is money and he thinks only about its increase."[22] Like Shelgunov, who may very well have drawn his conclusions from Engelgardt's account, Engelgardt argued that the *kulak* could thrive only in an environment of pervasive poverty, could only prosper where there was weakness to exploit, for "there is nothing for a *kulak* to take from a prosperous landed *muzhik*. . . . "[23]

It is worth stressing that at this point in the search for a definition of the *kulak* and his activities, the mere practice of hiring fellow peasants, and even of exploiting them as hired hands, did not necessarily earn a peasant the label of *kulak*. For Engelgardt, it was not the phenomenon of the peasant employer which was distasteful; it was the phenomenon of the peasant who did not work himself and whose sole aim was the accumulation of greater and greater sums of money. In other words, it was the peasant-capitalist, complete with the emblematic fat gut, who was a real *kulak*.

Other observers were also sensitive to the intrusion of money in the natural economy of the village as a catalyst for the appearance of the *kulak*. Zlatovratskii described the appearance of the enterprising peasant to be the "result of compromises between the peasant's outlook with external influences," suggesting that the urge toward profit conflicted with and threatened to overwhelm communal virtues as peasants struggled to adapt to a money economy.[24] Uspenskii also focused on the penetration of money as a new requirement and aspiration of village life. His description of the village of Slepoe Litvino in *From a Village Diary* included a tax profile: the village owed 1,082 rubles 3/4 kopek a year and the arrears for the village of sixty households had risen to 8,000 rubles by the time he arrived in 1877.[25] The constant need for money, he explained, drove the peasant into the arms of the *kulak*.[26] He also included in his *Diary* a sketch of descriptions of peasant daydreams about money, how to get it, and what to do with it once they had it.[27] Astyrev joined this chorus when he complained that in Kochetov, "everyone lives here by the ruble and for the ruble."[28]

Money became a symbol for evil and sin because the *kulak* could only acquire it through the victimization of his fellow peasants. Uspenskii made this clear in his apocalyptic vision in *The Power of the Earth*. In his account "The Past of Ivan Bosykh," he directly juxtaposed the drab *muzhik* as childlike victim and the *kulak* as mature exploiter. As Ivan Bosykh recounted the tale of his perdition, the themes of the dangers of money and vulnerability to negative actors merged. As the third Ivan of Uspenskii's peasant cycle, Bosykh appeared as a broken man who had fallen prey to drink in the post-Emancipation era, losing his vitality and peasant substance "because of the freedom."[29] In this later sketch, the reader discovered that not only freedom but also money and his fellow peasants had made him a victim.

Money, he explained, was a post-Emancipation phenomenon which disrupted his life. The first step along the path of destruction for him had been borrowing money from the village moneylenders. When he could not meet their terms, he hired himself out to a friend of his brother-in-law for low wages. He was certain that this peasant had made great profit from his labor. In addition, Ivan Bosykh's peasant employer had taken his calf and sold it at a high price. Finally, his employer had reclaimed a horse which Ivan Bosykh thought he was paying for over time. Overwhelmed, Bosykh became violent, took to drink, had numerous problems with the *volost'* court, and beat his wife. In sum, the *kulaks* had ruined him. And what contributed to his vulnerability? Uspenskii concluded, "I could only be amazed at what a childlike, naive soul was preserved in this . . . good man, in whose confused life gathered, for some reason, only evil, only indignation."[30] Each *kulak* required a victim on whom to feed and the mass of drab, dreary gray *muzhiks* produced a steady supply.

Outsiders in general, and Uspenskii in particular, took pains to convey the peasants' disapproval of the exploitative peasant, whom they were likely to call a *miroed*. In the sketch "Now and Before," Uspenskii described how a local *volost'* court ordered that one of the wealthy peasants of the village be beaten because he had sold a calf to buy a mirror, thus breaking village conventions on economic norms. He explained that the purchase of a watch would elicit a similar response. "Whereas an outsider might see a peasant with a silver watch, and see only a silver watch, another peasant sees not a watch but a horse or 100 puds of hay—in his pocket is a whole horse bought through the need of another and sold for a high price, and in no way sees a watch with two hands."[31] Luxury items in the possession of a wealthy peasant thus had the same connotation here as did the fat gut of the *kulak* for Engelgardt.

Uspenskii described a more spectacular instance of retribution against the *kulak*. He witnessed a forest fire which alarmed him but caused no stir in the village. Perplexed, he investigated the matter and discovered that the local peasants had set fire to a large store of hay owned by the elder. It seemed that the elder, who had formerly been a hardworking *muzhik* and respected member of the community, had begun to exploit his fellow peasants when he gained control over tax collection. Whenever a peasant could not pay his taxes, the elder seized hay as payment in kind, only to sell it at a profit for himself. The peasants' means of reestablishing what they considered to be a correct norm of equality was to destroy all of the hay he had taken from them.[32] This *muzhik* had become not only an elder *kulak*, but also a *miroed*. Peasants attributed power to the *kulak*, but exploitation to the *miroed*. On this aspect of the village strongman's makeup, peasants agreed with outsiders that it was wrong and unacceptable. Given adequate provocation, even as victims, they would seek retribution.

Two further contributions to the definition of the *kulak* as exploiter deserve mention. Both appeared in *The Cause* at the beginning of the 1880s, at a point when the morphology of the *kulak* was taking firm enough shape to serve as a basis for expansion and comparison. The first was an eyewitness account which described one Petr Ivanovich Skromnov, a *"kulak*-communalist" who the author asserted was "a real person, not a figment of my imagination."[33] He inhabited the village of Gabulino, where he lived well by charging exorbitant prices for rent on land and seed for grain to other peasants. He was thus a typical *kulak*-exploiter. He was equally, however, an *obshchinnik*, a man of his commune, because he exploited only peasants who lived outside Gabulino and used his wealth to aid the members of his own community. Thus, in his one person, he represented the "duality of soul and two-faced character" of peasant culture which often confounded outsiders.[34] Over the next twenty years, the study of customary law through ethnographic surveys and expeditions would convince outsiders that the peasants did indeed follow distinct moral codes for those within their immediate community and for those outside their community, making such an apparently contradictory figure less of a mystery.[35]

In September 1881, after the surge in pogroms in the south of Russia, B. Lenskii's article "The Jew and the *Kulak* (A Socio-Economic Parallel)" appeared. In the face of much talk of Jewish exploitation, and the "especially loud cries from patriots and nationalists," Lenskii asked, "But what of Russian exploitation of Russians in the form of *kulachestvo?*"[36] He went on to discuss *kulak* activity as peasants exploiting the labor of fellow peasants in much the same terms as other writings on the subject. His insistence, however, that the *kulak* was no better than the Jew and, in fact, was morally worse than the Jew because he exploited his own kind, made Lenskii's article one of the most scathing in the debate on the origins and nature of *kulachestvo*. It also had the effect of linking exploitation with the Russian national character, reversing the usual attribution of this quality to Jews, who supposedly fed off the Russian peasants.

By the 1880s, the term *kulak* had indeed become synonymous with the term *exploitation*. Both Engelgardt and Sharapov employed it in their discussion of gentry farming, but not to apply to peasants. Just as Engelgardt took the term *rational farmer* and gave it to the peasants, so he took the term *kulachestvo* and foisted it on the gentry in one of his more elegant trope reversals. One of the major contributions of his letters was an examination of gentry use of "cut-off lands," former pasture and forest cut off the maximum allotment of peasant lands as part of the Emancipation to keep peasants in debt and thus obligated to work much as they had under serfdom. This, and the purely exploitative attitude of absentee gentry landowners toward their land, that is, their exclusive focus on profit, led Engelgardt to conclude, "The entire system of current gentry farming is supported, properly speaking, by the harness, by *kulachestvo*."[37] In much the same way, Sharapov confessed that when he decided to return to his estate in Smolensk to practice rational agronomy, he was self-conscious among the intelligentsia because he always felt people were saying to themselves "*kulak*-exploiter, landlord."[38] This confession indicates the extent to which the term *kulak* had become a synonym for exploitation in Russian culture, and specifically exploitation in the agricultural setting.

Although exploitation was the most obvious feature of the *kulak* for contemporaries, and the element that has persisted most tenaciously to this day, largely because of Lenin's usage and its subsequent enshrinement in the Soviet worldview, contemporaries were equally sensitive to the *kulak's* role as village strongman, to his power to manipulate village politics, and to control, often to block, the access of outsiders and their institutions to the peasant community. Although outsiders may have displayed some unwitting discomfort in their description of the *kulak* as a stong individual or egotist, their resentment of the *kulak* as manipulator or schemer was conscious and, I would argue, the most important factor in the deterioration of positive myth making about the Russian peasant. Similarly, whereas their disapproval of the *kulak*-exploiter had the patina of moral superiority, their rejection of the *kulak*-strongman revealed their frustration as would-be reformers or protectors of the peasantry.

For outsiders, the *kulak* was first and foremost a by-product of economic differentiation in the village and the breakdown in the previously perceived homogeneity of peasant life. Approaching the village with the dual construct of Darwinism and the critique of capitalism, they expected and found competition and exploitation in every peasant relationship that contributed to or illustrated economic differentiation. Their confidence that differentiation equaled competition led them to see the *kulak* as the manifestation of intraspecific struggle, as the pike always and everywhere striving to devour the carp who was fleeing his destruction. Given this fundamental expectation, outsiders were perplexed by the attraction the *kulak* held for his victims and infuriated by his ability to entwine fellow peasants in a relationship that shut out the nonpeasants.

In an article in *Herald of Europe* in 1886, V. N. Nazar'ev offered his conclusions on the transformations he had observed in the countryside in the twenty-five years since the Emancipation. His focus was on economic differentation and its sources. In the village of Bol'shaia Kartsovka, where he had lived most of his life, he described the deterioration of the pre-Emancipation and immediate post-Emancipation uniform prosperity into extreme poverty and wealth, and the critical role of the "*kulaks,* that is, the leeches sucking the sweat and blood of their fellow villagers."[39] He went on to set up a series of dichotomies within the village, juxtaposing the extremes of *kulachestvo* on one hand and meek virtue on the other in changing rural Russia, adding to the now common apocalyptic view of the countryside and its inhabitants which issued from the acceptance of the inevitability of struggle and the relationship of the *kulak* and his victims.

Solicitous outsiders were thus quite logically dismayed when they found that the *kulak* was able to close ranks with his "victims" whenever he felt his position was threatened. Those individuals like Astyrev, Nazar'ev, and Ivanchin-Pisarev who worked with the *volost'* administration, with the *volost'* court, or as justices of the peace, as well as rural schoolteachers, often found that their success or failure in the village depended largely on the local strongman and their ability to work through or around him. The gifts they offered the peasantry, literacy and understanding of the law, were the very attainments the *kulak* was most anxious to exclude, for they would have undermined his ability to manipulate his neighbors. Reports from the countryside on the resistance of village strongmen to "enlightenment" added to the dark image of the *kulak*.

Outsiders discovered that the *kulaks* were eager to establish a cooperative relationship with state representatives in the person of *volost'* clerks and justices of the peace. The tactic was quite simple: bribery with money and liquor. Ivanchin-Pisarev found that peasants of the first district to which he was assigned were surprised and suspicious when he explained that he did not drink. As part of his duties, he worked with the elder to draw up a report on tax arrears for the regional administration and attended a meeting of other *volost'* clerks making similar reports. While at this meeting, he was shocked to observe that the other clerks had made no effort to survey their districts. Instead, they talked openly about the bribes they received from local *kulaks* and reported according to the wishes of the richer elements of the village.[40] He concluded that given the prevalence of these relationships, he understood why most peasants did not bother to attend the meetings he called, which, they explained, the *kulaks* would control and where they, the poorer peasants, would have no chance to be heard.[41] His experience thus confirmed the general impression of the manipulation of *volost'* clerks and judges by village strongmen that had emerged from the debate over the *volost'* court as a potential agent of enlightenment in the village.[42]

Astyrev explored the potential and failure of his position as *volost'* clerk to do good for Russia's rural inhabitants. He arrived in Kochetov with the best intentions of serving the peasants, whom he viewed with positive prejudice: "[I]n the beginning of my service, I did not know rural people and, under the influence of city-nurtured traditions about the *muzhik* in particular and the *narod* in general, I saw in everyone who wore a sheepskin coat an object for tenderness."[43] He explained to his readers that the *volost'* clerk could serve as an agent of cultural transformation because he worked with the adults, attended all meetings, interpreted all of the laws for the peasants, recorded all contracts, and became an integral actor in village affairs.[44] Such was the hope he held for his tenure as clerk. He would soon conclude, however, that it was a futile hope because of the overwhelming obstacles facing the sincere clerk, not the least of which was the "sly, evil, stupid, greedy . . . *kulak.*"[45] Astyrev's account of the *kulak's* activities was one of the lengthiest and most powerful contributions to the development of the image. By exploring this account, we are able to get a fair sense of the picture that was taking shape in the minds of educated Russians as they searched for an explanation of the phenomenon.

Astyrev introduced this figure to the readers of *Herald of Europe* through a case study of one of the major events which occurred during his service, the decision on whether to repartition the land. He selected this incident, he explained, because it "reveals the role of the *kulak vis à vis* the gray peasant."[46] Kochetov was due for a repartition because the most recent one had taken place in 1858. According to the Emancipation Edict, two thirds of the households had to vote in favor of a repartition before it could take place. The *kulaks* of Kochetov resisted the repartition because they controlled the cheapest land in the *volost'*. When Astyrev called an assembly to vote on the proposal to set a new repartition, the vast majority of the peasants abstained from the vote. He set a date for another vote two weeks later. Therein began the activity of the *kulaks*, who were determined to secure a majority vote against the repartition.

Astyrev explained that the *kulaks* consisted of the peasant-landlords in the *volost'*, approximately 80 of the 510 heads of households. They appointed one peasant, Moseich, to represent their interests to the clerk. Soon after the first assembly, he arrived at Astyrev's door and, after drinking a cup of tea, explained the situation to Astyrev. He drew one hundred rubles out of his pocket and offered them to Astyrev. These were contributions from the various peasant landowners, who offered two options to the clerk. The first was that the repartition go ahead as planned but that it exclude all of the land they leased to other peasants. The second was that the repartition be postponed for at least a year so that they could collect the rents on their land for the full season. Astyrev asked what would happen if he did not accept the money. Moseich explained, " 'Well, and what will happen? If you don't agree, I'll turn everyone against you, I'll say that I gave you the money, and the business will go my way after all. . . .' "[47]

Astyrev took not the entire packet of rubles, but only twenty-five, explaining that he would take the rest afterward, when the matter had been settled. At the second assembly, those voting for the repartition fell forty-nine votes short of victory. Rather than allow the issue to pass without some confrontation with the *kulaks,* Astyrev announced to all present that they had collected one hundred rubles for his influence. The crowd replied, "And who hasn't heard about that?" He told them that he had not taken one hundred, but only twenty-five rubles, which he then offered to the 291 peasants who had been defeated in the vote. " 'Drink to their health, to your benefactors . . . ,' " he said as he handed the rubles over. This led to general astonishment. The supporters of the repartition could not believe that Astyrev had either refused the bribe or given them the money. " 'Now that's a trick, brothers, did you see? . . . We thought they were going to take from us again, and now they're giving to us!' " Astyrev later discovered that no one believed his action but instead explained that he had indeed taken all the money, and only out of the "goodness of his soul" had decided to share with everyone in the village. He concluded that the peasants could not fathom that the tradition of the reign through bribery of the *kulaks* had been broken.[48]

Astyrev developed the image of the kulak not only by reporting on such schemes as obstructing the repartition but also by recording conversations with the strongman of his *volost',* whose name was Parfen. In building his case against the *kulak,* Astyrev clearly believed that nothing he could describe would be as effective as Parfen's own confident narration of his successful control of the power structure in Kochetov. The following extended quotation from one section of Parfen's account is typical of the six pages of confidences he shared with the clerk one evening. As this section indicates, liquor played a prominent role in Parfen's *kulachestvo.*

> With clerks, and with the elders, I mostly have lived in peace, because I
> don't meddle in their business, and they don't get into ours. Well, that
> means, we don't get in each other's way. Only once did I have to take on
> the clerk, the *volost'* clerk, and this is what it was about. Somehow I didn't
> suit him; he started to crowd me and just before the New Year, when we
> named candidates for the *volost'* council, he even got out of hand. He took
> me, that is, took my name off the list: "It's not appropriate," he says, "to
> have Parfen as a candidate, because he's always drunk; I've crossed him

off, choose someone else." Akh! . . . So that's the way you think—okay then! They started to elect someone else, so I said to the commune, "Old guys! Why should we bother to choose, we take people off the list according to what the authorities say—what we don't agree to choose ourselves, and let Mr. Clerk himself appoint whoever will be convenient for them as candidates, and who won't be. . . ." Then the old guys got the point of it, what it was I was gettin' at, and how they all shouted at once, "How's that! We choose, and he dismisses! We'll go around to all the houses and won't elect anyone if they bump Parfen. Let him report to a higher authority. That's what! . . ." Well, the elder began to get scared right off at this first trouble and began to ask the clerk not to take me off the list. He gave in. Only, I didn't forget this trick of his. Two weeks later, they called the *volost'* together to figure out how much salary to pay who and how much to collect from each soul. Right then, I gave everyone something to drink with three rubles of my own money—I told everybody what to say at the assembly. So, well they set a salary for the elder, just what it was before: 20 rubles a month; and now the clerk? "Take the clerk down!" my people began to shout. "And why?" asks the elder. "Because 35 rubles is very high," they answer. Then I say: "Just the other day I was in town at the market. There, three or so guys thrust themselves on me. . . . They'd be happy to serve for 15 rubles. I promise to bring you the three of them day after tomorrow. Choose whichever one you want." Such a noise broke out—my God! . . . Well, finally we settled: we took two bottles from him and left his salary at the 35 it was before; he gave me a bit. I didn't lose out. . . . After that we lived all right—peacefully, he didn't bother me anymore; and he didn't last much longer. About half a year, more or less.[49]

The *kulak* of Astyrev's account thus had several tools at his disposal in protecting his position against the outsider's attempt to diminish it: first, he knew how to use the bottle in gaining the support of the peasants in his village; second, he was able to play on the peasants' sensitivity to being controlled by outsiders, evoking memories of the landlord by referring to the clerk as Mr. Clerk (*gospodin pisar'*) and suggesting that the clerk considered them incapable of making mature judgments; finally, he was a member of the community, which seemed to appreciate his swaggering buffoonery. He knew how to "play a crowd." This final advantage confounded and frustrated Astyrev, especially in his analysis of the kulak's power. Note that he used Parfen's name as a label to refer to the *kulak* as a type.

But what always amazed me was the extremely benevolent relationship of the *mir* to its parasites. . . . I never detected any . . . enmity towards the Parfens; there were instances when the Parfens had to give in to the friendly criticism of the commune, but as soon as the dispute was over, the Parfens took up their role again as dictators, in no way embarrassed because of their temporary defeat, and the others observe the Parfens' dealings with the commune's property partially approvingly, partially with envy. "Well, okay, well, and he's really a dog! . . . Tell me, my brother, he gave a bit to drink, and that's how he set things right."[50]

This ability of the *kulak* to gain power over his fellow peasants without their full comprehension of their entanglement was an important theme in P. V. Zasodimskii's novel, *Chronicle of the Smurino Settlement* (1874). Zasodimskii was a Populist writer of Zlatovratskii's and Uspenskii's style, but very much their junior in his skills and reputation. Like other *raznochintsy,* Zasodimskii was of modest provincial origins; he was forced to abandon his university education because of lack of money; and he devoted his adult life to work among and writing about the peasantry. He also wrote numerous stories for children, which may have well been his natural genre, for all of his work has a heavily didactic tone. Unlike many of his fellow *raznochintsy,* Zasodimskii was rather ethereal, with an undiluted idealism and otherworldliness that pervaded his physical being and creative work.[51] He corresponded with his more famous peers, who adopted a very solicitous tone in their letters to him, again an indication of his very gentleness of spirit.[52] Zasodimskii idolized Zlatovratskii and followed his lead in idealizing the virtues of the simple peasantry.[53] His peasant writings were marked, and handicapped, by a uniformly stark division between the forces of good and evil in the Russian village, with the communal peasants on the side of good and the *kulaks* and *miroeds* on the side of evil.

Despite the evident weakness in his literary skills, Zasodimskii was a legitimate voice in the discourse on the peasant soul because of his tenure in the countryside, his experience as a rural schoolteacher, and his avowed sincerity and dedication to truth. These qualities lent authority to his description of the *kulak,* especially in the example of the major character in *Chronicle,* Grigorii Ivanovich Prokudov. In his introduction of Prokudov, Zasodimskii included all of the features of the *kulak* that were floating around in the search for a definition of the phenomenon. Like his fellow observers, he pointed to the strongman's wealth, his rational intelligence, his exploitation, and his insidious manipulation. The narrator described Prokudov's wealth in terms of the 1,000 to 1,500 rubles in cash he had managed to accumulate through his activities. He was the epitome of calculated, rational self-interest, and was described as having little conscience, for "he, it seemed, even lived only to make a fortune." His chief talent in accumulating that fortune, it turned out, was his ability to play on "both good and evil feelings, both virtues and vices, human stupidity and need." This had enabled him to "stuff his purse full" and to enter the iron trade. He profited from the labor of his fellow villagers by buying the nails and tacks they made and selling them at a profit in the city. "He provided the peasants with loans of money, grain, any kind of product, also on profitable terms." Zasodimskii also identified the *kulak* Prokudov's calculating mentality, "Every step, every movement of his hand was calculated with him, measured and carried out in the most appropriate manner." Thus, like the rational peasant, the *kulak* was a conscious actor, but an actor who used his reason for the purpose of exploitation and individual profit. Finally, this *kulak* had captured his fellow villagers without their noticing or understanding the source of their dependency: "He held his fellow villagers in his hands, not with an iron rod, but as if in chains. But he put these chains on them so gingerly and softly that those wearing them did not feel their arms bound at all: it seemed to everyone that not Grigorii Ivanovich, but some other evil man put them on them."[54]

Whether through the record of his own words in the shape of Astyrev's Parfen or in the fictionalized version of Grigorii Ivanovich Prokudov, the *kulak* both displayed the distressing features of profit, individualism, and cleverness and was able to control his community. He was the urge for profit and gain incarnate; he exhibited no natural generosity; he engaged in speculation and usury while capitalizing on the weaknesses of his fellow man. He exercised unbridled self-interest in a milieu where there were no competitors; the field was his and his alone to rake in money and goods as he saw fit.

The *kulak* increasingly became the symbol of peasant resistance to reform, reform that might loosen his hold on his unwitting victims. Although there is ample evidence that peasants recognized the worth of literacy and actively sought it in their own schools, there were also reports of *kulak* obstruction of outsiders who tried to introduce education to the village.[55] The final installment of Svetlin's (Reznikov's) cycle, "The Communal Soul, Sketches from the *Narod's* Daily Life," focused on this phenomenon. This sketch described the experience of a dedicated young rural schoolteacher. Remarkable in his generosity of spirit and commitment to both the school and the community of peasants, the teacher served them both in numerous ways. One service he provided was to write all of their correspondence for free, whereas the *volost'* clerk charged a fee for each letter. He also read and explained all announcements which arrived in the village. This activity gained him the resentment of the powerful peasants in the village, who objected to his disruption of the balance of power they had established. The *kulaks* appealed to the district authorities, who succeeded in removing him from his post for engaging in activities beyond his position as teacher and causing bad relations between the peasants and the local authorities.[56]

Nazarev's reminiscences of his experiences in the "backwoods" included his account of his efforts to introduce education to the area. In his overwhelmingly pessimistic report, he described his village school project as his one great success. He had built a two-story schoolhouse, which sixty students attended. He explained that the school was constantly under attack, however, from the *kulaks* and the *volost'* clerk, who resented the literacy of the peasants and teacher. Literacy threatened their control in the village and provided a target for their destructive machinations.[57] Despite his success, Nazar'ev had a dim view of the enterprise: "[A] school has no role or future in the village if the peasants resent and oppose it and it exists only by virtue of the support of a few good people."[58]

Conclusion

The message that these accounts of manipulative peasants sent to the capitals was that would-be reformers should be wary of any notions of giving enlightenment to Russian peasant culture. The most serious obstacle was possibly the peasant himself in the form of a powerful, clever *kulak*, who was able to block the intrusion of outsiders through effective control of the mass of gray peasants. Whether it took the form of Populist radicalism, the development of legal consciousness through the *volost'* court, connections with the other culture outside the village through the office of the *volost'* clerk, or literacy through rural education, enlightenment of the rural backwoods would not be easily imposed or readily accepted. The *kulak* as manipulator was an individual power of darkness whose very position as parasite depended on the ignorance and weakness of the gray peasant.

The image of the gray peasant was thus the symbiotic partner of the image of the *kulak,* for the strength of the latter depended on the absence of any countervailing forces. The degree to which outsiders dismissed the ability of the average peasant to stand up to the *kulak* is striking. This pairing revealed the force that the Darwinian metaphor of struggle held, as well as the accompanying sense of evolutionary inevitability with a sure ascent of the strong and an equally sure decline of the weak. It also revealed the continuing force of a patriarchal or paternalistic approach to the peasantry writ large. The transfer of the paradigm of exploitation from the gentry to the *kulak* and the assignment of the role of victimization to the vast majority of the peasantry rested on the conviction that the Russian peasant could not take care of himself. The logical conclusion for any well-meaning observer was that educated society should assume the role of protector, should reestablish the pre-Emancipation system of tutelage known as *opeka.* This was the central agrument of the liberal K. D. Kavelin's series of articles, "The Peasant Question," published in *Herald of Europe* in 1881. He wrote that the notion of the Manchester School that every man should pursue his own self-interest, unfettered, was fine in a world where everyone had equal strength, but not when social forces were unequal, as they so clearly were in rural Russia. In the event of great inequality of social forces, it was the proper role of educated society and the state to help the weaker elements. Thus, in Russia, it was the obligation of state and society to decide the critical questions that the Russian peasants could not decide for themselves.[59]

Kavelin's reference to the Manchester School was an explicit statement of the concern that informed the approach of educated society to the phenomenon of the *kulak* as peasant individualist and exploiter. Individualism and striving for personal gain combined in the image of the *kulak* as a symbol of the transformation of collectivist, communal, homogeneous Russia. Individualism both departed from the fond image of the *narod* and represented the money-based, money-oriented economy of the West. It eroded the natural harmonies of rural life; it caused the breakdown of the rural Eden which so many educated Russians held dear, despite the caveat of Saltykov-Shchedrin. As an anonymous contributor to *Russian Herald* observed as early as 1876:

> The thing is that until now, our *narod* has not given us the ideal of an active splendid personality. The beauty in our observations of them, and which our literature, to its great credit, accustomed us to love in them, appears merely on the plane of elemental existence, of an isolated, idyllic way of living, or of a passive life. Just as soon as an active, energetic personality emerges from the midst of the *narod*, its fascination usually vanishes, and more often than not, individuality assumes the unattractive features of a peasant bloodsucker, a *kulak*, a stupidly willful person.[60]

The fast coupling of individualism with the urge for gain in the *kulak* image equally suggested the extent to which outsiders considered both to be a travesty of the truly Russian national character, for these were the obvious features of the market-driven West. Yet, the resolution of the question of the origins of the *kulak* brought these undesirable traits home. The conclusion that every peasant was potentially a *kulak* meant that the innate qualities of the Russian peasant, and, by extension, of the national culture, included individualistic egotism, exploitation, and obdurate manipulation.

The image of the *kulak* sat at the opposite end of the spectrum from the concept of the *narod*, representing the distillation of the various images into one negative element. The fundamental conclusion that the activities of the *kulak* were indigenous to the Russian village returned to the assumption about the *narod* which had included belief in innate qualities of the Russian people. These two images were distinct from the other images in their ascription of inborn qualities of "peasantness." Whereas the qualities of the *narod*, however, had been sketched in broad strokes of minimal definition, reflecting the relative lack of concrete knowledge, those of the *kulak* were sharp, were detailed, and carried the authority of more than twenty-five years of firsthand observation and experience. This contributed to the authority and force of the image, and to its power to dismay and discourage educated Russia. Astyrev expressed the distress of his generation when he juxtaposed the two images in a passage of uncharacteristically florid rhetoric.

> Rise, rise, Russian *narod,* wake up, shake off this heavy sleep. . . . You sleep, bewitched hero, and poisonous spiders have wrapped you in the fetters of their web, parasites suck your blood, and heaps of frogs and toads have been littered on your chest. In your veins, healthy blood still flows, your heart still beats, but once-strong arms, terrible for enemies, lie helplessly lashed along your half-dead body, and only from time to time does a fleeting, momentary, and fruitless convulsion remind the parasites that you are still alive, and they begin to spin their snare even more quickly, to suck your blood more mercilessly. . . . Stand up, hero! Tear off these fetters, while you still have the strength to break them, crush the parasites, the scorpions and toads, before they poison your organism! . . . But, he sleeps. . . .[61]

The evil of the *kulak* went beyond such straightforward harm as usury, then, and took on the burden of disabling the heroic, formerly strong, but now passive and entangled *narod.* His lust for money, his unrestrained individualism, and his urge and ability to manipulate made him a parasite on Russian culture, an agent of Russia's ruin. The *kulak* did not stand alone in domination of the scene of the transforming village, however; he was not the sole character cast for the role of destroying the rural idyll. In the mental construct of educated observers, there was another strong individualist in the village who carried all the threats of the *kulak;* she was the peasant woman, the *baba,* Russia's rural Eve.

8

Baba: The Peasant Woman— Virago, Eve, or Victim?

My father-in-law
Scolds me for nothing;
My mother-in-law,
For every trifle.
I will flee, dart away;
In a cuckoo's shape:
I will fly to my father's home,
To his garden green
Will I take my place,
On the apple-tree
My mother loves.
I will cuckoo cry,
I will sadly wail,
Till my wailings sad
Make all eyes weep,
Till the garden is drowned
In bitter tears.
W. R. S. RALSTON,
The Songs of the Russian People

With images of the peasant woman, we come to the end of the search for the peasant soul and the climax of educated society's progressive disillusionment with the village as the taproot of Russian culture. The peasant woman who had served as the symbol of rural purity and essential national qualities at the end of the eighteenth century became a symbol by the end of the nineteenth century of the disintegration of traditional structures as well as of the victimization inherent to the patriarchalism of Russian society. To a much lesser extent, one image of the peasant woman offered an alternative symbol of an invigorated peasantry, and thus Russia, emerging from the broken traditions of patriarchy and communalism. The triple image of the peasant woman as rural Eve, victim, or virago was a highly contested one, just as the images of the male peasant as rational, communal, victimized, or exploitative were. She appeared as both a decisively active and conscious defender of her individual self-interest and a passive and helpless victim. She was presented as both a sly manipulator and an unconscious beast of burden. Each of these representations grew out of the concerns of the educated Russians who constructed the images, out of the aspects of village culture on which they chose to focus, and out of broader trends within the debate over the peasant soul which informed educated visions of peasant women as much as they had visions of peasant men. Whereas the search for the peasant had largely focused on the male peasant, the peasant woman could and did take center stage even in a climate where there was a pronounced tendency to look at the male-dominated public institutions of village life as decisive and operate on the assumption that "the rules and mores that governed men's lives were taken for the whole of peasant society."[1]

The peasant woman almost always appeared as a Janus-like figure, part victim and part Eve, part martyr of patriarchal rule and part agent of the destruction of that patriarchy. As the inevitable victim or as the selfish, often money-hungry individualist, she thus became the female expression of the gray peasant and the *kulak*. As with these two male images, the image of the peasant woman as *baba* became a filter for judgments about mutual aid and competition, about natural rural structures and the invasion of money, about individualism and independence. Like the term *muzhik*, *baba* was an ostensibly neutral term in the immediate post-Emancipation era, connoting a mature, married peasant woman.[2] In peasant speech, however, the term had a negative resonance due to the numerous pejorative sayings and proverbs in which the patriarchal dismissal of female worth was linked to the *baba*. Such sayings as "The *baba* raves, only the devil believes her"; "By day she steals, by night she squeals, yes she spits"; "The *baba* has long hair and a short brain"; "A *baba* is slyer than the devil"; and "Avoid a *baba* like the devil" suggested the reputation the peasant woman held in the village.[3] The term *baba* was also part of the name of the important figure in Russian folklore Baba Yaga, an old crone who combined elements of the wicked witch with the wise old woman in a fantastic house where she practiced her equally fantastic and frightening skills.[4] As Lynne Viola concluded, "The *baba* might best be seen as a colorful combination of the American 'hag,' 'fishwife,' and 'woman driver' all rolled into a peasant mold."[5]

The negative connotation of the term *baba* was well known to any observer of the Russian village, and for that reason, it is especially telling that many of them chose to refer to the Russian peasant woman as *baba* rather than as *krest'ianka* or *krest'ianskaia zhenshchina*. In fact, the vast majority of contributors to the discussion of the peasant soul did just that, with the notable, and perhaps logical exceptions of two female observers and advocates of the peasant woman, A. I. Efimenko and M. K. Gorbunova. The image of the Russian peasant woman took the name *baba* in public debate over the peasant soul, carrying with it all the patriarchal baggage of the village, implicating the constructs of hierarchy and patriarchy that resided in the unconscious of the educated observers who used it.[6]

The image of the peasant woman would have special significance because of the basic psychological association of woman and fertility. In an intellectual climate in which the peasant came to be synonymous with Russia itself, the female peasant bore the burden of representing the culture's fertility, nurturance, and purity. The image of the peasant woman would also merge with the image of the Russian land, the earth, the soil from which the most basic necessities for cultural survival must spring. The peasant as symbol of Russia and the convergence of woman and land were by no means unique to the post-Emancipation period. Earth, woman, and mother had merged in the popular imagination from the earliest times in Russian culture.[7] During the search for the folk in the eighteenth-century development of national consciousness, positive images of the peasant as symbol of Russia had centered more around peasant women than peasant men. Radishchev's Aniuta and Karamzin's Liza marked the beginning of the tradition of the peasant as a full character in Russian literature and were symbols of the larger themes that the genre treated.[8] When writers, journalists, ethnographers, legal scholars, rural doctors, lawyers, and schoolteachers of the post-Emancipation era spoke of the peasant woman as a symbol of Russia, they were part of a long and familiar tradition.

In the post-Emancipation context, the image of the peasant woman was striking for the absence of the very virtues formerly attached to her figure and anticipated in the mental construct of the feminine. Beauty, purity, nurturance, even fertility were lacking; the absence of the latter caused quite a disjunction between the image and the reality of the peasant woman, who could expect to bear seven children in her lifetime. The absence of these features in the image of the *baba* can be explained largely as a result of the discourse out of which the image emerged: a societywide debate about the nature of the patriarchal, extended peasant household and its fragmentation into numerous nuclear families. Whereas images of the peasant man took shape against the backdrop of public spaces, the image of the peasant woman was placed almost exclusively in the private domain of the family. Judgments about her position and role in this setting, in turn, became judgments of the institution in all its symbolic importance as the genome of Russian culture.

The *Baba* as Rural Eve

Beginning in the early 1870s, at the same time that the peasant judge was coming under scrutiny, the phenomenon of the peasant household division captured the attention of educated society and provoked almost universal alarm.[9] Most educated Russians found the breakup of the patriarchal household distressing because they viewed this institution as the most fundamental element, the basic unit, in rural society or economy, or both. As the smallest manifestation of a communal, patriarchal system and mentality, the extended family embodied all of the virtues that characterized the beloved image of native Russian culture. The threat of its demise undermined the very foundation of cultural distinctiveness. When observers offered explanations for the deterioration of the extended family, they presented peasant women as the primary culprits. This identification of the peasant woman as the source of division in rural society was expressed by both her critics and her apologists and constituted the central feature of her figure in the public's imagination.

We recall that as early as the publication of the Liuboshchinskii Commission report in 1873 and 1874, interested readers discovered the "litigious daughter-in-law," who took her grievances about her hard lot in the extended family to the *volost'* court.[10] Outsiders in the city and local eyewitnesses quickly identified the *baba* in the extended family as the figure most likely to be infected with a new post-Emancipation principle of existence: individualism. The *baba* individualist thus became the main catalyst for the disintegration of the collectivism of the peasant family in the form of the household division. Engelgardt was one of the most forceful advocates of this view, not only assigning the same destructive aspect to the individualist *baba* as to the *kulak*, but indeed linking them directly in his diatribe against the peasant woman. In his description, she was the great divider and manipulator in family life; she was the most ready partner to the activity of village usurers and strongmen; she was a full-blown individualist in a culture that required cooperation and mutual aid to survive; finally she was a creature of easy virtue. Engelgardt's unrivaled position as an authority on peasant culture ensured that this negative portrait of the peasant would become a standard image.

Engelgardt invariably used the term *baba* to refer to peasant women. Although his usage may be considered consistent with his tendency toward affectation of the peasant vernacular, which became more pronounced the longer he lived in the countryside, it also revealed his distaste for village women. His fullest description of the *baba* as a type was in his discussion of the peasant family. For Engelgardt, the extended patriarchal family offered one of the best examples of the advantages of mutual aid, of joint ventures over individual ones. Like most other observers, he argued that all large families prospered, regardless of the character of the individual members, whereas small ones were virtually guaranteed to fail.[11] The result of the breakup of the extended family would inevitably be poverty. Even the peasants recognized this, but, "even so, they divided, and from one 'rich' household, there were made three poor ones. Everyone knew this, everyone understood this, and even so, they divided, because each one wants to live independently in his own little house according to his own will, every woman wants to run her own household."[12]

Every large family carried within it, however, the incubus of fatal division in the form of competition and selfishness among the women. In response to the male peasants' assertion that the *baba* caused all divisions, Engelgardt concurred that they were, indeed, the source of individualism in the village. He observed, "[A]mong the *babas,* individualism is even more highly developed than among the *muzhiks, babas* are even more egotistical, even less capable of collective endeavor unless this is a general abuse of someone, less humane, more heartless."[13] In his description, the *baba* was the scourge of the Russian village. Her character was a curious mixture of evil vanity, moral weakness, and ability to manipulate others.

Unlike the *muzhik,* who "relied on his mind, on strength, on ability to work," the *baba* "places all of her hope on her beauty, on her femininity, and, if she succeeds in sensing her beauty—that's the end."[14] Thus, Engelgardt immediately connected any possible beauty in the peasant woman with vanity and manipulation, with seduction and evil power. She was typically driven by her lust for money. "The morals of rural women and girls are incredibly simple: money, some kind of scarf, under certain conditions, as long as nobody knew about it, as long as everything were kept secret, would take care of everything."[15] This lust for money both provided the *baba* with greater incentive and initiative than the *muzhik* and made her more susceptible to exploitation from within and outside the village. Within the village, she was easy prey for the *kulak,* who recognized her greed and easily controlled her. From outside the village, any amorous passerby who was willing to pay a bit more than the *baba's* daily earnings of twenty or thirty kopeks could enjoy her charms for a pittance by city standards.[16]

Ever the rationalist, Engelgardt went on to justify such behavior in the peasant woman in terms of her poverty and the low pay and physical difficulty of alternative wage labor available to her. Still, this moralistic outburst begs for some consideration of his view of women and his personal relations with them. Engelgardt was known as a supporter of women's rights; as rector at the Agricultural Institute, he was the first to admit women to the chemistry lab.[17] He was married to a prominent feminist, who was a translator of European works of fiction, primarily for the journal *Herald of Europe.*[18]

They were completely estranged during his twenty-two years on Batish-chevo, apparently through her choice rather than his. At one point, hearing of her dire economic straits, Engelgardt offered her a place on the estate, where she could live completely free of his interference. She refused.[19] In his first decade on Batishchevo, he welcomed Populist students who traveled to the estate to learn how to farm. Among these students, there were young women, of whom he demanded the same simple life and physical labor he demanded of the men.[20] In the early 1880s, when Engelgardt turned away from farming as his primary occupation and took up the study of phosphate fertilizers through extensive experimentation on his estate, he passed all farming matters to the management of his daughter, Vera. This decision, as well as the fond correspondence between them during occasional separa-tions, supports his reputation as a believer in the abilities of women.[21] Fur-thermore, in the figures of his housekeeper, Avdotia, and of the "Old Woman" who ran the dining hall and cared for the small livestock on his estate, peasant women emerged as positive figures essential to the success of his farming and equally sources of companionship and knowledge for him. In each of the relationships where he was in a position of stewardship or supervi-sion as teacher, father, or employer and model for the student workers on his estate, Engelgardt welcomed women's contributions and strengths. It seems that he may have faltered when he had to accommodate as well as instruct or guide, as in the case of his independent-minded wife. He also found that he had to accommodate the peasant women surrounding his estate, and this may have been the ultimate source of his resentment of them.

Like most men of his class and generation, Engelgardt was discreet about sexual matters. We are left only to wonder about his twenty-two years of solitude on Batishchevo and about the possibility of intimate rela-tions with peasant women. The only hint he offered was one comment in his discussion of the peasant woman that, despite her willingness to sell sex to anyone for a low price, "anyone who does not know how a village *baba* can love, sacrificing everything for her beloved, does not know, in general, how a woman can love."[22] What is interesting in Engelgardt's discussion of the *baba's* sexual morality is his linkage of sex and money, of the *baba's* use of feminine wiles to manipulate, perhaps to entrap. In this, he displayed the suspicion of money and gain characteristic of his era, while reinforcing his broader image of the *baba* as a rural Eve. He spoke of female ascen-dancy in the village in terms of a disease which, having struck in one household, "spreads to all the households in the village." So infectious was this rule of women that every new woman who arrived in the village fell victim to the "general tone" and insisted on a position of power herself. Soon it became readily apparent to everyone which villages were con-trolled by women and a sort of "natural selection" occurred through which strong women gravitated to villages where women were dominant.[23]

The women exercised their harmful influence not only on other women but also on the hapless *muzhiks,* who, in Engelgardt's description, seemed incapable of resisting them. The *muzhik,* he was certain, was characterized more by all the qualities he admired and considered necessary for communal agriculture "outside the household, beyond the influence of the *baba.*"[24] The peasant women in Engelgardt's world had the ability to frustrate his efforts at reform in the shape of agricultural innnovation. He explained to his readers that the success of his pet project of cultivating flax as a commercial crop depended entirely on the willingness of peasant women in neighboring villages to take on the processing of the flax. He found that he had to set terms for work that were favorable to the women in peasant households, for if the terms did not serve women's individual interests, they would prevent the men from taking on the cultivation and processing of flax as sharecroppers. This ability of the peasant women to spoil his plans added to Engelgardt's distaste for their power in the countryside, which he attacked through the label of selfish, even stupid individualism.[25]

Engelgardt's allergic reaction to the figure of the combative and self-interested peasant woman was shared by many of his peers. This figure attracted the attention of outsiders, who took pains to introduce her to the reading public, who thus began to include this element in the image of the *baba.* As early as 1862, one eyewitness account of the post-Emancipation village included the sketch "The Battle of the Amazons," in which women from two communities were at each other's throats over wage labor. The women on the author's estate refused to take on work for him because they considered his wages too low; women from a neighboring village agreed to his terms. The final scene in the conflict, reported in detail, was a fistfight among all of the women from both communities outside the baths, naked women and girls going at each other at full force.[26] Again, the issue of money entered the scene, driving peasant women to violence against each other in the crudest of forms.

In a study of the position of women in the Russian family that was part of the larger enterprise of exploring customary law, I. Kharlamov discussed the image of the strong peasant woman in Russian culture. In her traditional form, he found the "*boi-baba*"—the energetic, manlike woman, the virago—to be a positive figure. Of this image he wrote, "The chief features of her character were practical quickness developed by family concerns and matters, a strong will, and a large dose of pluck and even cunning."[27] In Kharlamov's view, however, the peasant virago was a positive figure only so long as she was embedded in the system of mutual aid and mutual respect he described as characteristic of the Slavic family. When she exercised her qualities outside the family, in pursuit of interests not dedicated to the family or even against the family, Kharlamov no longer found her a positive figure. Thus, of the contemporary *boi-baba* he wrote that she was indeed "fighting a battle of the individual for her own preservation and development."[28] The Russian peasant woman could be both strong and good within the patriarchal family, but only strong and evil outside it.

Even Zlatovratskii fell prey to this mentality and contributed to the image of the strong *baba* as somehow unnatural. In one of his more successful pieces, "The Village King Lear," he described the daughter of the old peasant man she cared for in his madness as becoming harsh because she never married. When Zlatovratskii asked her why she had never married, she replied that she remained a spinster because she did not want to be a *baba*. His reaction was, "In this sharp, abrupt tone it was already apparent how the last traces of femininity had disappeared and that there had arisen that original, severe type of '*baba-muzhik*' which the Russian village has created in its age-old struggle."[29] Outside the natural order of things, that is, the patriarchal family, the woman became a man, the *baba* became a *muzhik*. Again and again, articles and accounts such as these revealed the incompatibility of the woman as feminine and virtuous and the woman as strong individualist in the post-Emancipation image of the *baba*. This is not to say, however, that these men were ignorant of or even blind to the existence of strong women, of the pivotal role women played in the rural economy, or of the phenomenon of whole villages' being run by women after their men left for wage labor elsewhere. Zlatovratskii wrote an entire sketch on *Bab'e tsarstvo,* the rule of the *babas,* in one such village; Uspenskii explicity recognized the force of women within the household and especially in areas of male out-migration; Engelgardt equally stressed the essential contributions of women within the family economy and their decisive roles in the economy of his region.[30] It was one thing, however, to acknowledge the strength and influence of women; it was quite another to embrace it. That would be left to female observers of the village.

The pervasiveness of the evil *baba* in reports from the village or in fiction set in the village is also striking. Although not every peasant woman who appeared in publicistic or strictly fictional writing was an agent of evil, many of them were. From the *raznochintsy* writers in the 1860s to Tolstoy and Chekhov thirty years later, Russian authors of the post-Emancipation era seemed very far indeed from the tradition of Karamzin and Radishchev in which peasant women embodied all that was good and pure. Everywhere we encounter murderous wives and mothers, jealous lovers, conniving and abusive mothers-in-law.

When we return to the story "Two Murders" written by Selivanov and published in *The Contemporary* in 1861, we meet a seventeen-year-old girl who schemes with her brother to murder his wife and an unfortunate witness to the crime.[31] The evil stepmother appears in V. I. Roskovshenko's "Marus'ia'. A Ukrainian Legend," vying with her stepdaughter for the love of a young man, then trying to kill the boy and having the girl

locked up when she discovers their involvement.[32] In Uspenskii's Agrafen'ia Petrov, the *baba* prostitutes herself to visiting urbanites in exchange
for the money and status wealth will bring.[33] In "The Victory of Father
Ivan," published anonymously in *Russian Wealth* in 1881, a village priest
triumphs over his evil, money-hungry, nagging wife ("this resolute individual of the female sex") by learning to ignore her completely, thus freeing
himself from the degradation that interaction with her brings.[34] V. Bystrenin's "Disorder" describes a tormenting mother-in-law, a village slut,
and a victimized wife who finally poisons her husband and mother-in-law to
break the triangle of evil that surrounds her.[35] Minor authors and more
established literary journalists produced these vignettes of the *baba* as the
incarnation of vice, pettiness, and greed. This was not great literature by
any means, but it entered the discourse all the same and added to the
construction of the image of the evil *baba*.

The evil *baba* found her fullest expression in Tolstoy's *Power of Darkness*, his morality play of peasant life, published in 1887. Here Tolstoy
turned full attention to the character of the Russian peasant and the tenor
of village culture. His concern in this play, as in his other writings, was
moral redemption, in this case examined through the figure of a peasant
man, Nikita. Tolstoy gave to his work not only his own reflections and
development on the question of redemption and resurrection, however,
but also a cast of peasant characters taken directly from the public debate
over the peasant soul. Contemporary critics were quick to recognize the
connection between this play and the works of writers like Uspenskii. As
the liberal critic Skabichevskii explained, the public expected to find the
peasant portrayed as the carrier of the moral ideal, as a continuation of
such characters as Karataev and Levin's Fedor. Instead, they found "rural
life depicted in the drama with the same photographic precision and deep,
realistic accuracy as it was depicted . . . by such connoisseurs as Gleb
Uspenskii."[36] Indeed, Uspenskii and Tolstoy debated the significance of
the powers each believed ruled the Russian village during a chance meeting
on a train. During this conversation, Tolstoy scorned Uspenskii's assertion
that the entire worldview of the peasant was shaped by the power of the
land. He argued that peasants had no such worldview and lived only to
"steal firewood, horses, to drink to excess and to beat their wives."[37]
Although this remark is typical of Tolstoy the enfant terrible, it is consistent
with his message that moral darkness dominated the Russian village.

The central action of moral darkness in the play was infanticide. An
illegitimate newborn is crushed beneath the floorboards until his skull
cracks. Although it is the father who actually places the child under the
board and crushes him, Tolstoy is quite clear in presenting the women as
responsible for planning the murder and forcing the father to commit it.[38]
So much were the women in this work the source of evil that Skabichevskii

suggested that *The Power of the Babas* would have been a more appropriate title.[39] Here the rural Eve appears in the characters of the grasping Anisia and the murderous Matrena. The coarseness of their speech, the premeditated evil of their deeds, and their lust for money make them part of the chorus line of evil *babas* familiar to educated society by the mid-1880s. Again, as in Engelgardt's description and in other writings, sexuality becomes a catalyst for sin and greed a motivation for evil deeds.

In the characters of Akim and Matrena, elderly husband and wife, Tolstoy followed the paradigm of the hapless *muzhik,* the communal peasant who fails to stand up to the challenge of the strong individual, the manipulator, the exploiter. For as the populist critic L. Obolenskii recognized, these two characters represented the two competing trends in Russian culture, the old agricultural patriarchal Russia and the new, developing, money-run Russia. "Akim is the representative of the best principles of the old life, of its agricultural, highest instincts and feelings. Matrena, on the other hand, represents the type of the new epoch, of the new temporary moral crisis that we are living through."[40] Obolenskii's quick appropriation of Tolstoy's characters as symbols of Russia's social and economic transformation points to the extent that peasant images had become cultural emblems. His identification of the source of this crisis followed the writings of Uspenskii, Zlatovratskii, and other eyewitnesses very closely. He declared that the crisis stemmed from "the shift from almost exclusively agricultural communal labor to individual labor, factory labor, the labor of the hired hand, labor on railroads and in cities. In the life of the village which has almost exclusively known the sacred labor of the land, this new principle of so-called bourgeois production made its entrance unnoticed with its *kulaks,* money and factories."[41] The result was "new forms of life, torn away from the land, from the family, the village and tradition."[42] In Tolstoy's *Power of Darkness,* the character responsible for this breakdown of the rural idyll was a *baba,* Matrena, emblem of "that deformed, vulgar progress which is destroying the village and communal existence."[43] That a Populist critic would excoriate the appearance of money and the *kulak* in the village is no surprise; that Tolstoy would link the forces of moral darkness with the *baba* and that the critic would accept that linkage underscore the extent to which the peasant woman had become the recognized culprit in the disintegration of patriarchal family structures in the village.

One of the most famous and successful genre paintings of the Itinerants offered a visual representation and confirmation of this construction. V. M. Maksimov's *Family Division* depicted the scene of the formal allocation of property within a peasant hut during a division. He captured a moment of acrimony between the old woman who thrusts her face forward accusingly at a young woman whom most viewers would recognize as her daughter-in-law. The men in the picture look bewildered or concerned, but not able or likely to intervene in this woman's quarrel. The message the canvas conveyed was, thus, that divisions did indeed come "from the *babas.*"

The various genres of eyewitness accounts, literary-journalistic sketches, Tolstoy's peasant morality play, and a major Itinerant painting played off each other in a multipart chorus proclaiming the peasant woman a *baba*-individualist and rural Eve who was breaking up most structures of traditional Russia, and particularly of patriarchal Russia. The distress this image reflected suggests that educated Russian men, however unconsciously, were themselves threatened by the peasant woman's strength and thus tended to see evidence of it everywhere in their discussion of the fission of extended households. Just as they were anxious about the peasant's selective respect of the principle of private property, so were they alarmed by the peasant woman's ability to challenge patriarchy.

The *Baba* as Victim

Despite the preponderance of examples of the *baba* as virago turned Eve, there was a sympathetic image of the peasant woman in the discourse on the peasant soul. The image of the peasant woman as victim was a comfortable one for members of educated society; in this form, she elicited concern and the urge to protect. She fed into the deep-seated expectation of tutelage over the peasantry and also fit into the model of passivity associated with the image of the *narod* and the gray peasant. This image of the Russian peasant woman of the post-Emancipation period is perhaps the most familiar one. This figure appeared frequently in published accounts or literary interpretations of peasant culture. She was defenseless in the face of difficult economic conditions, the rule of men in the village, the structure of the patriarchal household, and, most of all, the drunkenness of the *muzhik* himself. She was a victim of the poverty, ignorance, and dissipation of the Russian village. Like the images of the *baba* as virago and Eve, that of the *baba* as victim appeared against the backdrop of the private space of the patriarchal family. To identify her as victim meant to admit the failings of the patriarchal family. As the image of the victim emerged, it took two forms. The first, and more typical, one presented the peasant in all her suffering and left her there. The second, exceptional in the larger discourse but consistent among women reporters from the village, presented the victim who fought back, who challenged the patriarchy of family and community successfully, who assumed the mantle of virago once more.

From the twentieth-century perspective, Rose Glickman has neatly summarized the forms of victimization of peasant women in the family as exclusion, dependence, and subordination to men and "imbalance between their contribution to survival and their rewards," and Christine Worobec has explored the impact of patriarchal structures on peasant women.[44] Contemporaries were aware of these patterns as well, and some were willing to label them injustices. In the 1860s, V. K. Rzhevskii called them "absolute family slavery,"[45] Pecherskii echoed this sentiment in his depiction of one young girl's struggle against patriarchy,[46] and Selivanov presented one of the most graphic images of their effects. The elderly mother of the duo of criminal children in "Two Murders" bore the scars of passive suffering:

> [V]estiges of that suffering, passive obedience with which women of her
> position bear the slavery of married life. Her bent back, her lifeless eyes,
> her deeply wrinkled face show that a lot of labor has passed over this back,
> that much sorrow has created these wrinkles. This woman is the incarnation
> of suffering and physical labor; everything in her is crushed: both joy and
> sorrow, so crushed that she is equally incapable of feeling one or the other;
> it is difficult to decide whether this is a human being or a workhorse.[47]

Nazar'ev's reports from his position as justice of the peace in the 1870s also included evidence on the suffering of peasant women. One of the first impressions which shook him upon his arrival in the village was the number of "women with battered, beaten faces" who appealed to him for assistance.[48] He found that the male peasants resented him and the institution he represented because they were the product of those "New laws! and the women thank you for them, because they can come to you now when we beat them . . . we never hear the end of their threats to go to the justice of the peace if we beat them."[49]

But beat them they did. Nazar'ev offered three examples of the widespread phenomenon of the abuse reported in all the serious publications of the day, serving as the most consistent and disturbing testimony to the peasant woman's victimization. In one case he handled, father and son-in-law argued over who should have to feed the daughter/wife during the winter months when she was not laboring in the fields. Both men spoke of her to Nazar'ev as if about "a cow or a horse."[50] Another daughter was the victim of her drunken father's constant beatings, which intensified on his discovery of her pregnancy out of wedlock.[51] In a third case, a peasant patriarch drove his daughter out of the house into a cold December night as the time of her confinement drew near.[52] Such eyewitness accounts from the village entered the mental construct of the *baba* as authoritative material on her position in village culture and also explain why it could be to a woman's advantage to be married to a man who left the village to work elsewhere.[53]

Dostoevsky offered one of the most chilling scenes of wife beating, for his explanation made the act one of laconic entertainment. In *Diary of a*

Writer, he commented on the recent publicity surrounding the suicide of a peasant woman who saw death as the only escape from her husband's incessant beatings.

> Did you ever see how a *muzhik* whips his wife? I have. He begins with a rope or a strap. Peasant life is devoid of aesthetic delights—music, the-atres, magazines; naturally one has to fill it in somehow. Tying up his wife or thrusting her legs into the opening of a floorboard, our good little *muzhik* began, probably, methodically, coldbloodedly, even sleepily, with measured blows, not listening to the screams and entreaties. That is, really listening to them, listening with delight, or what pleasure would there be for him in the whipping? . . . Blows fall more and more frequently, more sharply, more countless; he is getting excited; he begins to savor it. He has already become a beast and he realizes this himself. The animal cries of the tortured woman go to his head like liquor. . . . Suddenly, he throws away the strap; like a madman, he grabs a stick, a bough, anything, and breaks it over her back with three final, terrific blows.—No more! He quits, sits down at the table, sighs, and turns to his kvass.[54]

These and other similar depictions of the peasant woman as victim left the reading public with an image of a broken figure, a battered figure, a moan-ing heap of bruised flesh. She was no more attractive a character than *baba* as Eve; indeed she contributed to the general disillusionment with the village and the peasantry. For in this form, the *baba* represented all of the horror of rural life, the underside of patriarchy, the disease within the idyll itself. Just as the gray peasant as victim within the village required the companion image of the *kulak* as the exploiter, so the *baba* as victim required a victimizer who was identified as the male peasant and patriarch.

It was difficult for many observers to incorporate this aspect of the patriarchal household into their concept of the post-Emancipation peasant family. As early as 1867, Elenev was prepared to declare that the slavery of the peasant woman was approaching its end.[55] Even someone as clear-eyed as Sharapov turned away from the position of the peasant woman. He argued, "The absence of any kind of despotism in the relations between the household head and the male members of the family was characteristic for the Great Russian family." Then he continued, "The relations to the women were somewhat different, but we will not pause on that question here."[56] In Sharapov's case, one can speculate that he veered away from this aspect of the Great Russian family because its implications would have threatened the image of the patriarchal household as a model of harmony and prosperity emerging from traditional structures. It was one thing to construct an image of the *kulak*-exploiter as an agent of disruption, for he was broadly perceived to be a symptom of transformations and specifically of the intrusion of a money economy and economic differentiation in the village. But to explore fully why the patriarchal household created its own victims among its women without the intrusion of external forces was more than Sharapov—the gentry landowner, agricultural editor of the Slavophile journal *Rus'*—could afford psychologically to do.

The *Baba* as Virago

In stark contrast to the presentation of the peasant woman as inevitable victim or the tendency to avoid the topic altogether stood the studies of two female observers of rural life who examined the lives of rural women and offered an alternative image and a more positive potential outcome of the disintegration of rural community and family traditions.

A. I. Efimenko and M. K. Gorbunova took up the study of peasant women at roughly the same time, Efimenko in Arkhangel'sk Province and Gorbunova in Moscow Province. Of the numerous observers and students of rural life, Aleksandra Efimenko was perhaps the strongest and most eloquent advocate of the peasant woman. She took up an intensive study of rural folkways in Arkhangel'sk during her husband's exile there, working with the records of local *volost'* courts in addition to observing life in the villages nearby. The most important of Efimenko's publications resulting from this research was her *Studies of the Life of the Folk,* which appeared in 1884. One of the major essays in this volume was a lengthy piece on the life of peasant women.

In this study, Efimenko confirmed the image of the peasant woman as the agent of disruption in patriarchal society but did not condemn her for her influence in that role. Throughout her discussion, she preferred the term *zhenshchina* to *baba,* using the latter only when she was reporting peasant conversation. Her central thesis was that the fundamental principle at the base of customary law was labor. She argued that Russian peasants had shared the principle of kinship ties with their fellow Slavs until the midnineteenth century, when the labor principle began to dominate economic, social, and family relations.[57] Labor equally shaped the peasant's legal consciousness and influenced his concept of justice, determining such issues as inheritance. Efimenko approached the study of the position of the peasant woman "exclusively as it is determined by the peasants' concepts about justice through their customary law."[58] Furthermore, because "the woman always appears only as a member of the family," her position could be understood only as a product of the principles of family life.[59] Efimenko argued that the intrusion of the labor principle, and its increasing dominance over the principle of birth, was profoundly altering the traditional patriarchal structure of the family unit. The peasant woman, as the weakest and least powerful member of the patriarchal household, stood only to gain from its demise. For this reason, Efimenko said, "[T]he folk are correct when they say that the woman is an enemy of the old order," who was engaged in fierce struggle to "destroy the patriarchal family."[60]

Efimenko explained that the woman's weak position in the family resulted from the fact that she was never a full member of the family and had no say in family decisions. Her burden consisted of providing whatever labor the family enterprise required, whether working in the fields or tending livestock and poultry, and taking care of all the domestic responsibilities of cooking, cleaning, and child care. In addition to her contributions to the economy of the extended family, she had to dress, feed, and care for her nuclear family. In sum, "she must only work, work, and work. Every man in the family is her superior" in her "almost slavish position."[61]

Efimenko reported that not all peasant women submitted to their slavery; some took advantage of changes in the village to wage a protest against patriarchy. She argued that peasant women could begin to struggle only when "the patriarchal family was already wavering," when "the principle of the individual has begun to develop."[62] She observed that these two processes were both possible and evident in post-Emancipation Russia as the larger economy pressed on the autarkic peasant economy and wrought changes in the family as a social and economic unit. As soon as the peasant woman sensed that there were cracks in the structure that oppressed her, she became a bitter and determined opponent who used every tool available to her to fight for a less dependent role in the household. In describing the peasant woman's struggle, Efimenko did not idealize or romanticize her; instead she described the lengths—or depths—to which she would go to secure every minor, even petty victory. Her portrait of the Russian peasant woman was thus more sympathetic in its explanation of why she behaved as she did. She could be a virago on her own terms.

Efimenko described the peasant woman as an "evil opponent" of the patriarchal system. The weapons in her arsenal of domestic struggle included "slyness, slander, constant arguments over the merest trifles. . . ." Her goal was to make life in the extended household unbearable for everyone, while she constantly exerted pressure on her husband to break out on his own. In Efimenko's opinion, the peasant woman had earned the village sobriquets about the *baba*. Freed from the extended household, however, the peasant woman blossomed. Despite the probability of some economic insecurity in the new nuclear family, the woman's responsibilities earned her a different, improved position. If the labor principle continued to determine her role, as Efimenko asserted it did, then the woman as worker shifted in her relationship to her husband. Although he may have persisted in his notions about who should rule the roost, economic necessity required that he assign his wife, now his sole co-worker, a larger and more independent role. Such families predominated in the Arkhangel'sk region, where

Efimenko observed that the peasant woman developed her own sphere of activity, with which her husband had neither the time nor the inclination to interfere. Her position was thus transformed as her husband "involuntarily had to look at his wife as a partner, with whom he worked together for the achievement of their common well-being."[63] The peasant woman knew this instinctively, Efimenko claimed, and it was this goal of greater independence and expanded individual worth which motivated her negative, destructive behavior within the context of the traditional peasant household.

Efimenko's definition of the peasant woman thus supported the view that she was a shrewd, sly being who aimed at the manipulation of others for her own ends. She was an individualist in the fight of her life against patriarchy. We should pause to note at this point that Efimenko offered one of the very few positive prognoses, and certainly the most extensive one, for a future rural Russia beyond the traditional structures and roles of patriarchy and collectivism. Her peasant woman, while a true Eve in her tactics, retained the virtues of the virago, the *boi-baba,* and as an individual emancipated from the rule of the extended household, if not of patriarchy necessarily, she was able to play a positive, productive, and contributing role in her nuclear family and, by extension, the community.

This view had also found expression in the reports of M. K. Gorbunova published in *Notes of the Fatherland* in 1881 and 1882. Gorbunova, as a member of the Commission on the Investigation of Cottage Industry in Russia (1874–1879), traveled around Moscow Province gathering information from peasant women about their crafts. The purpose of her ten articles was to report on cottage industry, but their effect was to offer a series of fond vignettes of independent peasant women who found themselves, for one reason or another, outside the patriarchal household and supporting themselves through cottage industry. The portrait she painted of Russian peasant women was a positive one and complemented Efimenko's work in that it offered a detailed description of the lives of several women who had broken free of the extended household. Her reports offered evidence that the peasant woman could be resourceful and creative given the opportunity. Each of Gorbunova's peasant women displayed initiative and talent, an ability to meet the challenge of supporting herself and her family in the event of the loss of support of husband or extended family. The main figures in her account did not seek their independent position but managed all the same to make the best of it. In developing their craft, they mastered the system of supply and demand, they participated in the market, and they worked long hours. Given the choice of demanding independence and passive dependence, one woman concluded to Gorbunova, "Sometimes it has been very hard . . . but even so it is better to be alone than to be married. When you are alone, you can live however you like. . . ."[64]

Interestingly, Gorbunova assigned the virtuous symbols of rustic nobility to these women in a way that was absent from other reports. These were long-suffering, industrious women. They were excellent homemakers, generous hostesses, gentle in spirit, wise in experience. She offered one of the very rare—indeed, exceptionally rare—scenes of domestic warmth, of exemplary "hearth and home" to be found in contemporary reports from the village. Of one woman she wrote,

> And Marfa Egorovna turned out to be a good, concerned homemaker. She heated up her little iron stove in her simple, clean izba; she gave me her felt boots, explaining that they were soft, good, not like store-bought ones, but made from her own wool—she even has her own lambs. She gave me her new coat to put on, she started the samovar, she ran after some milk, in a word, she did everything she could to warm and welcome me.[65]

Gorbunova thus gave back to the peasant woman, now on her own and distinct from patriarchy, the strength and sanctity that she had held in her eighteenth-century symbolism. "Look at what a saint, what a good woman you are!" she exclaimed to one of her respondents and equally exclaimed for the benefit of her urban readers.[66]

Like Efimenko, Gorbunova stepped out of the mainstream of educated society's attitudes toward the social and economic transformations they observed. Where Efimenko had hailed individualism, Gorbunova sanctioned the pursuit of profit. Her women were indeed "torn from the earth": they were engaged in nonagricultural labor that took them into the market and the money economy. What Engelgardt had found distasteful, she was able to appreciate. Somehow Gorbunova was less sensitive to the hint of *kulachestvo* associated with any money-making enterprise, any tendency toward entrepreneurial behavior.[67] Perhaps because she recognized the necessity that motivated her money-making women, she was able to embrace their businesslike life without attaching the label of exploitation to it.

Uspenskii's "Varvara"

As tempting as it is to conclude on this positive note—on the image of the *boi-baba* in her reincarnation outside the patriarchal family—it would be incorrect to leave the impression that this view was anything other than exceptional in the discourse. Such wholly positive image making was not to be found elsewhere. Outsiders simply could not, as a rule, recognize a beautiful, virtuous, energetic, nurturant peasant woman or endow the *baba* with those features. Although Tolstoy himself offered the briefest glimpse of one such woman in Levin's elegiac description of peasants mowing in the fields in *Anna Karenina*,[68] his own Matrena and Anisia were more typical of the era. Ironically, it was Gleb Uspenskii, whom Wortman has described as being incapable of seeing anything of beauty, who created the most fully developed, positive female peasant character outside Gorbunova's and Efimenko's accounts. When we examine his portrait closely, we find, however, that Uspenskii shared the same prejudices about sexuality and money in association with the peasant woman as most of his peers.

Uspenskii's "Varvara" appeared in the story "It Came to My Memory, From Reminiscences of the Countryside," published in *Notes of the Fatherland* in 1881. The fiction is typically strained and overdrawn, and I must beg my readers' forgiveness for subjecting them to it in detail, even secondhand. The story warrants this lengthy explication because it draws together much of what was in the air at the time and also points to some of the important lacunae in the image of the *baba*. The theme of the larger narration of which Varvara's tale was only a part was the breakdown of traditional rural life, symbolized by migrant workers and field hands. Varvara was one such field hand, whom Uspenskii described in the opening lines of the sketch with the words "This was the ideal worker and in everything else—nothing."[69]

In Varvara, urban readers found the female embodiment of the raw physicality and power of the Russian peasant. Uspenskii described her as the poetry of agricultural labor incarnate. At twenty-five years of age, she had no definitive features when she was idle; only manual labor activated her body and spirit. "Yes, reader, work excites Varvara just as a formal dance excites a great beauty. . . . Only at work did she know what she was, 'why she was on the face of the earth and what she was worth.' "[70] Unlike the other women who worked beside her, Varvara was pure, in Uspenskii's terms, because money did not enter into her relationship to land and labor; "in her whole life, she had not known what money was."[71] She worked instead only for bread at the end of the day and, more importantly, for the pleasure that labor gave her.

Varvara was not only a willing but also an exceptionally able worker for whom all tasks of sowing and harvesting came easily and naturally. When she moved along the rows of wheat, swinging her scythe in consistent arcs, her body became poetry in motion, even, rhythmic, and accurate: "Easily she walks across the cut hay, easily she cuts with the sharp end of the shaft along the surface of the strip of hay, and the hay drops at her feet from right to left and from left to right; it falls not in clumps, does not drag along the earth, but flutters in thin, alternating streams."[72] Her total absorption in the routine of agricultural labor gave Varvara unbroken tranquility of spirit which acted on all who surrounded her. She was curiously unconscious of her effect on others, however, and insensitive to the subtleties of human intercourse and emotion. Whereas her figure and physiognomy were animated and lovely as she worked in the field, her face was always impassive, blank, stupid when she did not have any manual occupation.

Varvara unwittingly became the tragic heroine in a petty human drama orchestrated by her employer's wife, who was jealous of her. When Varvara realized that the wife had made her the butt of a cruel joke, she was distraught and felt betrayed by her fellow workers, who joined in the laughter at her expense. In a flash of cognition, Varvara became no longer simple, departed for St. Petersburg, and was never heard from again.

Uspenskii at first glance seems to have created a *baba* who incorporated many of the elements of the peasant woman as symbol of all that was desirable in rural culture. Unlike her forebears, Aniuta and Liza, Varvara was not, however, a noble savage, but a noble beast. Uspenskii denied this positive female figure any true humanity, any intellect, any spirituality, any sexuality. It was Varvara's very lack of thought, of perception, of understanding which recommended her. As soon as she understood the sexual implications of the joke at her expense, she saw herself and her world differently. Indeed, she became like the other *babas,* conscious of the monetary value of her labor. What had been sacred then became profane. She left for the most profane of settings, St. Petersburg. Like Uspenskii's male peasants, she could be a positive cultural image only so long as she lived within the unconscious regimen of the cycle of labor and land.

In Varvara, as in the rural Eves discussed earlier, sensuality, sexuality, and indeed fertility were absent. There were no voluptuous peasant women like Emile Zola's Françoise in *The Earth* in the Russian post-Emancipation discourse on the peasant soul. Communal, saintly figures were largely old women, beyond the temptations or bounty of the flesh.[73] The figure of the nurturant mother, the truly maternal *baba,* is also missing. Indeed, when mothers did appear, they often as not practiced infanticide or displayed disconcerting nonchalance over the death of their children.[74] Given the very high rates of infant mortality among the peasantry, maternal resignation over infant deaths should not have been surprising, but it was. The outsiders' choice to report this attitude, rather than its opposite, was consistent with the bleak image of the peasant woman current in educated society.[75] This lacuna in the image of the *baba* was undoubtedly a reflection of the harsh world of rural Russia. Engelgardt and Gorbunova offered their examples of "failed" mothers to illustrate the cold reality of marginal existence in the village. Uspenskii's and Tolstoy's women were the incarnation of moral darkness in the countryside. Peasant women were thus symbols of rural Russia, but almost solely of its darker elements.

Of all the elements of life in rural Russia, only the land received an equally poor review and there was surely a psychological connection between the vision of the land and the vision of woman. In early Russia, woman and earth shared images of bounty, moistness, and fertility,[76] and among the peasants, moist Mother Earth was long considered a pure force, out of which nothing evil could spring.[77] Yet in the late nineteenth century, woman and earth shared images of dry sterility. This convergence of desiccated female images for land and woman was most obvious in the work of Gleb Uspenskii.

We should recall that the critical question for Uspenskii in the relationship between man and the land was mastery. Would the land master the peasant or would the peasant master the land? Uspenskii's earth was selfish and unyielding. He frequently expressed perplexity over the peasant's gratitude for the meager fruits which the land offered him as compensation for his ceaseless toil.[78] His earth lacked elements of eroticism and fecundity. It was alternatively a wet nurse or something like, but not quite, a wife. In Uspenskii's writings, there was no concept of bounty in rural life, but rather a grim, sparse, gray world of subsistence and hunger. In fact, Uspenskii eschewed physical descriptions of the landscape altogether.[79] The absence of the elements of beauty and fertility in his image of Mother Earth joined his dismissal of the same in the *baba*, leaving her a barren figure indeed.

The disjunction between the image of the *baba* which lacked the maternal element and the reality of childbearing patterns of peasant women[80] alerts us to the importance of perception and prejudice among the outsiders who constructed that image. In the image of the *baba* the frustrated longings of educated society are laid bare as they invested peasant women with their disappointment and disillusionment with rural society. The dialogism of the image of the *baba* was a manifestation of the conflicting hopes and fears among educated Russians hoping to redefine their culture. For those who still idealized the extended patriarchal family as the seedbed of collectivism, the peasant woman represented the pernicious influence of individualism in the post-Emancipation village. For those who rejected money and the urge for profit as a part of Russian life, the peasant woman was a major agent for their appearance in the village. For those who found sexuality disconcerting, the peasant woman was a seductive, manipulative creature. For those who recognized the potential tyranny and abuse in the patriarchal household, the peasant woman symbolized the victims of patriarchy and paternalism writ large. Only for the exceptional observers of Efimenko's and Gorbunova's type could the Russian peasant woman embody a positive future for transforming Russia. In the discourse on the peasant soul, in the search for cultural self-definition through the construction of images of the peasant, the *baba* as virago, Eve, or victim was the consummate manifestation of the distress that was taking hold in educated society about Russia's future course by the end of the 1880s.

9

Conclusion

It is impossible, it is true, not to agree that for a rather long time, . . .
in Russian journals and in Russian books . . . in all forms of literary
creativity, in idylls and elegies, in near odes of the old style, and especially in sketches, sketches and sketches, the *narod* appeared. . . .

A. VVEDENSKII, "Literary Perspectives (A Word About Literary Populism)"

After the mood of joy, bright hopes and bubbling activity which filled
the epoch of reform, there followed years of complete and bitter disappointment. The joyful mood turned into a gloomy, ironic mood, which
for some reached despair or extreme bitterness.

K. D. KAVELIN, "Topics of the Day"

In society and in the press, more and more strikingly, a very bad
phenomenon has lately begun to reveal itself, to which the expression
"it is pure fantasy and difficult to believe" fully applies. We are talking
about that pessimistic attitude toward the *narod* and the characteristic
peculiarities of their life, which rings sharply even among the ranks of
people who have placed the well-being of the Russian people as the top
priority. It is as if they have lost faith in the *narod:* their life and those
fundamental principles which not long ago were the beacon of a better
future, have become the subject of skepticism, a completely logical
phenomenon, but, unfortunately in the current case, exaggerated,
senseless, and crossing over into pessimism. . . .

F. ANDREEV, "A Word about the *Muzhik* and
Pathological Pessimism about the *Muzhik*"

By the late 1880s, the search for an understanding of rural culture through
a definition of the peasant soul and the construction of the images that had
characterized that search came to an end. A critical phase in the experience
of post-Emancipation Russian society wound down, giving way to the development of alternative approaches to the free peasantry and to new defini-

tions of authority and legitimacy of knowledge about the peasants and their world. It was a phase that ended on a note of discouragement, bitterness, and pessimism as educated Russians fulfilled Dostoevsky's prophecy that if the peasantry turned out to be "not as we imagined," their educated admirers would "renounce them without regret."[1] A generation of educated Russians had gone through a schooling in the nature of the peasant and village culture, had engaged in a sincere and assiduous exploration of the mentality and morality of rural man and woman, and had experienced the reversal of hopes and illusions attached to fond visions of rural Russia as both pure Eden and seedbed of renewal and redemption. The loss of those visions contributed to a societywide fin de siècle despondency over the combined forces of resistance to progressive reform from above in the government of Alexander III and from below in the very population educated Russians had hoped to uplift and engage.

At the same time, however, the search for the peasant soul had generated images of the peasant which offered compelling models for further inquiry. They were compelling for apparently contradictory reasons. The first was that they did represent fragments of rural reality, however much they were constructed by members of educated society. The second was that these images issued from the concerns and anxieties of the writers, painters, journalists, and local observers who captured the spirit of the era through their responses to the question, Who is the Russian peasant? The interplay between the two contexts of the village and the intellectual world of the capitals produced texts and images that would hold force beyond the search for the peasant soul.

Not all the images that emerged from the discourse over the peasant soul held equal weight by the end of the 1880s. Out of the contest of representations, three images prevailed: the rational peasant as man of the land, the gray peasant as victim, and the *kulak* as manipulative exploiter. Of the three images of the peasant woman, the images of *baba* as rural Eve and victim paralleled the *kulak* and the gray peasant, conforming to the conclusions about peasant culture that granted these images of the male peasant the authority they held. The triumph of these images at the expense of those of the *narod* and the communal peasant reflected the terms of the debate over the peasant soul. It equally left a legacy of further distance and division in Russian culture, placing peasant culture outside Russia's potential progress and thus contributing to a tendency in educated society and government circles to consign the peasant to a position of perpetual tutelage.

The image of the *narod* was the essential first casualty of the search for the peasant soul. It served as the established master image in educated society's conception of the simple folk of Russia at the time of the Emancipation. It carried over from the pre-Emancipation era, and particularly the late eighteenth century, when it had served as a major element in Russia's national self-definition in the face of official Europeanization of high culture. In the immediate post-Emancipation era, it served as the question mark, the general shared notion of what the peasants were, but one that invited investigation and eventual dismantling. In this period of self-conscious "newness," the old concept was sure to give way before new definitions. Further, as the insistence on empirical observation as the sine qua non of any true or legitimate definition of the peasant took hold, the open and vague definition of the *narod* gave way to new "scientific" or "realistic" images. Finally, the components of the image itself did not lend themselves to this period of progressive reform and the expectation of further transformations. The distinctive features of the image of the *narod* were the very opposite of those that might engender elements of development and progress, the wishful thinking of radical Populists and neo-Slavophiles alike notwithstanding. Simplicity, intellectual benightedness, cultural homogeneity, and submersion of the individual into the collective were appealing to creators of this image by virtue of the qualities they excluded: diversity, independence of thought, and complexity of interests and needs. The *narod* existed either as a tabula rasa for reformers who saw great opportunities for raising these childlike adults according to their political ideals or as a repository of the obscurantist faith of Russian Orthodoxy and martyrdom. In either case, the image of the *narod* was, as Dostoevsky had recognized, a theory, not the product of scientific approaches or quasi-sociological study. By 1881, Vvedenskii would dismiss Dostoevsky's own vision of the *narod* by saying, "there is no other word for this except fantasy," while the experience of the radical Populists offered graphic testimony to the futility of their image making.[2]

The feebleness of the image of the communal peasant in the debate over the peasant soul stemmed from similar sources. This image highlighted the paradox inherent in the requirement of scientific approaches to the definition of the peasant soul. True to those principles, writers and observers like Zlatovratskii and Kishenskii looked to the peasant's social environment to identify the commune as the most influential institution in shaping the peasant's mentality and behavior. They thus sought sociological explanations rather than describing the peasant's values as somehow inborn or essential. Because they were seeking a definition of the peasant soul and were focusing on moral values as a product of communal structures, they did not concentrate on the economic functions of the commune, but rather on aspects of communal life that defied quantification or scientific methods of description and analysis. This diminished the authority of the image in the discourse, because it enabled critics to charge that Zlatovratskii was insufficiently realistic in his appraisal of village culture. The fact that the image of the communal peasant took shape within the framework of the Darwinian model also contributed to its weak performance in the discourse. The communal peasant was represented as a symbol of failing traditions, a species that was dying out in the era of contest and struggle in Russia. Moral anchors were giving way under the force of individualism, self-interest, and lust for money. The notion of natural selection as an inevitable process joined with the consciousness of new beginnings to undermine the strength of the image of the communal peasant. The absence of any young communal peasants in the various contributions to the debate pointed to the growing conclusion that this was a type slated for extinction.

The failure of the images of the *narod* and the communal peasant robbed educated Russians of the alternative sources of moral strength that many sought as an antidote to the encroachment of values associated with the secular, individualistic, and competitive West. Neither the possibility of rapprochement with the peasant nor that of redemption through association with his moral community found much promise in these two images. This conclusion contributed to a search for other sources of national definition and rejuvenation, which I will discuss.

The images of the rational peasant, the gray peasant, and the *kulak* dominated the discourse because they were most obviously the product of new approaches. Specifically they resulted from emphasis on economic structures within the peasant's environment as the key to his mentality and behavior. The penetration of the peasant's relationship to the land and of the constraints of subsistence farming was a revelation for Engelgardt and Uspenskii and equally for their readers. It explained much of what had mystified observers in the early 1860s and landowners who had struggled to set the terms of their individual Emancipation land settlements on their estates. It also explained the source of peasant resistance to agricultural innovation and to so-called gentry rational agronomy. The image of the peasant as a rational economic actor within his own environment rested on the kind of information and reporting that held full authority in the debate over the peasant soul. Furthermore, the central drama of the peasant's struggle with the material conditions of his labor fit the paradigm of the struggle for existence and was thus one which much of educated Russian society was intellectually prepared to accept. These aspects of the image made it legitimate and compelling within the debate over the peasant soul, but also acceptable and useful for specialists and professional students of the peasants who would participate in the next generation's various debates over peasant farming, family structures, customary law, labor patterns, and, ultimately, political attitudes.

The symbiotic images of the gray peasant as victim and the *kulak* as victimizer or exploiter also resulted from emphasis on economic structures in the village and conformed to the model of the struggle for existence.

They also confirmed the general sense of transformations and new phenomena in the post-Emancipation era, because the *kulak* was so often identified as a product of the new village and the gray peasant as the victim of new economic relations and possibilities in the countryside. One might even argue that the *kulak* was an example of educated society's projection of its own anxieties on the village. The image of the *kulak* implied that every peasant wanted to be the village strongman, to be the pike, not to eliminate him. Every peasant was born with the desire to exploit and manipulate others, to join that group of uncultured peasants who drove outsiders to distraction. Exploitation was not, thus, the exclusive sin of the gentry or of the educated, but a universal tendency in Russian culture. The *kulak's* swaggering individualism, self-interest, and unabashed pleasure in accumulation became the repository of educated society's aversions as much as the *narod's* qualities had been the repository of their longings.

Not only did these images offer explanations of rural culture to educated Russian society. They also provided a prediction of what part the peasant might play in Russia's future development. Indeed, the answers to the question, Who is the Russian peasant?, did suggest answers to the question, What will Russia be? The answers they suggested were discouraging, for the cumulative effect of these images was to deny the possibility of genuine engagement, one might even use the term *assimilation*, of the peasant in Russia's developing culture as active agents in her progress.

The concept of the *kulak* as the true Russian peasant presented no hope for this figure as a participant in Russia's progress. His innate urge to exploit and to manipulate placed him firmly in the camp of opponents of a general improvement in the economic or social condition of his fellow villagers. He was the beneficiary of their lack of development, their economic instability, their illiteracy, and their vulnerability to temptations of the spirit and the flesh. His power in the rural community presented would-be enlighteners with the disconcerting possibility that the early steps toward progress might strengthen his position even further. As one contributor to *The Week* lamented in 1880, "We assumed literacy was a totally desirable end. Instead, we discovered it was a means, an instrument which could be evil in the hands of a literate *kulak* . . . who takes advantage of the illiterate peasants in his village."[3] The power of the *kulak,* according to his image makers, resulted not only from the difficulties of the peasants' economic situation and the pervasive weakness of Russian culture but equally from every peasant's admiration of his power and aspiration to emulate him.

The images of the rational and communal peasant also precluded any plan to engage the peasant. The basic principle in the rational peasant's culture was autarky, whereas that in the communal peasant's was tradition. The entire logic of the peasant as rational agronomist depended on the self-sufficiency of his subsistence economy, and thus resistance to any efforts

which might transform local agriculture for the benefit of national agriculture. Similarly, Uspenskii's dire predictions of what would become of Russia in the event of intellectual or emotional individuation of the peasant
separate from his natural environment also blocked any vision of a reinvigo-
rated peasantry. One of Uspenskii's critics cried foul on this account: "It is
terrible to think that education and everything else the thinking public is
doing to try to bring progress to the *narod* turns the *muzhik* into some kind
of beast having neither conscience nor honor!"[4] The image of the peasant
as definitively communal, and thus a product of the traditions of strict
egalitarianism, implied that no exceptional performance among the peasants would be tolerated within the community. Thus community mores
could stifle any moves toward economic improvement or signs of individual
initiative.

The final approach to defining the peasant soul offered a vision of the
village not as a source of potential strength, but as a scene of fratricidal,
enervating strife, of intraspecific struggle between the *kulak* and his victim,
the gray peasant. The combination of the passive image of the dreary
muzhik who offered little or no resistance to either the pressure of the
outside world or the machinations of his peasant exploiter and the frustrated resignation of such would-be village activists as Nazar'ev and
Astyrev, who granted the *kulak* victory, effectively denied the ability of the
Russian peasant to struggle through a transitional period toward dynamic
development. Certainly their concession to the *kulak* reflected their impa-
tience as reformers, but the effect of their articulation of the peasant as
either exploiter or victim was to discourage others from taking up the next
position in the relay of development.

All of these discouraging images came together in the striking image of
the Russian peasant woman. The conceptual proximity of the images of the
boi-baba (virago) and Eve with the *kulak* and of the peasant woman as
victim with the gray peasant made the incarnation of educated society's
anxieties in their peasant constructs especially vivid here. The figure of the
peasant woman, so fully the repository of sentimentalist ideals and the
search for the folk in the eighteenth century, now joined the *kulak* in
character and in actions as the strong individualist, the selfish egotist who
threatened the rural Eden. "Every woman wants to run her own household," Engelgardt declared, with all of the power that implied. While the
kulak with his fat gut and piles of money threatened the harmony and
equilibrium of the natural economy, symbolizing the sin of profit against
the sacred labor of the pure agriculturalist, the *baba* threatened the sacred
institutions of collectivism and patriarchy for those who still held these
principles dear, consciously or unconsciously.

Similarly, in an era when the members of educated society were fully
absorbed with larger social issues and committed to the mass of the *narod*,

the undeniable presence of a peasant protester for the rights of the individual against the crowd, against the community, against the justification of the larger good, called their own self-abnegation into question. Finally, with the clear exceptions of Efimenko and Gorbunova, outsiders wanted progress and uplift to be generated through their own individual or institutional agencies, primarily education and "legal consciousness." It was unnerving to observe the individual struggle of peasant women taking place beyond the reach of educated society's assistance.

This is why the image of the peasant woman as victim, although obviously grounded in reality, took up such a large space in the public discourse. Victims call for protectors, and in a society where the educated were so imbued with the sense of either gentry-paternal obligations or guilt-ridden urges to compensate the sacrifices of the peasantry in the past, the peasant woman as victim fulfilled the same function as her forebears had in the eighteenth-century search for purity by Westernized—and thus tainted— intellectuals from Moscow and St. Petersburg. Just as Aniuta and Liza were the epitome of native Russia, so the peasant women in Lud'mer's, Nazar'ev's, and countless other accounts were the epitome of the peasantry as the exploited and the victimized.

For those who had set out to discover the peasant soul, who contributed to this discourse, for whom indigenous cultural traits and potential were the decisive agents of Russia's continued development and reform in the spirit of the 1860s, the combination of these images was simply overwhelming. The utter dreariness of the world they now perceived in the village left them deflated and drained. By the late 1880s, such a longtime observer as Astyrev could describe to his readers with full confidence of their comprehension and recognition the following scene from rural Russia.

> I was traveling on business when I suddenly, by chance, had to sit in a village I did not know for a couple of hours, absolutely not knowing what to do with myself. The weather had become disgusting; a fine, light autumn rain was drizzling. I did not even want to look out the window, the views outside were so sad and ugly: an empty, dirty street, cut up by enormous tracks, izbas blackened by the rain with straw roofs dank with moisture, naked fields in the second plane, and on the third, a sparse wood that looked as if it had been shaved except for one tuft of hair. . . . These were all too familiar pictures of filth, want, and a depressing, monotonous life.[5]

This and similar reports confirmed the observation that for those who had gone to the village with high hopes of rapprochement and renewal, "the rural paradise bit by bit began to turn into rural Hell; the result: weariness, coolness, apathy, disillusionment, vague skepticism, and pathological pessi-

mism over the *muzhik* [muzhikovstvuiushchii pessimizm]."⁶ The perceived
reality, the images as they had been constructed, the stock characters in the
rural drama were too much to bear, and educated Russia "turned its back
in contempt on the *muzhik.*"⁷

The extent to which these stock characters had become part of the
national idiom can be seen in Anton Chekhov's short story of 1897, "Peasants [*Muzhiki*]". Although Chekhov's depiction of the peasants of the
village of Zhukovo does not convey contempt for peasants, and instead
stresses the force of poverty in determining their unlucky and distasteful
fate, he does construct a milieu which is consistent with the image making
of the previous generation and the despair over the countryside it engendered. When the peasant–turned–hotel waiter Nikolay Chikildeyev re-
turns home from Moscow to his native village to die, he finds not the cozy
hearth of his youth but a hut that frightens him, because "it was so dark and
crowded and squalid."⁸ Inside the hut lives an extended family dominated
by women whose characterization follows the pattern of the image making
of the *baba* in the 1870s and 1880s. The mistress of the house is a quarrel-
some old shrew who torments everyone else in the household. One
daughter-in-law, Marya, is a typical victim, the abused wife of a drunken
gray *muzhik,* Kiryak. Interestingly, Chekhov also refers to this peasant
mother's equanimity toward her children's deaths. He explains that "[t]he
poorer peasants did not fear death" and says of Marya that she, "far from
dreading death, regretted that it was so long in coming, and was glad when
her children died."⁹

The other daughter-in-law, Fyokla, is a foul-mouthed Eve who engages
in sexual relations with men on a gentry estate across the river and wallows
with pleasure in the filth of daily life in the village and the hut. She "found
everything in this life to her taste: the poverty, the filth, the incessant curs-
ing. She ate whatever was given her indiscriminately, slept anywhere and on
whatever came to hand. She would empty the slops just at the porch, would
splash them out from the doorsill, and then walk barefoot through the
puddle."¹⁰ Both Marya and Fyokla displayed a lack of consciousness; they
"were exceedingly backward and dull-witted."¹¹ The drunken Kiryak shared
the features of Uspenskii's distorted gray *muzhiks.* He "looked terrifying,"
"growled like a beast," and generally exhibited no signs of humanity except
the pain of hangovers after his brutal bouts of drinking.

After the death of Nikolay Chikildeyev, his wife and daughter leave
Zhukovo. The wife, Olga, had arrived with Nikolay only months before as
a sedate, God-fearing woman, capable of compassion and radiance. As she
set off on the road out of Zhukovo, she carried marks of the village with
her. She had grown thin and plain, she had gone gray, "and instead of her
former attractive appearance and pleasant smile, her face now had the sad,
resigned expression left by the sorrows she had experienced, and there was

something obtuse and wooden about her gaze, as though she were deaf."[12] Chekhov suggests that through her experience in the village and close association with the peasants there, Olga had begun the process of dehumanization that would have eventually made her their equal.

Olga leaves the village behind with the following reflection on her experience with the peasants.

> During the summer and the winter there had been hours and days when it seemed as though these people lived worse than cattle, and it was terrible to be with them; they were coarse, dishonest, dirty, and drunken; they did not live at peace with one another but quarreled continually, because they feared, suspected, and despised each other. Who keeps the tavern and encourages drunkenness? The peasant. Who embezzles and drinks up the funds that belong to the community, the schools, the church? The peasant. Who steals from his neighbors, sets fire to their property, bears false witness at court for a bottle of vodka? . . . The peasant. Yes, to live with them was terrible. . . .[13]

Chekhov goes on to find justification for these features of peasant life in their poverty, their humiliation at the hands of local officials, and the corruption of the peasants who were prosperous, "themselves coarse, dishonest, drunken. . . ."[14] Chekhov's peasants thus stepped easily into the roles cast for them two decades earlier: victim, shrew, Eve, dehumanized gray beast, and corrupt exploiter. His portrait of the village and its inhabitants was of a piece with the conclusions of the debate over the peasant soul.

When "pathological pessimism over the *muzhik*" had possessed educated society in the late 1880s, the question, Who is the Russian peasant?, was replaced in serious journals by the question, What is the intelligentsia? Attention shifted from the peasantry as the key to Russian culture and development to the educated, critically thinking elements of society as the decisive actors. Articles on the intelligentsia became as prominent as articles on the peasantry had been a decade earlier.[15] At the same time, there emerged a defense of individual interests, a warning of the need to work on one's own ills before looking after others', an elevation of personal and private concerns over public ones.[16] So much was this the case that Kavelin opened his analysis of social thought over the previous forty years in *Russian Thought* in 1888 with the declaration "[T]he fundamental reason for our current mental and moral apathy lies in the low level of our spiritual and moral development of the individual personality."[17] In a curious double reversal, educated society turned its back on the strong individuals of the village, the *kulak* and the *baba,* and retreated to the educated and enlightened, yet did so proclaiming that the time had come for reassertion of individual interests.

Interest in and debate over the Russian peasant did not end in the late 1880s, of course. In the twenty years or so before the fall of autocracy, the peasant question continued to be at the center of public discourse. In publicism and in literature, however, exploration of the peasant and his world departed in aims and method from the first post-Reform generation. Whereas investigators from various perspectives and from various disciplines had converged on the topic of the peasant soul or the peasant mentality with a shared ethos of positivism, empiricism, and realism, writers in the late 1880s began to reject pure realism in favor of romance and idealization, while the state and the *zemstva* undertook major statistical studies. A sedimentation of approaches to the peasant occurred, reflecting on one hand the greater sophistication of such scholarly disciplines as ethnography, demography, statistics, and jurisprudence, and on the other hand, a redefinition of the function of literature and the appropriate treatment of rural themes in the arts.

In literature, a shift away from photographic realism, positivism, and naturalism led authors to proclaim the primacy of moral concerns and the poetic and inspirational requirements of fiction. As early as 1881, Kishenskii had declared that the writer should strive to uplift, to improve, to contribute to progress, goals which, he claimed, the realists of Uspenskii's type missed entirely.[18] In 1885, Vvedenskii concluded that the Populist-realist literature of the previous decade had failed to produce any great work, largely because "it did not reflect the poetic side of the *narod's* daily life."[19] The editors of *The Northern Herald* announced their views on literature in their first number as excluding "the pathological phenomenon of naturalism," because, "for us the literary and scientific points of view are diametrically opposed to each other." Indeed, by moving away from a purely empirical, scientific, positivist approach, literature could and should return to its moral foundations, "the idea of good, the idea of eternal good."[20] Similarly, Obolenskii distinguished between science and literature, denying that positivism was equally applicable to both fields. Whereas positivism was appropriate for purely scientific investigation, it failed to illuminate the essentially human aspects of life.

> But the world which a man sees and feels both within himself and outside of himself seems much more complicated to him than it appears in experience and in scientific experience in particular. For example, within himself he knows sensations, feelings, consciousness, ideals of the supreme truth and good, love and self-sacrifice, questions and dreams about the goal and meaning of life, invincible strivings toward goals which are higher than ordinary, animal-vegetative daily life.[21]

These aspects of life, inaccessible to positivism, constituted the proper domain of literature. In much the same spirit, a rising star of the next generation of writers, A. I. Ertel', explained to Zlatovratskii that Russian authors should avoid the failings of naturalism and always keep the moral element and the "dream" at the center of their work.[22]

Ertel' went on to make explicit the new moral and political task facing Russian authors in the era of reaction under Alexander III, a struggle against the arbitrariness of rigid autocracy which required active engagement.[23] Given the prevailing mood of pessimism, largely generated as much by the depressing depiction of the mass of the Russian people as by the oppressive rule from above, authors could no longer afford to indulge in "insistent realism." Their task now was to inspire, and to inspire, they needed not to depict peasant exploiters and victims but to create peasant heroes and saints. Ertel' would rise to the challenge, as did his peer V. G. Korolenko, who was praised in this spirit for avoiding overly realistic characterizations while clearly demonstrating his sympathies with the downtrodden.[24] His forte was the depiction of heroic, active peasant figures who contrasted with the inert mass of gray *muzhiks* of Uspenskii and even Zlatovratskii.[25] This he did through what he called a "synthesis of realism and romanticism," and worked against the influence of naturalism in Russian literature in his position as editor at *Russian Wealth*.[26]

In painting as well, the Itinerants shifted away from critical realism to a more nostalgic, romantic treatment of rural life. They moved out of the izba into the fields surrounding the village street, to the natural setting which began to gain on peasant portraiture as the focus of their work. As field, flower, sun, and sky emerged as the principal elements in the image of rural Russia, the psychological portrait receded. G. G. Miasoedov's *Mowers* of 1887 illustrates this shift, for here the peasant figures are only one element in a scene of harvesttime in the setting of wheat, flowers, sunshine, and blue sky. The painting is diffuse, bathed in an even distribution of light with the principal figure attracting the viewer's eye not through any exceptional detail within the composition, but merely because of his size and placement. This example of Miasoedov's work was typical of the Itinerants' shift toward a more idealized vision of rural Russia. I. I. Levitan produced landscapes which depicted the rural world as nature, with the peasants as incidental in the frame. In *March* (1895), the peasant is absent, as is narrative content. Instead we find a lyrical scene of the natural world executed in a style that has moved away from photographic precision toward impressionism. In works where peasant figures appeared, they were more a part of the landscape than the focus of the painting. V. A. Serov's *October in Domotkanovo* (1895) places a peasant boy amid the straw, emphasizing his position as one of the several natural elements in the scene by using both the same range of colors and the same brush stroke for his figure as for the straw, horses, shed, and trees. This is equally true of A. E. Arkhipov's *The Return Trip* (1896), where the peasant is turned away from the viewer. V. A. Serov's *Peasant Woman in a Cart* (1896) illustrates the distance Russian painters had traveled away from critical realism by the turn of the century.

This shift away from critical realism in the treatment of strictly rural scenes by the Itinerants was all the more striking because it contrasted so sharply with the treatment of urban, industrial, or migratory life at the end of the century. In the factory yard in Arkhipov's *Day Laborers* (1896) or in the laundry in his *Washerwomen* (1901), critical realism held firm, complete with attention to the psychology of the characters and to the details of their setting. Here the harsh scrutiny of the painter provided illustrations of the dark side of modernization in Russian culture. In national self-definition, the countryside became the opposite, the subject of nostalgic and gentle treatment in the juxtaposition between Russia's rural past and her modernizing, industrializing, urban present. This demise of the genre of literary journalism and of the critically realistic approach to the rural theme in painting at the end of the 1880s was one marker of the end of the discourse on the peasant soul. New definitions of the legitimate functions and styles of artistic creation reflected both aesthetic judgments and concerns about a different kind of social and economic transformation from that of the 1860s through 1880s. Whereas the free peasantry had seemed to be the most compelling new element in Russian society after 1861, by 1890 factory laborers and peasant migrants to the cities were beginning to loom large as both the victims of industrialization and a potentially threatening by-product of urbanization and development. In them, writers and painters found new subjects for examining the essence and drama of contemporary Russian life. Further examination of the peasant and his culture would take place not through art, but through science. This division of labors, as it were, was a manifestation of the growing complexity of Russian intellectual life, of the rise of professions, and of the greater sophistication of scholarly disciplines.

The empirical study of the peasant increasingly took place under the auspices of state commissions, scholarly societies, and *zemstvo* statistical boards. Primarily under the Ministry of the Interior, the state would continue to gather information from local officials on population, family patterns, land distribution, and local institutions of justice. The Imperial Free Economic Society, the Imperial Russian Geographic Society, the Society of Naturalists, Anthropologists, and Ethnographers, as well as wealthy individuals such as Prince V. N. Tenishev and A. N. Pypin, would sponsor ethnographic expeditions and surveys with the goal of establishing a large body of materials on rural customs and attitudes. *Zemstvo* statistical boards would continue and expand their household census and other studies of the village. These undertakings marked a new level of sophistication in educated society and among state officials in their methods and questions in regard to the village and the peasant. Moreover, they represented a more institutionalized approach and a search for a different set of signposts than those in the search for the peasant soul. Numbers, data, hard facts would replace characterizations, eyewitness accounts, image making. The goals of rapprochement and redemption fell away in these approaches, and the peasantry became its own, separate, distinct object of study, more other culture than ever before, indeed more alien and curious.

In the study of the peasant as judge, customary law dominated the debate and underscored the distance between village attitudes toward justice, crime, and punishment and the concepts of legality wrapped up in the term *legal consciousness. Samosud,* the practice of peasant righting of wrongs completely outside the legal system, persisted and captured the full attention of *obshchestvo.*[27] The pessimistic conclusions about the competency of the *volost'* court judges to stand up to powerful figures in village politics led to the introduction of the Land Captain in 1889, a noble agent of administrative tutelage over the peasants whose mandate was to order village life and protect the peasant from himself or his neighbor. Distress over the persistence of the breakup of extended families through household divisions led the state to expand the restrictions on these fissions by law in 1886. Thus, although the peasantry was certainly under scrutiny, they were seen as both peculiar and in need of tutelage.

In the two areas of activity where educated members of society continued to work intimately with the village, education and public health, one can argue that an attitude of tutelage was equally dominant: *zemstvo* schoolteachers went to teach the peasants, while *zemstvo* doctors went to cure them. Rural education programs rested both on faith in the power of education itself and in a belief that the peasant was educable. Liberal faith in the universal potential of intellectual development and specific programs for the spread of literacy supported the belief of such men as Baron N. Korf in the eventual enlightenment of the Russian village. Korf published two remarkable articles in late 1881 to shore up faith in rural education by reporting on the peasant's retention of literacy. He wanted to demonstrate that peasants not only had learned to read but also were reading to learn as long as five years after their schooling. He did this by reporting on his survey of about five hundred peasants who had studied for at least three winter sessions previously. He reported that more than 90 percent read well and with comprehension, while 80 percent were able to solve simple problems involving addition and subtraction.[28] He offered these results as evidence of the rewards teaching in the village could bring and supported the value of education as the path to true progress.

Zemstvo physicians acted out of a similar faith in science and medical knowledge. Because of the predominance of the "filth theory" on the origins of disease in this period, their approach to the village was directed at cleaning it up and striving to "fight the ignorance of the popular masses and to change the entire aspect of their world view."[29] *Zemstvo* medicine rested on a quite negative perception of the peasant and on elite notions of eliminating sources of contamination born of ignorance and superstition. Frieden argues that even genuine altruism and populism were very rare among *zemstvo* doctors who, she says, were drawn to *zemstvo* medicine "because its scientific achievements enhanced their public image as educated individuals with valuable skills."[30]

For the most part, educated society found itself in much the same position vis à vis the peasants in 1890 that it had been in 1861: distant from the village, viewing the peasantry as the other, and assuming the role of the sole active agents in Russian culture who would bear the responsibility for moving it forward. The conclusion of the broad search for the peasant soul as an effort to close the gap between educated society and the peasantry through personal experience and shared knowledge of the village was thus a reassertion of the polarity of Russian society. The binary division in the consciousness of educated Russians between *obshchestvo* and *narod* reappeared in a stubborn reincarnation of this aspect of Russian culture. If we consider the collection of images to be an iconostasis of sorts, we find that it fulfilled its function of division between the sanctuary and the nave—here the village and the world of educated Russians—while failing to achieve the second function of creating in "one whole an image which reflects a state of the universe where all separation is overcome, where there is achieved a reconciliation between God and the creature, and with the creature itself."[31] Instead the peasant icons of the late 1880s were the fruit of failed rapprochement and reconciliation which reinforced profound division and alienation. Yet this position in 1890 was a more pernicious one for Russian culture because that distance rested on confident knowledge of the Russian peasant and frustration at the resistance of village culture.

A contributor to *Week* captured that frustration when he wrote, "People are turning away from work in the village, they say it is useless, that there are no positive results, that it is just pouring water on concrete."[32] Active engagement within the systems of village culture and work with those systems seemed, this metaphor suggested, impossible as educated members of society rolled off the surface of a solid, impermeable society made up of the peasant types associated with the images that the search for the peasant soul had created. The authority of these images and their negative messages in the figures of the gray peasant, the *kulak,* and the *baba* encouraged the well-established tradition of *opeka,* of tutelage, to take a more aggressive turn, not only to foster the urge to supervise and protect the peasants but also to control and act on them. In a passage that was characteristic of the new defense of individualism and initiative and gave testimony to the impact of the very images he had himself contributed to, Uspenskii described a group of settlers in New Russia in 1888: "Looking at these healthy, free people who were neither hungry nor cold, who were dressed well, warmly and attractively in clothes they wove and made themselves, listening to their expansive, intelligent speech, I completely forgot the word *muzhik*. Yes, these were *authentic free people,* precisely *people.* . . . These were not *muzhiks.* . . ."[33] The peasant had become so much the other by the end of the decade that in his realistic depiction, he had ceased even to be human.

As the curtain dropped on the drama of post-Emancipation *obshchestvo*'s eager rush to the village and on the cast of peasant characters who were left standing on stage, it marked a new and intensified phase of cultural division. The milling crowd of the silent and sympathetic *narod* had left the stage. In their place, the rational peasant of the land ploughed steadily on his little plot, absorbed in the land, sweating from his labor, occasionally pausing to thank God for the few grains the miserly earth yielded him. The communal peasant in his enfeeblement stood at the center of a communal circle that was melting away, while the gray peasant lay prostrate with a bottle in hand, sat staring blankly at the figures leaning over him, or stood with plank raised to strike his wife. The *kulak* strutted with a bag of money around his neck and a fat gut bulging under his shirt. He thumped his fellow peasants on the back while waving his backside at the outsiders who had arrived to watch his show. The *babas* either lay moaning and helpless, searching the crowd for a savior, or sashayed with scheming faces, whispering in the ear of the *kulak* or the gray peasant. Only the *boi-baba* on her own, separated from the crowd and turned away from their antics, offered the prospect of vigor and virtue. It was a sad ending to the promise of the hopeful search for the peasant soul and for national self-definition in the village. The urge for rapprochement had led to rejection; the hope for renewal and redemption had ended in recrimination. As the public filed out of the theater, they left resigned to their own exceptional humanity within the culture.

Notes

Introduction

1. Vasilii Evgrafovich Cheshikhin-Vetrinskii, *Gleb Ivanovich Uspenskii: Biograficheskii ocherk* (Moscow, 1929), 302–3.

2. Leonid Ouspensky and Vladimir Lossky, *The Meaning of Icons*, G. E. H. Palmer and E. Kadloubovsky, trans., URS Graf-Verlag, Olten Switzerland, ed. (Boston, 1952), 16.

3. Dominick LaCapra, *Rethinking Intellectual History: Texts, Contexts, Language* (Ithaca, 1983), 36–60.

4. David A. J. Macey, *Government and Peasant in Russia, 1861–1906: The Prehistory of the Stolypin Reforms* (Dekalb, Ill., 1987).

5. Marc Raeff, "The Peasant Commune in the Political Thinking of Russian Publicists: Laissez-faire Liberalism in the Reign of Alexander II" (Ph.D. Diss., Harvard University, 1950); Steven Alan Grant, "The Peasant Commune in Russian Thought" (Ph.D. diss., Harvard University, 1973).

6. Ben Eklof, *Russian Peasant Schools: Officialdom, Village Culture, and Popular Pedagogy, 1861–1914* (Berkeley, 1986); Nancy Mandelker Frieden, *Russian Physicians in an Era of Reform and Revolution, 1856–1905* (Princeton, 1981).

7. Thomas S. Pearson, *Russian Officialdom in Crisis: Autocracy and Local Self-Government, 1861–1900* (Cambridge, 1989); Francis William Wcislo, *Reforming Rural Russia: State, Local Society and National Politics, 1855–1914* (Princeton, 1990); George L. Yaney, *The Urge to Mobilize: Agrarian Reform in Russia, 1861–1930* (Urbana, Ill., 1982).

8. LaCapra explored the importance of contexts for understanding texts further in his *History, Politics and the Novel* (Ithaca, 1987). For a useful examination of LaCapra's position in comparison with that of Hayden White, see Lloyd S. Kramer, "Literature, Criticism, and Historical Imagination: The Literary Challenge of Hayden White and Dominick LaCapra," in Lynn Hunt, ed., *The New Cultural History* (Berkeley, 1989), 97–128.

9. Mikhail M. Bakhtin, *Problems of Dostoevsky's Poetics*, Caryl Emerson, ed. and trans. (Minneapolis, 1984), 6–7.

10. Ibid., 27.

11. Ibid., 29.

12. Ibid., 203.

13. Hayden V. White, *Tropics of Discourse: Essays in Cultural Criticism* (Baltimore, 1978), 2.

14. Ibid., 21.

15. Jeffrey Brooks, "Readers and Reading at the End of the Tsarist Era," in W. M. Todd, ed., *Literature and Society in Imperial Russia, 1880–1914* (Stanford, 1978), 99–100; R. J. Ware, "A Russian Journal and Its Public: *Otechestvennye zapiski*, 1868–1884," *Oxford Slavonic Papers* n.s. 14 (1981): 130.

16. V. Leshkov, "Obshchestvo i vospitanie, lichnost' i narodnoe prosveshchenie," *Den'* no. 21 (May 23, 1864), 8.

17. So A. N. Pypin described it in a letter to N. G. Chernyshevsky, January 16, 1883. Tsentral'nyi Gosudarstvennyi arkhiv literatury i iskusstva (hereafter TsGALI), fond 395, opis' 1, delo 225, l.3.

18. For information on these reforms see: S. Kucherov, *Courts, Lawyers, and Trials under the Last Three Tsars* (New York, 1953); Richard Wortman, *The Development of a Russian Legal Consciousness* (Chicago, 1976); Forrest A. Miller, *Dmitrii Miliutin and the Reform Era in Russia* (Nashville, Tenn., 1968); Terence Emmons and Wayne Vucinich, eds., *The Zemstvo in Russia: An Experiment in Local Self-Government* (Cambridge, 1982).

19. Skaldin [F. P. Elenev], "V Zakholust'i i v stolitse, V," *Otechestvennye zapiski* 185 (November 1869): 1:151.

20. LaCapra, *Rethinking Intellectual History*, 49.

21. Iurii M. Lotman and Boris A. Uspenskii, "Binary Models in the Dynamics of Russian Culture (to the End of the Eighteenth Century)," in Iurii M. Lotman, Lidiia Ia. Ginsburg, and Boris A. Uspenskii, *The Semiotics of Russian Cultural History*, Alexander D. Nakhimovsky and Alice Stone Nakhimovsky, eds. (Ithaca, 1985), 30–66.

22. N. a., "Sovremennaia khronika Rossii," *Otechestvennye zapiski* 137 (August 1861): 39–40.

23. For a discussion of this term, see Abbott Gleason, *Young Russia: The Genesis of Russian Radicalism in the 1860s* (New York, 1980), 2–3.

24. Taken from n. 15 in John Gooding, "Toward *War and Peace:* Tolstoy's Nekhliudov in 'Lucern'," *The Russian Review* 48 (October 1989): 390.

25. G. Eliseev, "Proizvoditel'nye sily Rossii," *Otechestvennye zapiski* 180 (February 1868): 407–8.

26. White, *Tropics*, 151–52.

27. Ibid., 152.

28. Richard Wortman's study of the psychology of four prominent Populists, three of whom are important in this study also, provides a thorough analysis of the individual needs that propelled many figures to the village in this period. Richard S. Wortman, *The Crisis of Russian Populism* (Cambridge, 1967).

29. For a discussion of developments in science, the emergence of scientific societies, and efforts to make science accessible to the public, see Alexander Vucinich, *Science in Russian Culture, 1861–1917* (Stanford, 1970).

30. Daniel P. Todes focuses on the resistance of Russian biologists to the Malthusian elements in Darwin's theory in his *Darwin without Malthus: The Struggle for Existence in Russian Evolutionary Thought* (Oxford, 1989). Alexander Vucinich

explores Darwin's influence in Russian thought, broadly defined, in an encyclopedic study. Alexander Vucinich, *Darwin in Russian Thought* (Berkeley, 1988).

31. See Frieden, *Russian Physicians;* Richard Wortman, *The Development of a Russian Legal Consciousness* (Chicago, 1976); Harley Balzer, ed., *Professions in Russia at the End of the Old Regime* (Ithaca, forthcoming).

32. LaCapra, *Rethinking Intellectual History,* 313.

33. R. J. Ware, "A Russian Journal and Its Public: *Otechestvennye zapiski,* 1868–1884," *Oxford Slavonic Papers* n.s. (1981): 121–46; M. V. Teplinskii, "*Otechestvennye zapiski*" *(1868–1884) Istoriia zhurnala: Literaturnaia kritika* (Iuzhno-Sakhalinsk, 1966), 107–9.

34. TsGALI, fond 572, opis' 2, delo 27, contains a series of letters from Sharapov to Engelgardt in February and March 1881. Aksakov withdrew the offer to Engelgardt after the assassination of Alexander II.

35. TsGALI, fond 202, opis' 1, delo 205, includes a letter from A. I. Ertel' to Zlatovratskii bemoaning the divisiveness among writers in St. Petersburg who had fallen out with each other since the closing of *Notes on the Fatherland.* Letter of March 1890, ll. 3–4.

36. TsGALI, fond 572, opis' 1, delo 142, l. 5, includes a letter to Engelgardt from his former colleague, P. A. Lachinov, reporting a conversation between the chemist, Mendeleev, and Loris-Melikov in which the Minister of the Interior indicated his familiarity with Engelgardt's work.

37. See n. 15.

38. Dominick LaCapra, *Soundings in Critical Theory* (Ithaca, 1989), 137.

39. G. I. Shchetinina, "Revoliutsionnaia publitsistika 80-kh–nachala 90-kh godov xix v. o polozhenii russkogo krest'ianstva," in S. L. Tikhvinskii, ed., *Sotsial'no-ekonomicheskoe razvitie Rossii: Sbornik statei k 100-letiiu dnia rozhdeniia Nikolaia Mikhailovicha Druzhinina* (Moscow, 1986), 247.

40. K. D. Kavelin, *Krest'ianskii vopros: Issledovanie o znachenii u nas krest'ianskogo dela, prichinakh ego upadka, i merakh k podniatiiu sel'skogo khoziaistva i byta poselian* (St. Petersburg, 1882), 31.

41. Franco Venturi, *Roots of Revolution,* Francis Haskell, trans. (New York, 1960); Andrzej Walicki, *The Controversy over Capitalism: Studies in the Social Philosophy of the Russian Populists* (Oxford, 1969); Petr Andreevich Zaionchkovskii, *Provedenie v zhizn' krest'ianskoi reformy 1861 g.* (Moscow, 1958), and *The Russian Autocracy in Crisis, 1878–1882,* Gary A. Hamburg, trans. (Gulf Breeze, Fla., 1979); Macey, *Government and Peasant in Russia;* Arthur P. Mendel, *Dilemmas of Progress in Tsarist Russia: Legal Marxism and Legal Populism* (Cambridge, 1961); Norman M. Naimark, *Terrorists and Social Democrats: The Russian Revolutionary Movement under Alexander II* (Cambridge, 1983).

42. Ben Eklof, *Russian Peasant Schools;* Jeffrey Brooks, *When Russia Learned to Read: Literacy and Popular Literature, 1861–1917* (Princeton, 1985); Emmons and Vucinich, eds., *The Zemstvo in Russia;* Roger Bartlett, ed., *Land Commune and Peasant Community in Russia* (London, 1990); Andrei Matveevich Anfimov, *Ekonomicheskoe polozhenie i klassovaia bor'ba krest'ian evropeiskoi Rossii, 1881–1904* (Moscow, 1984), and *Krest'ianskoe khoziaistvo evropeiskoi Rossii, 1881–1904* (Moscow, 1980); Steven L. Hoch, *Serfdom and Social Control in Russia: Petrovskoe, a Village in Tambov* (Chicago, 1986); Christine D. Worobec, *Peasant Russia:*

Family and Community in the Post-Emancipation Period (Princeton, 1991); Timothy Mixter and Esther Kingston-Mann, *Peasant Economy, Culture and Politics of European Russia, 1800–1921* (Princeton, 1991).

43. Jean Blankoff, *La societé russe de la seconde moitié du xixe siècle* (Brussels, 1972); Jean Lothe, *Gleb Ivanovic Uspenskii et le populisme russe: Contribution à l'histoire de la pensée et de la littérature populistes en Russie (1870–1890)* (Leiden, 1963); Nikita Ivanovich Prutskov, *Gleb Uspenskii Semidesiatykh—nachala vos'midesiatykh godov* (Gorkii, 1955), and *Tvorcheskii put' Gleba Uspenskogo* (Moscow, 1958); Konstantin Grigor'evich Semenkin, *N. N. Zlatovratskii: Ocherk Zhizni i tvorchestva* (Iaroslavl', 1976).

44. Richard S. Wortman, *The Crisis of Russian Populism* (Cambridge, 1967); Daniel Field, *Rebels in the Name of the Tsar* (Boston, 1976); Andrew Donskov, *The Changing Image of the Peasant in Nineteenth-Century Russian Drama* (Helsinki, 1972).

45. Wortman, *Crisis of Russian Populism*, 33.

46. Field, *Rebels*, 212–13.

47. Esther Kingston-Mann, *Lenin and the Problem of Marxist Peasant Revolution* (New York, 1985), 19–38.

48. Teodor Shanin, *The Roots of Otherness: Russia's Turn of the Century*, vol. 1, *Russia as a "Developing Society"* (Houndmills, Basingstroke, Hampshire, 1985), and vol. 2, *Russia, 1905–1907: Revolution as a Moment of Truth* (New Haven, 1986), and *The Awkward Class: Political Sociology of the Peasantry in a Developing Society: Russia 1910–1925* (Oxford, 1972).

Chapter 1. The 1860s: Setting the Stage

1. Hans Rogger, *National Consciousness in Eighteenth-Century Russia* (Cambridge, 1960).

2. Donald Fanger, "The Peasant in Literature," in Wayne Vucinich, ed., *The Peasant in Nineteenth Century Russia* (Stanford, 1968), 231–62.

3. Judy Woodhouse, "A Landlord's Sketches? D. V. Grigorovič and Peasant Genre Fiction," *Journal of European Studies* 16 (1986): 271–94.

4. F. B-a, " 'Muzhik' s tochki zreniia liudei 40-kh godov," *Delo* (June 1881): 25–33.

5. N. V. Shelgunov, "Narodnyi realizm v literature," *Delo* (May 1871): 6.

6. Ronald D. LeBlanc, "Teniers, Flemish Art, and the Natural School Debate," *Slavic Review* 50 (Fall 1991): 576–89; Ronald D. LeBlanc, "Tenierism: Seventeenth-Century Flemish Art and Early Nineteenth-Century Russian Prose," *The Russian Review* 49 (1990): 19–41; and Jurij V. Mann, "The Natural School as a Stage in the Development of Russian Literature," *Neohelicon* 15 (1988): 89–99.

7. N. V. Uspenskii, "Ocherki narodnogo byta," *Sovremennik* 85 (January 1861): 241–48; and 86 (April 1861): 369–82.

8. Edward J. Brown, "So Much Depends . . . Russian Critics in Search of 'Reality'," *The Russian Review* 48 (October 1989): 363.

9. N. V. Uspenskii, "Iz dnevnika neizvestnogo," *Sovremennik* 91 (January 1862): 241–48.

10. I. Selivanov, "Dva ubiistva," *Sovremennik* 87 (May 1861): 5–42, with these characterizations on p. 7.

11. See, for example, V. A. Sleptsov, "Kazaki: Derevenskie stseny," *Sovremennik* 100 (February 1864): 555–70; Rodimyi, "Kolodez: Rasskaz," *Otechestvennye zapiski* 171/7 & 8 (1867): 808–14.

12. F. M. Reshetnikov, "Podlipovtsy: Etnograficheskii ocherk, I," *Sovremennik* 101 (March 1864): 155–89.

13. Rose Glickman, "An Alternative View of the Peasantry: The Raznochintsy Writers of the 1860s," *Slavic Review* 32 (December 1973): 693.

14. See Louis Chevalier, *Laboring Classes and Dangerous Classes in Paris during the First Half of the Nineteenth Century* (New York, 1973), for an examination of this process in Paris during a period of rapid urbanization when the bourgeois citizens of Paris suddenly had to share space and culture with the working poor.

15. M. E. Saltykov-Shchedrin, "V derevne: Letnii fel'eton," *Sovremennik* 97 (August 1863): 2:173–98.

16. N. B., "Iz Kashiry: Pis'mo 2-oe," *Den'* no. 4 (November 4, 1861): 8.

17. Ibid., 9.

18. V., "Nasha sel'skaia zhizn': Zametki literatora-obyvatelia," *Otechestvennye zapiski* 170/3 & 4 (1867): 394.

19. A. Skabichevskii, "Kritika: Zhivaia struia (Vopros o narodnosti v literature) in "Sovremennoe obozrenie," *Otechesvennye zapiski* 177/4 (1868): 161–62.

20. See, for example: S. Bezymennyi, "Proshloe leto v derevne," *Russkii vestnik* 37 (February 1862): 664–701; continued in *Russkii vestnik* 38 (March 1862): 380–416; 39 (May 1862): 42–76; 39 (June 1862): 509–51; 40 (July 1862): 67–115; 40 (August 1862): 610–58; Vol. 41 (September 1862): 197–237; A. A. Fet, "Iz derevni," *Russkii vestnik* 50 (April 1864): 575–626; Kniaz' V. P. Meshcherskii, "Eshche o volostnykh sudakh," *Russkii vestnik* 51 (June 1864): 765–82; Mirovoi posrednik A. Vas'kov, "Iz Nerekhotskogo uezda," *Den'* no. 4 (Nov. 4, 1861), 12; N. Pirogov, "Pis'mo iz Kamenets—Podol'skoi gubernii, mirovogo posrednika Vinnitskogo uezda," *Den* no. 6 (Nov. 18, 1861), 7–8; Dmitrii Samarin, "Pis'mo mirovogo posrednika: iz Samarskoi gubernii," *Den'* no. 8 (Dec. 2, 1861), 9; Pavel Bats, "Iz Kozlova," *Den'* no. 27 (Apr. 17, 1862), 10–11; Mirovoi posrednik Nik. Tsiolkovskii, "Iz Orenburgskogo uezda," *Den'* no. 31 (May 12, 1862), 14–15; S. Protopov, "Dve pedagogicheskie ekskursii v derevniu," *Den'* no. 13 (Mar. 28, 1863), 15–17; P. B., "Iz Balakhninskogo uezda," *Den* no. 16 (Apr. 20, 1863), 12–13; Mirovoi posrednik, "Iz zapisok mirovogo posrednika," *Den'* no. 43 (Oct. 26, 1863), 4–6; M. Iu-n, "Iz derevni, I," *Den'* no. 34 (Aug. 22, 1864), 11–13, continued in no. 35 (Aug. 29, 1864), 5–7, and no. 36 (Sept. 5, 1864), 3–6; K. D. Kavelin, "Pis'ma iz derevni," in *Sobranie sochinenii* 663–87 (first appeared in *Moskovskie vedemosti,* 1860, nos. 192 and 194).

21. Dmitrii Samarin, "Pis'mo," 9.

22. Mirovoi posrednik, "Iz zapisok," *Den'* no. 43 (Oct. 26, 1863): 5.

23. Sergei Aleksandrovich Tokarev, *Istoriia russkoi etnografii* (Moscow, 1966), 282.

24. A. N. Afanas'ev, *Russkie narodnye skazki.* 8 vols. (Moscow, 1861–1863). See also Maria-Gabriele Wosien, *The Russian Folk-Tale: Some Structural and Thematic Aspects* (Munich, 1969), 14–16.

25. Catherine Black Clay, "Ethos and Empire: The Ethnographic Expedition of the Imperial Russian Naval Ministry, 1855–1862" (Ph.D. diss., University of Oregon, 1989).

26. Abbott Gleason, *Young Russia: The Genesis of Russian Radicalism in the 1860s* (New York, 1980), 226–89. These were also the years when P. N. Rybnikov was gathering and publishing Russian folk songs: P. N. Rybnikov, *Pesni, sobranniia P. N. Rybnikovym* (Moscow, 1861–1867).

27. P. N. Rybnikov, *Pesni: Chast' 1: Narodyne byliny, stariny i pobyval'shchiny* (Moscow, 1861); P. V. Kireevskii, *Pesni* (Moscow, 1860–1861); P. V. Shein, *Russkie narodyne byliny i pesni* (Moscow, 1859), reviewed in 137 (July 1861), "Kritika," 1–79.

28. V. P. Bezobrazov, "Iz putevykh zapisok, I–II," *Russkii vestnik* 34 (July 1861): 265–308; V. I. Dal', "Kartiny russkogo byta: Seren'kaia—samorodok—Ianvar'," *Russkii vestnik* 67 (January 1867): 318–53 (a fictionalized ethnographic sketch); V. I. Roskovshenko, "Marusia: Malorossiiskoe predanie," *Russkii vestnik* 69 (May 1867): 357–88 (similarly fictionalized).

29. Ardamon R——skov, "Iz derevenskoi glushi: zametki o khlystovskoi i skopecheskoi sekte," *Den'* no. 24 (June 13, 1864), 7–10; F. Gur'ev, "Zimnee delo: kartina krest'ianskoi zhizni," *Den'* no. 51 (December 21, 1863), 12–14.

30. P. I. Iakushkin, "Velik Bog zemli russkoi!" *Sovremennik* 94 (January 1863): 1:5–54, and "Nebyval'shchina," *Sovremennik* 111 (November–December 1865): 1:5–21; E. D., "Posidenok i svad'ba (Posv. N. D. Dmitrievu)," *Sovremennik* 97 (July 1863): 1:5–48; Vlad. A. Aleksandrov, "Derevenskoe vesel'e v Vologodskom uezde: Etnograficheskie materialy," *Sovremennik* 103 (July 1864): 1:169–200; N. S. Preobrazhenskii (pseud. N. Pr——skii), "Bania, igrishche, slushan'e i shestoe ianvaria: Etnograficheskie ocherki Kadnikovskogo uezda (Stat'ia pervaia)," *Sovremennik* 104 (October 1864): 1:499–522, and "Sel'skii prazdnik: Etnograficheskie ocherki Kadnikovskogo uezda (Stat'ia vtoraia)," *Sovremennik* 106 (February 1865): 1:409–45.

31. A. N. Pypin, "Kak ponimat' etnografiiu? (Posviashchaetsia "Dniu")," *Sovremennik* 106 (February 1865): 2:173–84.

32. Alexander Vucinich, *Social Thought in Tsarist Russia: The Quest for a General Science of Society, 1861–1917* (Chicago, 1976), 3.

33. Ibid., 15–18.

34. Ibid., 24–5.

35. Ibid., 26.

36. See such articles as V. Lesevich, "Positivizm posle Konta," *Otechestvennye zapiski* 182 (April 1869): 363–99; P. L. Lavrov, "Antropologi v Evrope i ikh sovremennoe znachenie," *Otechestvennye zapiski* 182 (March 1869): 2:1–51; M. A. Antonovich, "Teoriia proiskhozhdeniia vidov v tsarstve zhivotnom (O proiskhozhdenii vidov v tsarstvakh zhivotnom i rastitel'nom putem estestvennogo podbora rodichei, ili o sokhranenii usovershenstvovannykh porod v bor'be za sushestvovanie. Sochinenii Charl'za Darvina. Perevel s Angliiskogo S. Rachinskii. (SPb

1864)," *Sovremennik* 101 (March 1864): 2:63–107; G. O. Gel'mhol'ts [Helmholtz], "O vsaimodeistvii sil prirody: Publichnaia lektsiia," *Sovremennik* 101 (April 1864): 1:449–76; P. D. Iurkevich, "Iazyk fiziologov i psikhologov," *Russkii vestnik* 38 (April 1862): 912–35; K. P. Pobedonostsev, "Mestnoe naselenie Rossii," *Russkii vestnik* 40 (July 1862): 5–34 (a review of two volumes of statistical information with heavy praise for the statistical method); D. N. Abashev, "Agronomicheskie uchenie Libikha (Liebig)," *Russkii vestnik* 52 (July 1864): 170–245; n.a., "Istochniki narodnogo sueveriia," *Otechestvennye zapiski* 179 (August 1868): 129–43, for a sense of the dominance of scientific methods and discoveries in social thought. See also Alexander Vucinich, *Science in Russian Culture, 1861–1917* (Stanford, 1970).

37. A. N. Pypin, "Umstvennoe razvitie russkogo naroda: Sotsial'no-pedagogicheskie usloviia umstvennogo razvitiia russkogo naroda: Sochinenie Afanasiia Shchapova. SPb, 1870," *Vestnik Evropy* 1 (January 1870): 332.

38. See, for example, Bezymennyi, "Proshloe leto v derevne," *Russkii vestnik* 116 (April 1875): 664; Gleb Ivanovich Uspenskii, *Sobranie sochinenii* (Moscow, 1956), 4:8; Nikolai Nikolaevich Zlatovratskii, *Derevenskie budni* (St. Petersburg, 1882), 6; A. N. Engelgardt, "Iz derevni, I," *Otechestvennye zapiski* 202 (May 1872): 30.

39. A. Skabichevskii, "Kritika: Protivopolozhnaia krainost'" (Sochineniia Marko-Vovchka. Tom I. Rasskazy iz Ukrainskogo byta. Izdanie I. Papina. SPb. 1867)," *Otechestvennye zapiski* 179 (July 1868): 19–50; N. V. Shelgunov, "Narodnyi realizm v literature," *Delo* (May 1871): 6.

40. White, *Tropics*, 3.

41. Gary Marker, *Publishing, Printing, and the Origins of Intellectual Life in Russia, 1700–1800* (Princeton, 1985), 121.

42. The number of newspapers published in Russia leaped from 36 to 125 in this period. Vera Romanova Leikina-Svirskaia, *Intelligentsiia v Rossii v vtoroi polovine xix veka* (Moscow, 1971), 217.

43. Gosudarstvennaia Ordena Trudovogo Krasnogo Znameni Publichnaia Biblioteka imeni M. E. Saltykova-Shchedrina, Otdel rukopisei (hereafter referred to as GPB-OR), fond 621 (A. N. Pypin), d. 1021, l. 5 (letter of March 17, 1881, to Pypin by A. I. Ertel'); also P. Zasodimskii, "Iz literaturnykh vospominanii," *Russkoe bogatstvo* (December 1881): 1:99–128.

44. K. D. Kavelin, *Sobranie sochinenii K. D. Kavelina*, vol. 2, *Publitsistika* (St. Petersburg, 1904), 405.

Chapter 2. *Narod:* Passive, Benighted, and Simple

1. Akademiia nauk, *Slovar' akademii rossiiskoi po azbuchnomu poriadu raspolozhennyi*, chast' 3 (St. Petersburg, 1814), 1176.

2. Vladimir Dal', *Tolkovyi slovar' zhivogo velikorusskogo iazyka*, tom 2 (1881; Moscow, 1955), 461.

3. On Germany, see John G. Gagliardo, *From Pariah to Patriot: The Changing Image of the German Peasant, 1770–1840* (Lexington, Ky., 1969).

4. Hans Rogger, *National Consciousness in Eighteenth-Century Russia* (Cambridge, 1960), 173.

5. Abbott Gleason, *Young Russia: The Genesis of Russian Radicalism in the 1860s* (New York, 1980), 2.

6. Konstantin Sergeevich Aksakov, "On the Internal State of Russia," in Marc Raeff, ed., *Russian Intellectual History: An Anthology* (New York, 1963), 249.

7. Alexander Herzen, *From the Other Shore and the Russian People and Socialism* (Cleveland, 1963), 166.

8. Ibid., 189.

9. Ibid., 194.

10. Ibid., 180.

11. I. S. Aksakov, "Moskva 10-ogo marta," *Den'* no. 22 (March 10, 1862), 1–2.

12. Ibid., 2. The adjective *tsel'noe*, here translated as integral, may also mean undiluted. By referring to the *narod* as a *tsel'noe iavlenie*, Aksakov thus combined the concepts of unity and purity in his image.

13. M. Koialovich, "Gde nashi sily?" *Den'* no. 31 (August 3, 1863), 6–9.

14. N. Pirogov, "Pis'mo iz Kamenits—Podol'skoi gubernii, . . . ," 8.

15. Skaldin [Elenev], "Iz zakholust'i, III," *Otechestvennye zapiski* 181/11 (1868): 279.

16. Ibid.

17. Ibid., 279–80.

18. M. N. Protopov, "Gleb Uspenskii, Prodolzhenie," *Russkaia mysl'* (September 1890): 2:155–56.

19. Lev Nikolaevich Tolstoy, *Vonia i mir*, tom 5 (Moscow, 1869), 227.

20. Ibid., 233.

21. Ibid., 234.

22. Ibid.

23. Ibid., 236.

24. Ibid., 296.

25. Daniel Field, "Peasants and Propagandists in the Russian Movement to the People of 1874," *Journal of Modern History* 59 (September 1987): 415–38.

26. A. P. Pribyleva and V. N. Figner, *Narodovolets Aleksandr Dmitrievich Mikhailov* (Leningrad, 1925), 107.

27. A. O. Lukashevich, "Nechto iz popytochnoi praktiki (K materialam oshibochnykh i nadlezhashchikh formakh, sposobakh, priemakh i ppr.)," *Krasnyi arkhiv* 15 (1926): 2:127–28.

28. S. A. Viktorova-Val'ter, "Iz zhizni revoliutsionnoi molodezhi 2-i poloviny 1870-kh godov," *Katorga i ssylka* 4 (1924): 67.

29. Nikolai Aleksandrovich Morozov, *Povesti moei zhizni*, vol. 1 (Moscow, 1947), 90.

30. Ibid., 77–78.

31. Ibid., 91.

32. Sergei Filippovich Kovalik [Starik], "Dvizhenie semidesiatykh godov po Bol'shomu protsessu (193-kh)," *Byloe* (October 1906): 61.

33. Aleksandra Efimenko, "Odno iz nashikh narodnykh osobennostei," *Nedelia* (April 15, 1876), 118.

34. Morozov, 90.

35. V. Bogucharskii, *Aktivnoe narodnichestvo semidesiatykh godov* (Moscow, 1912), 200–201.

36. V. A. Kr——g, "Kratkii ocherk ekonomicheskogo polozheniia sel'skogo naseleniia Orlovskogo uezda Viatskoi gubernii," *Delo* 3 (March 1871): 132.

37. Ibid., 133.

38. Osip A. Aptekman, *Iz istorii revoliutsionnogo narodnichestva: "Zemlia i volia" 70-kh godov* (*Po lichnym vospominaniiam*) (Rostov-na-Don, 1906), 46.

39. E. Breshko-Breshkovskaia, "Vospominaniia propagandistki," *Obshchina* 6 and 7 (June–July 1878): 26.

40. N., "Narodoliubtsy," *Nedelia* (February 7, 1882), 190.

41. V. V. Bervi-Flerovskii, *Izbrannye ekonomicheskie proizvedeniia v dvukh tomakh*, vol. 1 (Moscow, 1958), 270 and 291.

42. Akademiia nauk SSSR, *Revoliutsionnoe narodnichestvo 70-kh godov xix veka: Sbornik dokumentov i materialov v dvukh tomakh*, vol. 1 (Moscow, 1964), 260–61.

43. B. Bazilevskii, *Gosudarstvennye prestupleniia v Rossii v xix veke*, 3 (Paris, 1905), 87.

44. Ibid., 131.

45. Pribyleva and Figner, 89.

46. *Revoliutsionnoe narodnichestvo*, 360.

47. Field also concedes that in their approach to the peasantry, the propagandists displayed a "naive faith" in radical literature's appeal to the peasants. He rightly distinguishes between naivete about *what* would appeal to the peasants and *growing* sophistication in comprehending the depth of the "cultural gulf between educated society and the common people." Field, "Peasants and Propagandists," 434.

48. Morozov, 91.

49. A. O. Lukashevich, "V narod! . . . ," *Byloe* no. 3 (1907): 14; and V. Debogorii-Mokrievich, *Vospominaniia* (St. Petersburg, 1906), 219–20.

50. Morozov, 106.

51. *Revoliutsionnoe narodnichestvo*, 273.

52. James C. Scott, *The Moral Economy of the Peasant: Rebellion and Subsistence in Southeast Asia* (New Haven, 1976).

53. K. D. Kavelin, *Krest'ianskii vopros: Issledovanie o znachenii u nas krest'ianskogo dela, prichinakh ego upadka i merakh k podniatiiu sel'skogo kkhoziaistva i byta poselian* (St. Petersburg, 1882).

54. Morozov, 118, 222.

55. *Revoliutsionnoe narodnichestvo*, 182.

56. Ibid., 132.

57. Ibid., 132–33.

58. From 1871 to 1874, Samara Province experienced widespread crop failure and its usual companion, famine. Arcadius Kahan, *Russian Economic History: The Nineteenth Century*, Roger Weiss, ed. (Chicago, 1989), 110–14.

59. *Revoliutsionnoe narodnichestvo*, 134.

60. Vera Filippovna Zakharina, *Golos revoliutsionnoi Rossii: Literatura revoliutsionnogo podpol'ia 70-kh godov xix v.* (Moscow, 1971).

61. "Chto takoe narodnichestvo," *Nedelia* (August 3, 1880), 985.

62. Sergei Mikhailovich Kravchinskii, *The Russian Peasantry: Their Condition, Social Life, and Religion* (New York, 1888), 76–77.

63. Aptekman, 69.

64. Lukashevich, "Nechto," 130–31.

65. Pribyleva and Figner, 116–17.

66. Kravchinskii, *Peasantry*, 89. This was a sentiment expressed most eloquently by one such village priest, Belliustin. See a translation of his thoughts on this subject in I. S. Belliustin, *Description of the Clergy in Rural Russia: The Memoir of a Nineteenth-Century Parish Priest*, Gregory L. Freeze, trans. (Ithaca, 1985).

67. Boris Samuilovich Itenberg, *Dvizhenie revoliutsionnogo narodnichestva: Narodnicheskie kruzhki i "khozhdenie v narod" v 70-kh godakh xix v.* (Moscow, 1965), 312–13.

68. Field points out that the peasants' ambivalence toward questions of faith led some propagandists to limit their criticism to remarks that were "anticlerical rather than irreligious." Field, "Peasants and Propagandists," 435.

69. Morozov, 120–21.

70. Bazilevskii (1903), 328.

71. F. M. Dostoevskii, *Polnoe sobranie sochinenii v tridtsati tomakh*, vol. 26 (Leningrad, 1984), 170.

72. Idem, *Polnoe sobranie sochinenii v tridtsati tomakh*, vol. 22 (Leningrad, 1981), 113.

73. Idem, *Polnoe sobranie sochinenii v tridtsati tomakh*, vol. 21 (Leningrad, 1980), 36.

74. Idem, *Polnoe sobranie sochinenii v tridtsati tomakh*, vol. 25 (Leningrad, 1983), 15.

75. The passage is quoted in Chapter 8. p. 173. Dostoevskii, *Polnoe sobranie sochinenii v tridtsati tomakh*, vol. 21 (Leningrad, 1980), 21.

76. Idem, *Polnoe sobranie sochinenii v tridtsati tomakh*, vol. 25 (Leningrad, 1983), 124.

77. Ibid., 123.

78. Ibid., 16.

79. Idem, *Polnoe sobranie sochinenii v tridtsati tomakh*, vol. 22 (Leningrad, 1981), 45.

80. Idem, *Polnoe sobranie sochinenii v tridtsati tomakh*, vol. 23 (Leningrad, 1981), 161.

81. Ibid., 103.

82. L. N. Tolstoy, *Anna Karenina*, tom 3 (Moscow, 1878), 398.

83. Tolstoy, *Anna Karenina*, tom 2 (Moscow, 1878), 7.

84. Ibid.

85. Ibid., 64.

86. Ibid., for one such scene, 163–66.

87. Ibid., 6.

88. Tolstoy, *Anna Karenina*, tom 3, 378–79.

89. Dostoevskii, *Polnoe sobranie sochinenii v tridtsati tomakh*, vol. 22 (Leningrad, 1981), 44.

90. Ibid.

Chapter 3. The Peasant as Judge

1. Andrzej Walicki's recent work, *Legal Philosophies of Russian Liberalism* (Oxford, 1987), examines the search for a "rule-of-law" state as one of the main goals of Russian liberals but does not fully explore the implications of that search in terms of the peasants. As the following discussion will demonstrate, liberals and others in search of a unified, national system of law looked both above at the need to establish legality as the principle of governance and below at the need to resolve the problems posed by the resilience of customary law as the most prevalent system of popular justice.

2. Studies of the Judicial Reform include Samuel Kucherov, *Courts, Lawyers, and Trials under the Last Three Tsars* (New York, 1953); Richard Wortman, *The Development of a Russian Legal Consciousness* (Chicago, 1976); William G. Wagner, "The Development of the Law of Inheritance and Patrimonial Property in Post-Emancipation Russia and Its Social, Economic and Political Implications" (D.Phil. thesis, Oxford University, 1980). See also Kucherov, "Sudebnaia reforma Aleksandra II (1864–1964)," *Novyi zhurnal* (The new review) 78 (1965): 231–52; I. V. Gessen, *Sudebnaia reforma* (St. Petersburg, 1905); N. V. Davydov and N. N. Polianskii, *Sudebnaia reforma,* 2 vols. (Moscow, 1915); G. A. Dzhanshiev, *Osnovy sudebnoi reformy (k 25-letiiu novogo suda): Istoriko-iuridicheskie etiudy* (Moscow, 1891); A. F. Koni, *Otsy i deti sudebnoi reformy (k piatidesiatiletiiu sudebnykh ustavov)* (Moscow, 1914); Ministerstvo iustitsii, *Sudebyne ustavy 20 noiabria 1864 g. za piat'desiat' let,* 2 vols. (Petrograd, 1914); B. V. Vilenskii, *Sudebnaia reforma i kontrreforma v Rossii* (Saratov, 1969).

3. Francis Wcislo examines these motives as central to the activities of the men involved in the preparation of the Emancipation itself, particularly in reference to rural society, in his *Reforming Rural Russia: State, Local Society and National Politics, 1855–1914* (Princeton, 1990), introduction and chap. 1.

4. For a description of the chief features of the jury system as part of the reform, see Samuel Kucherov, "The Jury as Part of the Russian Judicial Reform of 1864," *The American Slavonic and East European Review* 9 (1950): 77–90.

5. Harvard Law Library copy of materials from the commissions involved in designing the reform. Listed as *Sudebnaia reforma.* Handwritten vol. 12. Binding imprint vol. 10. *Zhurnal soedinennykh departmentov zakonov i grazhdanskikh del gosudarstvennogo soveta o preobrazovanii sudebnoi chasti v Rossia,* 184.

6. Ibid., 183; Dzhanshiev, *Sbornik statei* (Moscow, 1914), 405–7.

7. On Bludov's resistance to any reform that might threaten the tradition of autocratic control, surveillance, and the class system of justice, see Wortman, *The Development,* 163–64.

8. Koni, *Otsy i dety,* 18. The perception that peasants considered convicts and criminals as unfortunates to be pitied rather than punished was common. See, for example, S. V. Maksimov, "Narodnye prestupleniia i neschastiia (Chast' pervaia: Vstuplenie. 1. Ubiitsy.—II. Samoubiitsy)," *Otechestvennye zapiski* 182 (1869): 1, and V. K. Rzhevskii, "Vospitanie naroda," *Russkii vestnik* 55 (January 1865): 256.

9. *Sudebnaia reforma,* vol. 10, *Zhurnal soedinennykh,* 183; *Sudebnaia reforma,* vol. 12, *Zamechaniia o razvitii osnovnykh polozhenii preobrazovaniia sudebnoi chasti v Rossii,* chast' 2, 516; A. M. Unkovskii, "Novye osnovaniia

sudoproizvodstva, (I)," *Sovremennik*, nos. 1–2 (January–February 1863), 394–95; S. Barshev, "Zadacha prisiazhnykh v dele ugolovnogo prava," *Russkii vestnik* 45 (1863): 116–18.

10. *Sudebnaia reforma*, vol. 10, *Zhurnal soedinennykh*, 183–84.

11. Koni, *Otsy i dety*, 18–19. This practice would later become the center of debate over legal reform and consistently be referred to as *samosud*.

12. Ibid.

13. *Sudebnaia reforma*, vol. 10, *Zhurnal soedinennykh*, 317.

14. *Sudebnaia reforma*, vol. 12, *Zamechaniia*, chast' 1, 401.

15. Ibid., 681–82.

16. Ivan Sergeevich Aksakov, *Sochineniia*, vol. 4 (Moscow, 1886), 553–55.

17. *Sudebnaia reforma*, vol. 12, *Zamechaniia*, chast' 3, 249–50; chast' 4, 228, 336, 370–73.

18. Ibid., chast' 5, 129–30. A member of the Simbirsk nobility called for the same caution when dealing with Tatar jurors. He called for their exclusion or for limitation of their number to two or three per jury because of their dishonesty and prejudice in favor of fellow Tatars. Chast' 3, 113.

19. Nikolai Nikolaevich Zlatovratskii, *Sochineniia*, 3d ed. (Moscow, 1897), 32.

20. Ibid., 48.

21. Ibid., 55.

22. M. V., "Zhurnalistika," *Novosti*, no. 94 (April 5, 1875), 1–2, read in TsGALI, fond 202, opis' 1, d. 256.

23. A. M. Skabichevskii, "Mysli po povodu tekushchei literatury," *Birzhevye vedemosti* no. 8 (Jan. 10, 1875), 2, read in TsGALI, fond 202, opis' 1, d. 257.

24. N.a., "Novosti Russkoi literatury," *Novosti* no. 3 (Jan. 3, 1875), 1–2, read in TsGALI, fond 202, opis' 1, d. 256.

25. F. M. Dostoevsky, *The Brothers Karamazov*, Constance Garnett, trans. (New York, 1957), 683. Monika Greenleaf reminded me of this scene and its connection to the discourse on the peasant soul.

26. For a description of the court and an outline of its experience, see Peter Czap, Jr., "Peasant-Class Courts and Peasant Customary Justice in Russia, 1861–1912," *Journal of Social History* 1 (1967): 149–79.

27. See, for example, "Polez'nost' volostnogo suda," *Nedelia* (October 15, 1872), 712–16.

28. N. M. Druzhinin, *Gosudarstvennye krest'iane i reforma P. D. Kiseleva*, vol. 1, *Predposylki i sushchnost' reformy* (Moscow, 1946), and vol. 2, *Realizatsiia i posledstviia reformy* (Moscow, 1958).

29. Nikolai Petrovich Semenov, *Osvobozhdenie krest'ian v tsarstvovanie imperatora Aleksandra II*, vol. 2 (St. Petersburg, 1890), 474.

30. Ibid., 487. For a fuller description of desiderata of the reformers in relation to the *volost'* court, see C. A. Frierson, "Rural Justice in Public Opinion: The *Volost'* Court Debate, 1861–1912," *The Slavonic and East European Review* 64 (October 1986): 526–45; also S. F. Luginin, "Volostnye sudy," *Russkii vestnik* 50 (March 1864): 383–84.

31. *Trudy kommissi po preobrazovaniiu volostnykh sudov*, vol. 1 (St. Petersburg, 1873), 1.

32. Il'ia Grigor'evich Orshanskii, *Issledovaniia po russkomu pravu obychnomu i brachnomu* (St. Petersburg, 1879), 191; and Sergei V. Pakhman, *Obychnoe grazhdanskoe pravo v Rossii: Iuridcheskie ocherki,* vol. 1 (St. Petersburg, 1877), ix.

33. Pakhman, 392.

34. Ibid., 53.

35. P. P. Chubinskii, *Trudy etnografichesko-statisticheskoi ekspeditsii v zapadno-russkii krai* (St. Petersburg, 1872), 30.

36. In the report of the Valuev Commission in 1873, for example, question 80 addressed the issue of private property. Virtually every respondent stated that the peasants in his region had no concept of private property. *Doklad vysochaishe uchrezhdennoi komissii dlia issledovaniia nyneshnego polozheniia sel'skogo khoziaistva i sel'skoi proizvoditel'nosti v Rossii: Prilozhenie VI* (St. Petersburg, 1873).

37. Andrzej Walicki, *Legal Philosophies of Russian Liberalism* (Oxford, 1987), 3. The centrality of respect for property in legal consciousness was also apparent in the commission that designed the jury system as part of the Judicial Reform. Reservations about the suitability of the peasants as jurors were largely based on the fear that they would not respect property. To address that concern, the legislators established high property qualifications for potential peasant jurors. *Sudebnaia reforma,* vol. 10, *Zhurnal soedinennykh,* 318–19; A. A. Golovachev, *Desiat' let reform, 1861–1871* (St. Petersburg, 1872), 366.

38. Kavelin, *Sobranie sochinenii,* vol. 2, *Publitsistika,* 790–93. This came in an article first published under the title "Iz derevenskoi zapisnoi knizhki" in *Sankt Peterburgskie vedemosti,* nos. 259, 260, and 264.

39. Pakhman, 49.

40. Ibid., 355.

41. Chubinskii, 83.

42. This subject would continue to be prominent in the discussion of the peasant mentality through the end of the century. See my "Crime and Punishment in the Russian Village: Rural Concepts of Criminality at the End of the Nineteenth Century," *Slavic Review* 46 (1987): 55–69.

43. Pakhman, 62.

44. Ibid., 69.

45. Ibid., 120.

46. Ibid., 55–58.

47. Ibid., 193.

48. Ibid., 194.

49. Ibid., 199–201.

50. Chubinskii, viii.

51. Orshanskii, *Issledovaniia po russkomu pravu* (St. Petersburg, 1879), ix.

52. Ibid., 69.

53. Ibid., 70.

54. Ibid.

55. Ibid., 129–30.

56. Ibid., 146–47.

57. Ibid., 106–7.

58. See *Nedelia* (April 29, 1884), 622.

59. Aleksandra Iakovlevna Efimenko, *Issledovaniia narodnoi zhizni: Vypusk pervyl: Obychnoe pravo* (Moscow, 1884), 1.

60. Ibid., 171.

61. Ibid., 1.

62. Ibid., 9.

63. Ibid., 34–37.

64. Ibid., 179. See an early statement of the same sentiment in F. Sabaneev, "V zashchitu volostnykh sudov," *Den'* (November 9, 1863): 5–6.

65. V. N. Nazar'ev, "Sovremennaia glush': Iz vosponimanii mirovogo sud'i," *Vestnik Evropy* (March 1872): 142.

66. Ibid., 144.

67. Ibid. (March 1880): 69. Nazar'ev's sentiments were much the same in his "Noveishaia istoriia odnoi volosti'. Ocherk iz zhizni privolzhskogo zakholustiia," *Vestnik Evropy* 291 (January 1886): 217–56.

68. V. S. Krotkov, "Volostnye sudy (zametki provintsial'nogo advokata), I & II," *Otechestvennye zapiski* 208 (May 1873): 1–2.

69. Ibid., III & IV (July 1873): 3.

70. Ibid., 9.

71. Zh, "Nuzhno li sokhranit' volostnye sudy" *Iuridicheskii vestnik*, no. 2 (February 1873): 21.

72. T. A. Tergukasov, "O volostnykh sudakh," *Iuridicheshkii vestnik*, no. 5 (May/June 1873): 1–2.

73. *Trudy komissii po preobrazovaniiu* . . . , vol. 7 (St. Petersburg, 1874), 1–2, 183, for examples of these views.

74. N. Astyrev, "V volostnykh pisar'iakh: Zametki i nabliudeniia," *Vestnik Evropy* 288 (July 1885): 318–29.

75. For a discussion of alternative forms of rural justice to the *volost'* court, see Czap's article; Evgenii Ivanovich Iakushkin, *Obychnoe pravo; Materialy dlia bibliografii obychnogo prava,* vypusk 1 (Iaroslavl', 1875), xxiv; M. I. Zarudny, *Zakony i zhizn': Itogi issledovaniia krest'ianskikh sudov* (St. Petersburg, 1874), 173.

76. Beatrice Brodsky Farnsworth, "The Litigious Daughter-in-Law: Family Relations in Rural Russia in the Second Half of the Nineteenth Century," *Slavic Review* 45 (Spring 1986): 49–64.

77. Ibid., 49.

78. Ibid., 63–64.

Chapter 4. The Peasant as Rational Man of the Land

1. For full psychological portraits of Engelgardt and Uspenskii, see Richard Wortman, *The Crisis of Russian Populism* (Cambridge, 1967).

2. M. V. Teplinskii, *"Otechestvennye zapiski" (1868–1884) Istoria zhurnala: Literaturnaia kritika* (Iuzhno-sakhalinsk, 1966), 292.

3. Alexander Vucinich, *Science in Russian Culture, 1861–1917* (Stanford, 1970), 136–37.

4. *Istoricheskii ocherk razivitiia S. Peterburgskogo lesnogo instituta* (*1803–1903*) (St. Petersburg, 1903), 121–29.

5. A. N. Engelgardt, *Sbornik obshcheponiatnykh statei po estestvoznaniiu* (St. Petersburg, 1867).

6. A. N. Engelgardt, "Libikh v Russkom perevode," *Izbrannie sochineniia* (Moscow 1959), 625–33, first appeared in *Sankt-Petersburgskie vedomosti,* no. 272 (1863): 1–2.

7. Ibid., 627.

8. A. N. Engelgardt, "Po povodu knigi Darvina," *Sankt Peterburgskie vedomosti,* nos. 57, 65, and 70, discussed in L. L. Balashev, "Pervye shagi Darvinizma v Rossii i A. N. Engel'gardt," *Voprosy istoriia estestvoznaniia i tekhniki* (Moscow, 1959), 118–19.

9. See Daniel P. Todes, *Darwin without Malthus: The Struggle for Existence in Russian Evolutionary Thought* (Oxford, 1989), 24–44.

10. Rukopisnyi otdel, Pushkinskii dom, fond 577, opis' 1, delo 19, l. 37.

11. Rukopisnyi otdel, Pushkinskii dom, fond 572, opis' 1, delo 142, l. 5.

12. A. I. Faresov, *Semidesiatniki* (St. Petersburg, 1905), 6.

13. TsGALI, fond 572, opis' 2, delo 29, l. 9. The student offering this scenario was Vasilii Grigor's evich Kotel'nikov.

14. P. Ia. Nechuiatov, *Aleksandr Nikolaevich Engelgardt: Ocherk zhizni i deiatel'nosti* (Smolensk, 1957), 32–33.

15. Rukopisnyi otdel, Pushkinskii dom, fond 577, opis' 1, delo 19, l. 19.

16. TsGALI, fond 572, opis' 1, delo 174, l. 1.

17. A. N. Engelgardt, "Iz derevni, I," *Otechestvennye zapiski* 202 (May 1872): 30.

18. Ibid., 30–31.

19. Ibid., 41.

20. Ibid., 42–43.

21. Skaldin [F. P. Elenev], "V zakholust'i i v stolitse, III," *Otechestvennye zapiski* 181/11 (1868): 280.

22. Engelgardt, "Iz derevni, I," 46–47.

23. Engelgardt, "Iz derevni, V," *Otechestvennye zapiski* 228 (September 1876): 61.

24. Ibid., 62–64.

25. Engelgardt, "Iz derevni, IV," *Otechestvennye zapiski* 212 (February 1874): 276.

26. Engelgardt, "Iz derevni, III," *Otechestvennye zapiski* 206 (January 1873): 76–77.

27. Ibid.

28. Ibid., 79.

29. TsGALI, fond 572, opis' 2, dela 19 and 20. This two-volume diary is the true farmer's journal. Although it contains no record of Engelgardt's reflections and thus offers the historian little of his ideas about the peasantry, it is a very rich source on the practice of farming and on formal relations between the gentry farmer and his neighboring peasants. Here Engelgardt records all of the expenses and revenues of his estate, the log of his plantings and yields, the terms of his rental

and labor contracts with his peasants, a weather report for each day, and the births and deaths of livestock on the estate.

30. Engelgardt, "Iz derevni, IV," *Otechestvennye zapiski* 212 (February 1874): 269–333.

31. Engelgardt, "Iz derevni, VII," *Otechestvennye zapiski* 242 (January 1879): 101–2.

32. Ibid., 102–18.

33. Engelgardt, "Iz derevni, I," 48.

34. See n. 7.

35. Sharapov's account of his move to the countryside appeared in S. Sharapov, "Istoriia odnogo khoziaistva," *Rus'* no. 41 (August 22, 1881), 15–16; no. 42 (August 29, 1881), 14–16; no. 45 (September 19, 1881), 17–19.

36. Sergei Sharapov, *A. N. Engelgardt i ego znachenie dlia russkoi kul'turi i nauki* (St. Petersburg, 1893).

37. Engelgardt, "Iz derevni, XI," *Otechestvennye zapiski* 256 (February 1882): 353–56.

38. TsGALI, fond 572, opis' 1, delo 34, l. 2.

39. TsGALI, fond 572, opis' 2, delo 10, l. 1.

40. Ibid.

41. Joanna Hubbs has argued that this dual attitude toward the earth as both nurturant and potentially destructive was deeply embedded in the cultural history and consciousness of nineteenth-century Russians. Joanna Hubbs, *Mother Russia: The Feminine Myth in Russian Culture* (Bloomington, 1988).

42. Engelgardt, "Iz derevni, VII (Okonchanie)," *Otechestvennye zapiski* 242 (February 1879): 358.

43. Ibid., 358–61.

44. Ibid., 347.

45. V. E. Cheshikhin-Vetrinskii, *Gleb Ivanovich Uspenskii: Biograficheskii ocherk* (Moscow, 1929), 311.

46. This is clear from the nature of the correspondence with Saltykov-Shchedrin. See M. E. Saltykov-Shchedrin, *Sobranie sochinenii,* vol. 18, bk. 2 (Moscow, 1976), 133–34, 146–47; vol. 19, bk. 1 (Moscow, 1976), 35, 39, 79–80; vol. 19, bk. 2 (Moscow, 1977), 56, 127; and G. I. Uspenskii, *Sobranie sochinenii,* vol. 9 (Moscow, 1957), 251, 274, 310.

47. Cheshikhin-Vetrinskii, 32–50.

48. Ibid., 101.

49. Otdel rukopisei. Gosudarstvennaia Ordena Trudovogo Krasnogo Znameni Publichnaia biblioteka imeni M. E. Saltykova-Shchedrina, fond 621, opis' 1, delo 917, ll. 1–2. Reprinted also in G. I. Uspenskii, *Sobranie sochinenii,* (Moscow, 1957), 9:549–50.

50. V. E. Cheshikhin-Vetrinskii, 50.

51. Richard Wortman questioned both the veracity and the sincerity of Uspenskii's work in his study of Populism's "crisis," saying that "one can hardly accept Uspenskii as an objective reporter or his observations as indicative of general trends in the countryside" (*Crisis,* 70). Describing Uspenskii as the "populist 'martyr of the pen' whose personal disintegration epitomized the tragedy of a generation

whose ideals of life had proven false" (Ibid., 100), he interprets Uspenskii's forays into the village as outgrowths of a determination to find evil and disintegration everywhere. He describes him as "lapsing into myth and rhapsodic speculation, . . . in a world of hallucination" (Ibid., 92–93). This dismissal of Uspenskii's vision may be appropriate in a psychological prosopography of Populism, but it obscures the force that Uspenskii's image of the peasant held for contemporaries and for the development of approaches to study of the village in his generation and beyond.

52. Nikolai Prutskov, *Gleb Uspenskii semidesiatykh—nachala vos'midesiatykh godov* (Khar'kov, 1955), 38–39.

53. Uspenskii, *Sobranie sochinenii,* 4:43–44.

54. Ibid., 43.

55. Ibid., 97.

56. Ibid., 103.

57. Ibid., 109.

58. Ibid., 5:19.

59. Ibid.

60. Ibid., 25.

61. Ibid., 30.

62. Ibid., 31.

63. Ibid., 32.

64. Ibid., 40.

65. Ibid., 43.

66. Ibid., 48.

67. Ibid., 5:100.

68. Ibid., 115.

69. Ibid., 116.

70. Ibid., 128–30. Engelgardt also reported that the peasants had quite specific expectations about the amount of land each peasant would receive in the long-awaited Black Repartition.

71. Ibid., 131.

72. Ibid., 145–47.

73. Ibid., 177–78.

Chapter 5. The Communal Peasant

1. Steven Alan Grant, "The Peasant Commune in Russian Thought" (Ph.D. diss., Harvard University, 1973); and Marc Raeff, "The Peasant Commune in the Political Thinking of Russian Publicists: Laissez-faire Liberalism in the Reign of Alexander II" (Ph.D. diss., Harvard University, 1950). For discussion of the various forms of this institution, see Boris Mironov, "The Russian Peasant Commune after the Reforms of the 1860s," *Slavic Review* 44 (Fall 1985): 438–67; L. K. Kuchumova, "Sel'skaia pozemel'naia obshchina Evropeiskoi Rossii v 60–70 gody xix-go veka," *Istoricheskie zapiski* (Moscow, 1981), 333–35; and Moshe Lewin,

"The *Obshchina* and the Village," in Roger Bartlett, ed., *Land Commune and Peasant Community in Russia: Communal Forms in Imperial and Early Soviet Society* (London, 1990), 20–35.

2. For a discussion of the meaning and origins of these two terms, see Steven A. Grant. "*Obshchina* and *Mir,*" *Slavic Review* 35 (December 1976): 636–51.

3. Raeff, 29–30.

4. Grant, 70.

5. August von Haxthausen, *Studies on the Interior of Russia,* Eleanore L. M. Schmidt, trans. (Chicago, 1972), 288.

6. Grant, 85.

7. Raeff, 66, 100.

8. N. N. Zlatovratskii, "Ocherki derevenskogo nastroeniia, I" *Otechestvennye zapiski* 254 (February 1881): 225.

9. N. N. Zlatovratskii, *Vospominaniia* (Moscow, 1956), 39–45.

10. Richard Wortman, *The Crisis of Russian Populism* (Cambridge, 1967); A. M. Skabichevskii, "Mysli po povodu tekushchei literatury," *Birzhevie vedomosti* no. 332 (December 1, 1878), 1–2.

11. Like Uspenskii, Zlatovratskii was a recipient of assistance from the Society of Assistance for Needy Writers and Scholars. TsGALI, fond 202, opis' 1, delo 179, l.1 His daughter stressed the pressure of financial want and the limitations it imposed on her father's literary efforts. TsGALI, fond 202, opis' 2, delo 39, l. 7.

12. TsGALI, fond 202, opis' 2, delo 34, l. 1.

13. N. N. Zlatovratskii, *Sochineniia,* 3d ed. (Moscow, 1897), 128.

14. Ibid., 132–33.

15. N. N. Zlatovratskii, *Derevenskie budni* (St. Petersburg, 1882), 267.

16. N. N. Zlatovratskii, "Ocherki derevenskogo nastroeniia, III," *Otechestvennye zapiski* 255 (April 1881): 194.

17. Ibid., 196.

18. N. N. Zlatovratskii, "Ocherki derevenskogo nastroeniia, V," *Otechestvennye zapiski* 256 (May 1881): 83.

19. Zlatovratskii, *Derevenskie budni,* 332.

20. Ibid., 300.

21. Ibid., 339.

22. Ibid., 326.

23. Zlatovratskii, *Derevenskie budni,* 350.

24. Ibid., 351.

25. Ibid., 350.

26. Ibid., 5.

27. Zlatovratskii, *Sochineniia,* 104.

28. Ibid., 19.

29. TsGALI, fond 202, opis' 1, delo 205, l. 3.

30. Petr Chervinskii, "Ot sebia ili ot derevni?" *Nedelia* (January 11, 1876), 62.

31. Ibid.

32. S. M. Kravchinskii, *Russia under the Tsars,* William Westall, trans. (New York, 1885), 4.

33. S. Iuzhakov, "Voprosy obshchinnogo byta," *Otechestvennye zapiski* 269 (November 1883): 94–119.

34. Dmitrii Kishenskii, "Pis'ma o russkom krest'ianstve, I," *Rus'* (January 10, 1881), 16.

35. Kishenskii, "Pis'ma . . . , III," *Rus* no. 18 (March 14, 1881), 10.

36. Kishenskii, "Pis'ma . . . , III (Okonchanie)," *Rus'* no. 19 (March 21, 1881), 18.

37. Kishenskii, "Pis'ma . . . , IV (Okonchanie)," *Rus"* no. 30 (June 6, 1881), 15.

38. This was equally true for one I. Kh., who devoted an article in *Russian Wealth* to systems of mutual aid in the commune, only to lament at the end that these relations were fading, being replaced by those of the "employer to the employee, of capital to labor." I. Kh., "Pomoch'," *Russkoe bogatstvo* (January 1879): 66–74.

39. K. D. Kavelin, "Pozemel'naia obshchina v drevnei novoi Rossii," *Vestnik Evropy* 239 (May 1877): 211.

40. Ibid.

41. A. M. Skabichevskii, *Belletristy-narodniki* (St. Petersburg, 1888), 288.

Chapter 6. The Gray Peasant: Unadorned and Besieged

1. For recent studies of these processes and some of the discussion they generated, see: Robert E. Johnson, *Peasant and Proletarian: The Working Class of Moscow in the Late Nineteenth Century* (New Brunswick, N. J., 1979); Joseph Bradley, *Muzhik and Muscovite: Urbanization in Late Imperial Russia* (Berkeley, 1985); Barbara Alpern Engel, "The Woman's Side: Male Out-Migration and the Family Economy in Kostroma Province," *Slavic Review* 45 (Summer 1986): 257–71; Cathy A. Frierson, "*Razdel:* The Peasant Family Divided," *The Russian Review* 46 (January 1987): 35–51; and Patricia Herlihy, "Joy of the Rus': Rites and Rituals of Russian Drinking," *The Russian Review* 50 (April 1991): 131–47.

2. N. a., "Liberal o serom muzhike," *Nedelia* (February 19, 1878), 283.

3. P. Nikitin [P. N. Tkachev], "Muzhik v salonakh sovremennoi belletristiki," *Delo* (March 1879), 3.

4. G. I. Uspenskii, "Fedor Mikhailovich Reshetnikov (Biograficheskii ocherk)," *Sobranie sochinenii* 9:7–59.

5. A. Skabichevskii, "Neskol'ko slov o zhizni i sochineniiakh F. M. Reshetnikova," in F. M. Reshetnikov, *Polnoe sobranie sochinenii v dvukh tomakh* (St. Petersburg, 1904), x.

6. Reshetnikov, 2.

7. Ibid., 3.

8. Ibid., 11.

9. Ibid.

10. Ibid.

11. Ibid., 92–94.

12. A., "Real'naia belletristika," *Russkii vestnik* 116 (April 1875): 696.

13. Uspenskii, *Sobranie sochinenii,* 3:336.

14. Ibid., 337.

15. Ibid., 353.

16. Ibid., 357.

17. Uspenskii, *Sobranie sochinenii,* 5:103.

18. Ibid., 253.

19. Zlatovratskii, "Ocherki narodnogo nastroeniia," *Russkaia mysl'* I (January 1884): 94.

20. Ibid., 101.

21. Ibid., 102.

22. Ibid., 103.

23. Svetlin [E. I. Reznikov], "Mirskaia dusha (Ocherki narodnogo byta)," *Russkaia mysl'* 1 (January 1881): 71–88.

24. Engelgardt, "Iz derevni, VII (okonchanie)," 347–48.

25. A. I. Zabelin, "Vrachebnaia pomoshch' dlia naroda," *Russkii vestnik* 33 (May 1861): 68–78; G. N. Minkh, *Chuma v Rossii (Vetlianskaia epidemiia 1878– 1879 g.*), chast' 1 (Kiev, 1898); V. Portugalov, "Bolezni Russkogo naroda," *Russkoe bogatstvo* (November 1881): 1:11–47.

26. Nancy Mandelker Frieden, *Russian Physicians in an Era of Reform and Revolution, 1856–1905* (Princeton, 1981), 82–83.

27. N. Portugalov, "Sanitarnaia bezpomoshchnost' sela," *Nedelia* (September 5, 1875), 1006.

28. V. K. Rzhevskii, "Vospitanie naroda," *Russkii vestnik* 155 (January 1865): 246; Skaldin [Elenev], "V Zakholust'i i v stolitse," *Otechestvennye zapiski* 174 (September 1867): 325; M. Misha, "K risunku 'Na perelaze,'" *Rus'* (October 1878): 113–116; S. Rachinskii, "Iz zapisok sel'skogo uchitelia, II," *Russkii vestnik* 315 (August 1889): 113–26, for a sampling of these observations. For a discussion of the role drinking played in rural life, see Herlihy, "The Joys of Rus' . . ."

29. A. Aksakov, "O narodnom p'ianstve," *Russkii vestnik* 102 (November 1872): 142–201.

30. M. Leshchinskii, *O vlianii p'ianstva na obshchestvennoe zdorov'e, nrav- stvennost', deialtel'nie sily i merakh k ogranicheniiu ego* (St. Petersburg, 1873).

31. Elizabeth Kridl Valkenier, *Russian Realist Art: The State and Society: The Peredvizhniki and Their Tradition* (Ann Arbor, 1977); Alain Besançon, "The Dissi- dence of Russian Painting," in Michael Cherniavsky, ed., *The Structure of Russian History* (New York, 1970), 381–411; Alison Hilton, "Scenes from Life and Contem- porary History: Russian Realism of the 1870s and 1880s," in Gabriel P. Weisberg, ed., *The European Realist Tradition* (Bloomington, 1982), 187–214; Elizabeth Kridl Valkenier, *Ilya Repin and the World of Russian Art* (New York, 1990).

32. Tatiana Ivanovna Kurochkina, *Ivasn Nikolaevich Kramskoi* (Moscow, 1980), 7.

33. Ouspensky and Lossky, *The Meaning of Icons,* 24.

34. This is the central argument of Elizabeth Kridl Valkenier, "The Pered- vizhniki and the Spirit of the 1860s," *The Russian Review* 34 (July 1975): 247–65.

35. Besançon, 384.

36. Valkenier, *Russian Realist,* 95.

37. Besançon, 389.

38. Valkenier, *Russian Realist,* 47.

39. G. G. Miasoedov, *Pis'ma, dokumenty, vospominaniia* (Moscow, 1972), 185.

40. James Thompson, *The Peasant in French Nineteenth-Century Art* (Dublin, 1980); Raymond Grew, "Picturing the People: Images of the Lower Orders in Nineteenth-Centruy French Art," in Robert I. Rotberg and Theodore K. Rabb, eds., *Art and History: Images and Their Meaning* (Cambridge, 1988), 203–31; and Elizabeth Johns, "The Farmer in the Works of William Sidney Mount," ibid., 257–81.

41. Weisberg, vii.

42. Andrei Konstantinovich Lebedev and Aleksandr Vasil'evich Solodovnikov, *Vladimir Vasil'evich Stasov: Zhizn' i tvorchestvo* (Moscow, 1976), 104.

43. Ilia Efimovich Repin, *Dalekoe blizkoe*, 3d ed. (Moscow, 1949), 176–77.

44. Miasoedov, 182.

45. Kurochkina, 38. Kramskoi also praised Repin precisely because he "possesses the ability to make the Russian muzhik exactly what he is. . . ." S. N. Gol'dshtein, *Ivan Nikolaevich Kramskoi: Zhizn' i tvorchestvo* (Moscow, 1965), 186.

46. Ouspensky and Lossky, *The Meaning of Icons*, 29.

47. Ibid.

48. Ibid., 40.

49. Kurochkina, 122.

50. T. M. Kovalenskaia, ed., *Kramskoi ob iskusstve* (Moscow, 1960), 81.

51. Kurochkina, 121.

52. See Grew, 216.

53. Johns, 266.

54. Grew, 215–16.

55. Kurochkina, 172.

56. Ibid., 132, n. 116.

57. V. Savikhin, "Ded Sofron," *Russkoe bogatstvo* (March 1885), 1:475–509.

58. Savikhin, 491.

59. K. Arsen'ev, "Lesnaia pravda i vyshaia spravedlivost'," *Vestnik Evropy* 277 (October 1883): 671–72.

60. N. a. "Liberal" o serom muzhike. . . ," 285.

Chapter 7. *Kulak:* The Village Strongman

1. Engelgardt, "Iz derevni, X," *Otechestvennye zapiski* 254 (January 1881): 411.

2. Ibid.

3. See, for example, "The Pike with the Long Teeth," in A. Afanas'ev, *Russian Fairy Tales,* Norbert Guterman, trans. (New York, 1945), 54–55.

4. N. Astyrev, "V volostnykh pisariakh. Zametki i nabliudeniia," *Vestnik Evropy* (August 1885): 485.

5. N. K. Shelgunov, "Ocherki russkoi zhiznii. XXXII," *Russkaia mysl'* (January 1888), 2:175.

6. Ibid., 177.

7. Ibid., 178.

8. G. I. Uspenskii, *Sobranie sochinenii* (Moscow, 1956), 5:216.

9. N. N. Zlatovratskii, *Derevenskie budni* (St. Petersburg, 1882), 351.

10. V. I. Dal', "Kartiny russkogo byta: Seren'kaia—Samorodok.—Ianvar," *Russkii vestnik* 67 (January 1867): 336–38.

11. Andrei Pecherskii, "Za Volgoi, Rasskaz, Gl. I–IV," *Russkii vestnik* 75 (June 1868): 460.

12. Ibid., 461–62.

13. Pecherskii, "Za Volgoi, Rasskaz, Gl.VII–XVII," *Russkii vestnik* 76 (July 1868): 227.

14. For a discussion of Lenin's *Razvitie kapitalizma v Rossii,* see Esther Kingston-Mann, *Lenin and the Problem of the Marxist Peasant Revolution* (New York, 1985), 42–46.

15. Kingston-Mann, 226.

16. N. Naumov, "Krest'ianskie vybory, II," *Delo* 5 (May 1873): 181.

17. A. I. Ivanchin-Pisarev, *Khozh denie v narod* (Moscow, 1929), 148.

18. Ibid., 163.

19. Ibid., 172.

20. Engelgardt, "Iz derevni, X," *Otechestvennye zapiski* 254 (January 1881): 411–12.

21. Ibid.

22. Ibid., 412.

23. Ibid., 413.

24. Zlatovratskii, *Derevenskie budni,* 371.

25. Uspenskii, *Sobranie sochinenii,* 4:32–33.

26. Ibid., 33–34.

27. Ibid., 90–96.

28. Astyrev, 317.

29. Uspenskii, *Sobranie sochinenii,* 5:103.

30. Ibid., 158.

31. Ibid., 138.

32. Ibid., 376–84.

33. A. Sh., "*Kulak-obshchinnik,*" *Delo* 6 (June 1880): 177.

34. Zlatovratskii, *Derevenskie,* 370.

35. See Cathy A. Frierson, "Crime and Punishment in the Russian Village: Concepts of Criminality at the End of the Nineteenth Century," *Slavic Review* 46 (1987): 55–69.

36. B. Lenskii, "Evrei i kulak (Obshchestvenno-ekonomicheskaia parallel')," *Delo* 9 (September 1881): 28.

37. Engelgardt, "Iz derevni, XI," *Otechestvennye zapiski* 260 (February 1882): 370. The word *harness* in this passage refers to his earlier explanation that the gentry "harnessed" the peasantry through the use of cut-off lands.

38. S. Sharapov, "Istoriia odnogo khoziaistva," *Rus'* (August 22, 1881), 15.

39. V. N. Nazar'ev, "Noveishaia istoriia odnoi volosti: Ocherk iz zhizni privolzh-skogo zakhalust'ia," *Vestnik Evropy* 291 (January 1886): 218.

40. Ivanchin-Pisarev, 70–83.

41. Ibid., 22.

42. See Chap. 3. See, also, E. Iakushkin, "Volostnye sudy v Iaroslavskoi

gubernii," *Iuridicheskii vestnik* 3 (March 1872): 9; *Trudy,* 7:1–2, 8, 183; T. A. Tergukasov, "O volostnykh sudakh," *Iuridicheskii vestnik* 5 (May/June 1873): 1–2; V. Dmitrieva, "Svoim sudom: Iz vospominanii sel'skoi uchitel'nitsy," *Severnyi vestnik* (January 1888): 93–135; N. L——n, "Volostnoi sud," *Rus'* (December 1, 1883): 51–58; Derevenskii zhitel', "O nashem sel'skom samouprovlenii," *Rus'* (February 1, 1884), 50–56.

43. Astyrev, "V volostnykh pisariakh. . . ," *Vestnik Evropy* 288 (July 1885): 334.

44. Idem, "V volostnykh pisariakh. . . ," *Vestnik Evropy* 289 (August 1885): 521–22.

45. Idem, "V volostnykh pisariakh. . . ," *Vestnik Evropy* 288 (July 1885): 334.

46. Ibid., 331.

47. Ibid., 348.

48. Ibid., 349–51.

49. Idem, "V volostnykh pisariakh. . . ," *Vestnik Evropy* 289 (August 1885): 490–91.

50. Ibid., 499.

51. See, for example, Klavdiia Lukashevich, "Svetloi pamiati Pavla Vladimirovicha Zasodimskogo," *Rodnik* (1912): 675–79, read in TsGALI, fond 203, opis' 1, delo 198.

52. TsGALI, fond 203, opis' 1, dela 121a, 98, 76 (letters from A. I. Ertel', A. S. Prugavin, and A. I. Levitov).

53. Rukopisnyi otdel, Pushkinskii dom, fond 111, opis' 1, delo 110 (letters from Zasodimskii to Zlatovratskii, 1888–1910).

54. P. V. Zasodimskii, *Khronika sela Smurina* (Moscow, 1959), 7–8.

55. On peasant initiative in rural education, see Ben Eklof, *Russian Peasant Schools: Officialdom, Village Culture, and Popular Pedagogy, 1861–1914* (Berkeley, 1986).

56. Svetlin [Reznikov], "Mirskaia dusha. . . ," *Russkaia mysl'* 5 (May 1881): 58–78.

57. Nazar'ev (March 1876): 304–5. Eklof also makes this observation in his study of the position of the rural school teacher: Ben Eklof, "Face to the Village: The Russian Teacher and the Peasant Community, 1880–1914," In Roger Bartlett, ed., *Land Commune and Peasant Community in Russia: Communal Forms in Imperial and Early Soviet Society* (London, 1990), 351.

58. Nazar'ev (March 1876): 313.

59. Kavelin, *Sobranie Sochinenii,* 438.

60. A., "Opiat' o narodnosti i o kul'turnykh tipakh," *Russkii vestnik* 122 (March 1876): 372.

61. Astyrev, 500.

Chapter 8. *Baba:* The Peasant Woman—Virago, Eve or Victim?

1. Rose Glickman, "Women and the Peasant Commune," in Roger Bartlett, ed., *Land Commune and Peasant Community in Russia: Communal Forms in Imperial and Early Soviet Society* (London, 1990), 321.

2. See V. Dal', *Tolkovyi slovar' zhivogo velikorusskago iazyka* (1881; Moscow, 1955), 1:32.

3. A. Ia. Efimenko, *Issledovaniia narodnoi zhizni: Vypusk pervyi: Obychnoe pravo* (Moscow, 1884), 74; Dal', 1:32; and V. N. Dobrovol'skii, compiler, *Smolenskii etnograficheskii sbornik, chast' 3, Poslovitsy: Zapiski IRGO: Otdel etnografii,* vol. 23, vyp. 2 (St. Petersburg, 1894), 1.

4. For a discussion of Baba Yaga, see Joanna Hubbs, *Mother Russia: The Feminine Myth in Russian Culture* (Bloomington, 1988), 36–41.

5. Lynne Viola, "Bab'i bunty and Peasant Women's Protest during Collectivization," *The Russian Review* 45 (January 1986): 23.

6. On this point, Glickman notes, "The culture of the observers was, after all, similar in essence if not in detail to peasant culture in its patriarchal assumptions." Glickman, "Women and the Peasant Commune," 321.

7. James H. Billington, *The Icon and the Axe: An Interpretative History of Russian Culture* (New York, 1966), 20; and Hubbs, *Mother Russia,* 67–74.

8. Hans Rogger, *National Consciousness in Eighteenth-Century Russia* (Cambridge, 1960); and Donald Fanger, "The Peasant in Literature," in Wayne Vucinich, ed., *The Peasant in Nineteenth-Century Russia* (Stanford, 1968), 231–62.

9. One contemporary dated the outbreak of the furor over the family division precisely with the publication of the Valuev Commission's report in 1873. See O. E. Shmidt, "K voprosu o krest'ianskikh semeinykh razdelakh," *Russkaia mysl'* (January 1886), 2:21. There were occasional reports of increased numbers of fissions immediately after the Emancipation, but it was only in the 1870s that the phenomenon became one of the central issues within the "peasant question." For the early period, see M. Iu——n, "Iz derevni, I," *Den'* (August 22, 1864), 11–13; Skaldin [Elenev], "V zakholust'i i v stolitse," *Otechestvennye zapiski* 174 (1867): 678–80. For a discussion of the nature of family divisions and their impact on public opinion, and for their function in the commune, see Cathy A. Frierson, "*Razdel:* The Peasant Family Divided," *The Russian Review* 46 (January 1987): 35–51; and Frierson, "Peasant Family Divisions and the Commune," in Roger Bartlett, ed., *Land Commune and Peasant Community, in Russia: Communal Forms in Imperial and Early Soviet Society* (London, 1990), 303–20.

10. See Chapter 3, pp. 74–75.

11. See Frierson, "*Razdel,*" 39, n. 6.

12. Engelgardt, "Iz derevni, VII," *Otechestvennye zapiski* 242 (January 1979): 136.

13. Ibid., 138.

14. Ibid. A peasant woman would have to "sense" her beauty in a world where the mirror was a rarity.

15. Ibid., 139.

16. Ibid. Engelgardt's attribution of sexual license and greed as evidence of the peasant woman's moral weakness conformed to attitudes deeply embedded in Orthodox culture. See Eve Levin, *Sex and Society in the World of the Orthodox Slavs, 900–1700* (Ithaca, 1989).

17. Iu. S. Musabekov, "Pervyi russkii khimicheskii zhurnal i ego osnovateli," *Materialy po istorii otechestvennoi khimii: Sbornik dokladov na vtorom vsesoiuz-*

nom soveshchanii po istorii otechestvennoi khimii 21 26 aprelia 1951 g. (Moscow, 1953), 299.

18. Her name was Anna Nikolaevna Engelgardt. RO GPB, fond 621, opis' 1, delo 1018, contains her correspondence with A. N. Pypin about her translation work.

19. TsGALI, fond 572, opis' 1, delo 55 and delo 258.

20. TsGALI, fond 572, opis' 1, delo 37, l. 3.

21. See, for example, his letters to her during his visit to St. Petersburg in 1882 in TsGALI, fond 572, opis' 1, delo 60.

22. Engelgardt, "Iz derevni, VII," 139.

23. Ibid., 138.

24. Ibid.

25. Engelgardt, "Iz derevni, V," *Otechestvennye zapiski* 228 (September 1876): 28–37.

26. S. Bezymennyi, "Proshloe leto v derevne," *Russkii vestnik* 40 (July 1862): 81–93.

27. I. Kharlamov, "Zhenshchina v russkoi sem'e (opyt' po obychnomu pravu)," *Russkoe bogatstvo* (March 1880): 1:81.

28. Ibid., 95.

29. N. N. Zlatovratskii, "Derevenskii Lir (Rasskaz moego znakomogo)," *Russkoe bogatstvo* (January 1880), 1:201.

30. Zlatovratsakii, *Sochinenii,* 272–91; TsGALI, fond 513, opis' 1, delo 30; Engelgardt, RO PD, fond 577, opis' 1, delo 25; and for a discussion of women's rule in areas of male out-migration, see Barbara Alpern Engel, "The Woman's Side: Male Out-Migration and the Family Economy in Kostroma Province," *Slavic Review* 45 (Summer 1986): 257–71.

31. Selivanov, "Dva ubiistva," *Sovremennik* 87 (May 1861): 5–42.

32. V. I. Roskovshenko, "Marus'ia: Malorossiiskoe predanie," *Russkii vestnik* 69 (May 1867): 357–88.

33. Uspenskii, *Sobranie sochinenii,* 4:99–103.

34. Iu——ov, "Udacha otsa Ivana: Rasskaz," *Russkoe bogatstvo* (November 1881), 1:73–109.

35. V. Bystrenin, "Razlad: Derevenskaia byl'," *Russkoe bogatstvo* (September 1888), 1:37–66.

36. A. M. Skabichevskii, *Graf L. N. Tolstoi kak khudozhnik i myslitel'* (St. Petersburg, 1887), 217. Another critic at *Herald of Europe* also identified the style of this work with that of Uspenskii et al., adding that Tolstoy managed to capture the language and mood of the village better than his peers. R., "Edip v derevne," *Vestnik Evropy* 298 (March 1887): 426–32.

37. N. V. Uspenskii, *Iz proshlogo: Vospominaniia* (Moscow, 1889), 149.

38. L. N. Tolstoy, *Vlast' t'my ili "kogotok uviaz', vsei ptichke propast'"* (Moscow, 1887).

39. Skabichevskii, *Graf L. N. Tolstoi,* 232.

40. L. Obolenskii, "Psikhologiia i moral' v novoi drame Tolstogo ("Vlast' t'my ili kogotok uviaz' vsei ptichke propast' ")," *Russkoe bogatstvo* 3 (March 1887): 148.

41. Ibid., 148–49.

42. Ibid.

43. Obolenskii, 157.

44. Glickman, "Women and the Peasant Commune," 321; Christine D. Worobec, *Peasant Russia: Family and Community in the Post-Emancipation Period* (Princeton, 1991), 185–90.

45. V. K. Rzhevskii, "Vospitanie naroda," *Russkii vestnik* 55 (January 1865): 250.

46. Andrei Percherskii, "Za Volgoi, Rasskaz, Gl. VII–XVII," *Russkii vestnik* 76 (July 1868): 252.

47. Selivanov, "Dva ubiistva," 7. For later reports of victimization, see T. A. Kuzminskaia, "Bab'ia dolia: Iz narodnoi zhizni," *Vestnik Evropy* 292 (April 1886): 607–54; V. Dmitrieva, "Svoim sudom: Iz vospominanii sel'skoi uchitel'nitsy," *Severnyi vestnik* (January, 1888): 93–135.

48. V. N. Nazar'ev, "Sovremennaia glush'. Iz vospominanii mirovogo sud'i," *Vestnik Evropy* (February 1872): 610.

49. Ibid., 612.

50. Ibid., 620.

51. Ibid., 625.

52. V. N. Nazar'ev, "Sovremennaia glush'. Iz vospominanii mirovogo sud'i," *Vestnik Evropy* (March 1872): 151. Similar reports were to be found in Ia. Ludmer, "Bab'i stony (Iz zametok mirovogo sud'i)," *Iuridicheskii vestnik* no. 11 (November 1884): 446–67 and no. 12 (December 1884): 658–79.

53. Engel, "The Woman's Side," 257–71.

54. F. M. Dostoevskii, *Polnoe sobranie sochinenii v tridtsati tomakh,* vol. 21 (Leningrad, 1980), 21.

55. Skaldin [Elenev], 2:680.

56. S. Sharapov, "Chto takoe krest'ianskie razdely," *Rus'* (December 24, 1881), 16.

57. Aleksandra Iakovlevna Efimenko, *Issledovaniia narodnoi zhizni: Vypusk pervyi: Obychnoe pravo* (Moscow, 1884), 63.

58. Ibid., 49.

59. Ibid., 51.

60. Ibid., 89–90.

61. Efimenko, 74.

62. Ibid., 84. K. D. Kavelin had argued three years earlier that individualism was already the basic principle of the peasant household and that idealization of the patriarchal household was hindering state and society's resolution of the "peasant question." Kavelin, *Sobranie sochinenii,* 399–400.

63. Ibid., 92. On household patterns in Arkhangelsk, see Judith Pallot, "The Northern Commune: Archangel Province in the Late Nineteenth Century," in Bartlett, ed., *Land Commune and Peasant Community,* 86–105.

64. M. K. Gorbunova, "Po derevniam, I & II," *Otechestvennye zapiski* 257 (August 1881): 163.

65. Gorbunova, "Po derevniam, IV" (October 1881): 146.

66. Gorbunova, "Po derevniam, I & II": 186.

67. This was in contrast to the common linkage of cottage industry and

kulachestvo. See, for example, S. Shashkov, "Kustar i kulak," *Slovo* (February 1881): 25–52.

68. Tolstoy, *Anna Karenina,* vol. 2 (Moscow, 1878), 24–34.

69. Uspenskii, *Sobranie sochinenii,* 5:279.

70. Ibid.

71. Ibid.

72. Ibid., 280. Here, and in other passages in this piece, Varvara bears a striking, indeed a suspicious, resemblance to Zola's Françoise in *La Terre* (The earth). Of Françoise, Zola wrote, "Swinging her fork, she picked up the grass and flung it into the wind which carried it away in a pale golden shower. . . . As she walked along through this continual cloud of hay, she was very hot and full of high spirits." Emile Zola, *The Earth,* Douglas Parmee, trans. (Middlesex, England, 1980), 144. The resemblance is suspicious because Uspenskii was familiar with Zola's work not only through the latter's published works but also because he spent a great deal of time with Zola during his two trips to Paris in the mid-1870s. Uspenskii's wife also worked as Zola's secretary and translator. There are also passages in Uspenskii's *Power of the Earth* which sound remarkably like Zola's, especially on the land as the wet nurse. This topic begs for further exploration. See J. A. T. Lloyd, *Two Russian Reformers: Ivan Turgenev* (New York, 1911); G. I. Leshchinskaia, *Emil' Zolia: Bibliograficheskii ukazatel' russkikh perevodov i kriticheskoi literatury na russkom iazyke, 1865–1874* (Moscow, 1975); and M. K. Klemen, *Emil' Zolia: Sbornik statei* (Leningrad, 1934).

73. See, for example, A. I. Levitov, "Babushka Maslikha (Stepnye nravy)," *Sovremennik* (August 1864), 1:215–29. Similarly, the most positive female figures in Engelgardt's letters were his old housekeeper, Avdot'ia, and the cook, the "Old Woman." Zlatovratskii's female paragon of communal virtue, Ul'iana Mosevna, was also old, also a spinster and childless.

74. Uspenskii, 5:188–96; Engelgardt, "Iz derevni, III," *Otechestvennye zapiski* 206 (January 1873): 70; and "Iz derevni, VI," *Otechestvennye zapiski* 237 (March 1878): 42; Gorbunova, V (November 1881): 32–33; F. Tarasenko, "Greshnitsa," *Russkoe bogatstvo* (July 1886): 107–32.

75. On infant mortality, see Nancy M. Frieden, "Child Care: Medical Reform in a Traditionalist Culture," in David L. Ransel, ed., *The Family in Imperial Russia* (Urbana, 1978), 236–37.

76. James H. Billington, *The Icon and the Axe: An Interpretive History of Russian Culture* (New York, 1979), 20, and Hubbs's discussion of what she calls Mother Moist Earth. Joanna Hubbs, *Mother Russia: The Feminine Myth in Russian Culture* (Bloomington, 1988), 67–74.

77. S. V. Maksimov, *Nechistaia, nevedomaia i krestnaia sila* (St. Petersburg, 1903), 251.

78. Here again, Uspenskii resembles Zola, who wrote, "Yet how thankless and indifferent that land was! However much you adored it, its heart was never softened, it would not produce one single extra grain . . ." and one of whose peasants exclaimed, "It never gives you more than it wants, the crafty old bitch!" Emile Zola, *The Earth,* 93–95.

79. D. P. Shchestakov, "Sem'ia i narod v proizvedeniiakh Gleba I. Uspen-

skogo," *Chteniia v Obshchestve liubitelei russkoi slovesnosti v pamiat' A. S. Push-kina pri Imperatorskom Kazanskom universitete*, vyp. 24, 1902 (Karan, 1903), 24.
80. See Engel, 264–65.

Chapter 9. Conclusion

1. See Chapter 2, epigraph.
2. N. [Vvedenskii], "Literaturnye mechtaniia i deistvitel'nost': Po povodu li-teraturnykh mnenii o narode," *Vestnik Evropy* 266 (November 1881): 319.
3. N. a., "Intelligentsiia i narod," *Nedelia* (March 9, 1880), 309.
4. N. a., "Liberal o serom muzhike," *Nedelia* (February 19, 1878), 285.
5. N. Astyrev, "Ot kolyben'ka do mogilki: Etnograficheskii ocherk," *Vestnik evropy* 300 (July 1887): 48.
6. F. Andreev, "Nechto o muzhike i muzhikovstvuiushchem pessimizme," *Severnyi vestnik* (January 1889): 34.
7. Ibid., 30.
8. Anton Chekhov, "Peasants," in *The Portable Chekhov,* Avrahm Yarmo-linsky, ed. and trans. (New York, 1947), 312.
9. Ibid., 348.
10. Ibid., 334–35.
11. Ibid., 317.
12. Ibid., 351.
13. Ibid., 351–52.
14. Ibid.
15. Art. . . . , "Literaturnaia letopis' (Obozrenie zhurnalov i knig): Chto takoe intelligentsiia?" *Russkoe bogatstvo* 1 (January 1882): 82–99 (a review of numerous articles in other journals on the meaning of the term *intelligentsia*); n. a., "Po povodu tolkov o vzaimnom otnoshenii naroda i obshchestva," *Russkoe bogatstvo* ("Vnutrenee obozrenie") 9 (September 1887): 163–79; I. I. Ditiatin, "Kogda i pochemu voznikla rozn' v Rossii mezhdu 'kommanduiushchimi klassami' i 'narodom'," *Russkaia mysl'* 11 (November 1881): 303–82; n.a., "Intelligentsiia i narod," *Nedelia* (March 9, 1880), 308–13; N. N. Zlatovratskii, "Liudi starogo povedeniia," *Russkaia mysl'* 5 (May 1884): 307–35; Ivaniukov, "Unyne i pessimizm sovre-mennogo kul'turnogo obshchestva," *Severnyi vestnik* (October 1885): 36–50; Nor-man M. Naimark, *Terrorists and Social Democrats: The Russian Revolutionary Movement under Alexander II* (Cambridge, 1983), 781.
16. Ivaniukov, "Unyne. . . ," 48–50; N. Kapustina, "Pozdno," *Severnyi vestnik* 5 (May 1888): 159–83; A. Prugavin, "O mistitsizme v russkom narode i obsh-chestve," *Severnyi vestnik* 3 (March 1886): 193–215.
17. K. D. Kavelin, "Zloby dnia," *Russkaia mysl'* 3 (March 1888): 2.
18. D. Kishenskii, "Pis'ma o russkom krest'ianstve, I," 16.
19. Arsenii Vvedenskii, "Literaturnye perspektivy (nechto o literaturnym narodnichestve," *Severnyi vestnik* (September 1885): 196.
20. N.a. "Ot redaktsii," *Severnyi vestnik* 9 (September 1885): vi.

21. L. Obolenskii, "Osnovnaia oshibka sovremennogo materializma i pozitivizma," *Russkoe bogatstvo* 1 (January 1890): 79.

22. TsGALI, fond 202, opis' 1, delo 205, l. 2.

23. Ibid., l. 4.

24. K. K. Arsen'ev, "Novye literaturnye sily. V. Korolenko, *Ocherki i rasskazy* (Moscow 1887)," *Vestnik Evropy* 298 (March 1887): 285–301.

25. A. K. Kotov, *V. G. Korolenko: Ocherk zhizni i literaturnoi deiatel'nosti* (Moscow, 1957).

26. Kotov, 33; B. D. Letov, *V. G. Korolenko—redaktor* (Leningrad, 1961).

27. Stephen P. Frank, "Popular Justice, Community and Culture among the Russian Peasantry, 1870–1900," *The Russian Review* 46 (1987): 239–65; and Cathy A. Frierson, "Crime and Punishment in the Russian Village: Concepts of Criminality at the End of the Nineteenth Century," *Slavic Review* 46 (1987): 55–69.

28. Baron N. Korf, "Obrazovatel'nyi uroven' vzroslykh gramotnykh krest'ian," *Russkaia mysl'* 10 (October 1881): 2–13.

29. Nancy Mandelker Frieden, *Russian Physicians in an Era of Reform and Revolution, 1856–1905* Princeton, 1981), 91, n. 45.

30. Frieden, 104.

31. Leonid Ouspensky and Vladimir Lossky, *The Meaning of Icons,* URS Graf-Verlag, Olten Switzerland, ed. (Boston, 1952), 60.

32. N.a., "Stoit-li rabotat' v derevne?" *Nedelia* (October 13, 1885): 1109.

33. Uspenskii, "Pis'ma s dorogi," *Russkaia mysl'* 3 (March 1888): 161.

Selected Bibliography

In the following bibliography, I have not listed articles from the serious journals of the period. They constitute the majority of materials for the book and have been cited throughout the text.

Primary Sources

Archives

MOSCOW

TsGALI
    fond 572   A. N. Engelgardt
        202   N. N. Zlatovratskii
        513   G. I. Uspenskii
        203   P. V. Zasodimskii

LENINGRAD

Otdel rukopisei, GPB
    fond 621   A. N. Pypin
Rukopisnyi otdel, Pushkinskii Dom
    fond N. 2190 X C F. M. Reshetnikov and family
        111 N. N. Zlatovratskii
        577 A. N. Engelgardt

SMOLENSK

Gosudarstvennyi Arkhiv Smolenskoi oblasti
    fond 1   Records of the Governor's Chancellery (materials on surveillance of A. N. Engelgardt)

Materials

Harvard Law Library. *Sudebnaia reforma.* Vol. 10, *Zhurnal soedinennykh departmentov zakonov i grazhdanskikh del gosudarstvennogo soveta o preobrazo-*

vanii sudebnoi chasti v Rossia, and vol. 12, *Zamechaniia o razvitii osnovnykh polozhenii preobrazovaniia sudebnoi chasti v Rossii.*

Journals and Newspapers

Den', 1861–1865
Delo, 1870–1885
Iuridicheskii vestnik, 1872–1876
Nedelia, 1870–1885
Obshchina, 1878
Otechestvennye zapiski, 1861–1884
Rus', 1881–1884
Russkaia mysl', 1880–1890
Russkii vestnik, 1861–1890
Russkoe bogatstvo, 1879–1890
Severnyi vestnik, 1885–1890
Sovremennik, 1861–1866
Sudebnyi vestnik, 1872–1876
Vestnik Evropy, 1861–1890

Collected Works

Aksakov, I. S. *Sochineniia*. Vol. 4. Moscow, 1886.

Bervi Flerovskii, V. V. *Izbrannye ekonomicheskie proizvedeniia v dvukh tomakh.* Vol. 1. Moscow, 1958.

Dostoevskii, F. M. *Polnoe sobranie sochinenii v tridtsati tomakh.* Vols. 21–26. Leningrad, 1980–1984.

Engelgardt, A. N. *Izbrannye sochineniia*. Moscow, 1959.

Kavelin, K. D. *Sobranie sochinenii K. D. Kavelina.* Vol. 2, *Publitsistika*. St. Petersburg, 1904.

Reshetnikov, F. M. *Polnoe sobranie sochinenii v dvukh tomakh.* St. Petersburg, 1904.

Saltykov-Shchedrin, M. E. *Sobranie sochinenii.* Vol. 18, bk. 2, and vol. 19, bk. 1. Moscow, 1976.

Uspenskii, G. I. *Sobranie sochinenii.* Moscow, 1956.

Zlatovratskii, N. N. *Sochineniia.* 3d edition. Moscow, 1897.

Memoirs

Aptekman, O. A. *Iz istorii revoliutsionnogo narodnichestva. "Zemlia i Volia" 70-kh godov.* Rostov-na-Don, 1906.

Barannikov, A. I. *Narodovolets A. I. Barannikov v ego pis'makh.* Moscow, 1935.

Belousov, I. A. *Literaturnaia Moskva (Vospominaniia 1880–1928) Pisateli iz naroda: Pisateli-narodniki.* Moscow, 1928.

Berezin, V. P. *Mirovoi sud' v provintsii.* St. Petersburg, 1883.

Debogorii-Mokrievich, V. *Vospominaniia.* St. Petersburg, 1906.
Ivanchin-Pisarev, A. I. *Khozhdenie v narod.* Moscow, 1929.
Minkh, A. N. *Iz zapisok mirovogo posrednika A. N. Minkha, 1861–1866 gody.* Saratov, 1911.
Repin, I. E. *Dalekoe blizkoe.* 3d edition. Moscow, 1949.
Uspenskii, N. V. *Iz proshlogo: Vospominaniia.* Moscow, 1889.
Zlatovratskii, N. N. *Vospominaniia.* Moscow, 1956.

Books

Akademiia nauk. *Slovar' akademii rossiiskoi po azbuchnomu poriadu raspolozhennyi.* Pt. 3. St. Petersburg, 1814.
Akademiia nauk SSSR. *Revoliutsionnoe narodnichestvo 70-kh godov xix veka: Sbornik dokumentov i materialov v dvukh tomakh.* Vol. 1. Moscow, 1964.
Barykov, F. L., A. V. Polovtsov, and P. A. Sokolovskii, eds. *Sbornik materialov dlia izucheniia sel'skoi pozemel'noi obshchiny.* St. Petersburg, 1880.
Barykov, O. *Obychai nasledovaniia u gosudarstvennykh krest'ian.* St. Petersburg, 1862.
Bazilevskii, B. *Gosudarstvennye prestupleniia v Rossii v xix veke: Sbornik iz ofitsial'nykh izdanii pravitel'stvennykh soobshchenii.* Stuttgart, 1903.
Belliustin, I. S. *Description of the Clergy in Rural Russia: The Memoir of a Nineteenth-Century Parish Priest.* Translated by G. L. Freeze. Ithaca, 1985.
Berezinskii, P. *Gosudarstvennye prestupleniia v Rossii v xix veke.* Paris, 1905.
Bogucharskii, V. *Aktivnoe narodnichestvo semidesiatykh godov.* Moscow, 1912.
Burtsev, V., Comp. *Za sto let (1800–1896): Sbornik po istorii politicheskikh obshchestvennykh dvizhenii v Rossii.* London, 1897.
Chubinskii, P. P. *Trudy etnografichesko-statisticheskoi ekspeditsii v zapadno-russkii krai.* St. Petersburg, 1872.
Dal', V. *Tolkovy: slovar' zhivogo velikorusskogo iazyka.* 1881; Moscow, 1955.
Dobrovol'skii, V. N., comp. *Smolenskii etnograficheskii sbornik.* Chast' 3. *Poslovitsy: Zapiski IRGO: Otdel etnografii.* Vol. 23, vyp. 2. St. Petersburg, 1894.
Efimenko, A. Ia. *Issledovaniia narodnoi zhizni: Vypusk pervyi: Obychnoe pravo.* Moscow, 1884.
Engelgardt, A. N. *Iz derevni: 11 pisem: 1872–1882.* St. Petersburg, 1882.
———. *Iz derevni: 12 pisem: 1872–1887.* Moscow, 1960.
Golovachev, A. A. *Desiat' let reform, 1861–1871.* St. Petersburg, 1872.
von Haxthausen, A. *Studies on the Interior of Russia.* Translated by E. L. M. Schmidt. Chicago, 1972.
Iakushkin, E. I. *Obychnoe pravo: Materialy dlia bibliografii obychnogo prava.* Vyp. 1. Iaroslavl', 1875.
Illiustrov, I. I. *Iuridicheskie poslovitsy i pogovorki russkogo naroda.* Moscow, 1885.
Kalachov, N. V. *Ob otnoshenii iuridicheskikh obychaev k zakonodatel'stvu.* St. Petersburg, 1877.
———. *O volstnykh i sel'skikh sudakh v drevnei i nyneshnei Rossii.* St. Petersburg, 1880.

Korolenko, V. G. *Otoshedshie: Ob Uspenskom: O Chernyshevskom: O Cherkhove.* St. Petersburg, 1908.

Kovalenskaia, T. M., ed. *Kramskoi ob iskusstve.* Moscow, 1960.

Kravchinskii, S. M. *The Russian Peasantry: Their Condition, Social Life, and Religion.* New York, 1888.

———. *Russia under the Tsars.* Translated by W. Westall. New York, 1885.

———. *Underground Russia: Revolutionary Profiles and Sketches from Life.* Translated by P. Lavrov. 1883; Westport, Conn., 1973.

Leont'ev. A. A. *Krest'ianskoe pravo: Sistematicheskoe izlozhenie osobennostei zakonodatel'stva o krest'ianakh.* St. Petersburg, 1909.

———. *Volostnoi sud i iuridicheskie obychai krest'ian.* St. Petersburg, 1895.

P. L. *Zemlia i volia.* St. Petersburg, 1868.

Leshchinskii, M. *O vlianii p'ianstva na obshchestvennoe zdorov'e, nravstvennost', deiatel'nie sily i merakh k ogranicheniiu ego.* St. Petersburg, 1873.

Miasoedov, G. G. *Pis'ma, dokumenty, vospominaniia.* Moscow, 1972.

Ministerstvo Gosudarstvennykh Imushchestv. *Doklad vysochaishe uchrezhdennoi komissi: dlia issledovaniia nyneshnego polozheniia sel'skogo khoziaistva i sel'skoi proizvoditel'nosti v Rossii.* St. Petersburg, 1873.

Minkh, G. N. *Chuma v Rossii (Vetlianskaia epidemiia 1878–1879 g.).* Chast' 1. Kiev, 1898.

Orshanskii, I. G. *Issledovaniia po russkomu pravu obychnomu i brachnomu.* St. Petersburg, 1879.

Pakhman, S. V. *Obychnoe grazhdanskoe pravo v Rossii: Iuridicheskie ocherki.* Vol. 1. St. Petersburg, 1877. Vol. 2. St. Petersburg, 1879.

Priklonskii, S. A. *Narodnaia zhizn' na severe.* Moscow, 1884.

Semenov, N. P. *Osvobozhdenie krest'ian v tsarstvovanie imperatora Aleksandra II.* Vol. I. St. Petersburg, 1889. Vol. 2. St. Petersburg, 1890.

Sharapov, S. *A. N. Engel'gardt i ego znachenie dlia russkoi kul'turi i nauki.* St. Petersburg, 1893.

Skabichevskii, A. M. *Belletristy-narodniki: F. Reshetnikov, A. Levitov, Gl. Uspenskii, N. Zlatovratskii i pr. Kriticheskie ocherki.* St. Petersburg, 1888.

———. *Graf L. N. Tolstoy kak khudozhnik i myslitel'.* St. Petersburg, 1887.

Smirnov, A. *Ocherki semeinykh otnoshenii po obychnomu pravu russkogo naroda.* Moscow, 1878.

Suvorin, A., ed. *Ivan Nikolaevich Kramskoi: Ego zhizn', perepiska i khudozhestvenno-kriticheskie stat'i, 1837–1887.* St. Petersburg, 1888.

Tenishev, V. V. *Pravosudie v russkom krest'ianskom bytu.* Briansk, 1907.

Tolstoy, L. N. *Anna Karenina.* Moscow, 1878.

———. *Vlast' t'my ili 'kogotok uviaz', vsei ptichke propast'."* Moscow, 1887.

———. *Voina i mir.* Moscow, 1868–1869.

Tolstoy, L. N., and V. V. Stasov. *Perepiska, 1878–1906.* Leningrad, 1929.

Trudy kommisii po preobrazovaniiu volostnykh sudov. Vols. 1–7. St. Petersburg, 1873–1874.

Umanets, F. M. *Iz moikh nabliudenii po krest'ianskomu delu.* St. Petersburg, 1881.

Vasil'chikov, A. I. *O samoupravlenii: Sravnitel'nyi obzor russkikh i inostrannykh zemskikh i obshchestvennykh uchrezhdenii.* St. Petersburg, 1869.

———. *Sel'skii byt i sel'skoe khoziaistvo v Rossii.* St. Petersburg, 1881.

Vtoroe otdelenie Sobstvennoi E. I. V. Kantseliarii. *Otchet po glavnomu komitetu ob ustroistve sel'skogo sostoianiia za deviatiletie 19 fevralia 1861 po 19 fevralia 1870 g.* St. Petersburg, 1870.

Zasodimskii, P. V. *Khronika sela Smurina.* Moscow, 1939.

Zlatovratskii, N. N. *Derevenskie budni.* St. Petersburg, 1882.

Secondary Sources

Aleksandrov, V. A. *Obychnoe pravo krepostnoi derevni Rossii xviii–nachalo xix v.* Moscow, 1984.

Anfimov, A. M. *Ekonomicheskoe polozhenie i klassovaia bor'ba krest'ian evropeiskoi Rossii, 1881–1904.* Moscow, 1984.

———. *Krest'ianskoe khoziaistvo evropeiskoi Rossii, 1881–1904.* Moscow, 1980.

Bartlett, Roger, ed. *Land Commune and Peasant Community in Russia: Communal Forms in Imperial and Early Soviet Society.* London, 1990.

Belova, N. M. *Khudozhestvennoe izobrazhenie naroda v russkoi literature serediny xix v.* Saratov, 1969.

Berezina, V. G., ed., *Ocherki po istorii russkoi zhurnalistiki i kritiki.* Vol. 2. *Vtoraia polovina xix veka.* Leningrad, 1965.

Besançon, Alain. "The Dissidence of Russian Painting." In Chernviasky, Michael, ed., *The Structure of Russian History.* New York, 1970, 381–411.

Bezhkovich, A. S., ed. *Khoziaistvo i byt russkikh krest'ian: Pamiatniki material'noi kul'tury.* Moscow, 1969.

Billington, James H. *Mikhailovsky and Russian Populism.* Oxford, 1958.

———. *The Icon and the Axe: An Interpretive History of Russian Culture.* New York, 1979.

Blankoff, Jean. *La société russe de la seconde moitié du xixe siècle.* Brussels, 1974.

Blum, Jerome. *Lord and Peasant in Russia from the Ninth to the Nineteenth Century.* Princeton, 1971.

Brooks, Jeffrey. "Readers and Reading at the End of the Tsarist Era." In Todd, William Mills, ed., *Literature and Society in Imperial Russia, 1880–1914.* Stanford, 1978, 97–150.

———. *When Russia Learned to Read: Literacy and Popular Literature, 1861–1917.* Princeton, 1985.

Bush, V. V. *Ocherki literaturnogo narodnichestva 70–80 gg.* Leningrad, 1931.

Chernukha, V. G. *Krest'ianskii vopros v pravitel'stvennoi politike Rossii.* Leningrad, 1972.

Cheshikhin-Vetrinskii, V. E. *Gleb Ivanovich Uspenskii: Biograficheskii ocherk.* Moscow, 1929.

Czap, Peter. " 'A Large Family: The Peasant's Greatest Wealth': Serf Households in Mishino, Russia, 1814–1858." In Richard Wall, ed., *Family Forms in Historic Europe.* Cambridge, 1983, 105–152.

———. "Peasant-Class Courts and Peasant Customary Justice in Russia, 1861–1912." *Journal of Social History* 1/2 (1967): 149–79.

Davydov, N. V., and N. N. Polianskii. *Sudebnaia reforma.* 2 vols. Moscow, 1915.

Donskov, Andrew. *The Changing Image of the Peasant in Nineteenth-Century Drama.* Helsinki, 1972.

Druzhinin, N. M. *Gosudarstvennye krest'iane i reforma P. D. Kiseleva.* Vol. 1. *Predposylki i sushchnost' reformy.* Moscow, 1946. Vol. 2. *Realizatsiia i posledstviia reformy.* Moscow, 1958.

———. *Russkaia derevnia na perelome 1861–1880 gg.* Moscow, 1978.

Dunham, Vera Sandomirsky, "The Strong Woman Motif." In Cyril E. Black, ed. *The Transformation of Russian Society.* Cambridge, 1960, 459–483.

Dzhanshiev, G. A. *Osnovy sudebnoi reformy (k 25-letiiu novogo suda): Istoriko-iuridicheskie etiudy.* Moscow, 1891.

Eklof, Ben. *Russian Peasant Schools: Officialdom, Village Culture, and Popular Pedagogy, 1861–1914.* Berkeley, 1986.

Emmons, Terence, and Vucinich, Wayne, eds. *The Zemstvo in Russia: An Experiment in Local Self-Government.* Cambridge, 1982.

Engel, Barbara Alpern. "The Woman's Side: Male Out-Migration and the Family Economy in Kostroma Province," *Slavic Review* 45 (Summer 1986): 257–71.

Faresov, A. I. *Semidesiatniki.* St. Petersburg, 1905.

Farnsworth, Beatrice Brodsky. "The Litigious Daughter-in-Law: Family Relations in Rural Russia in the Second Half of the Nineteenth Century." *Slavic Review* 45, (Spring 1986): 49–64.

Fedorov, V. A. "Semeinye razdely v russkoi poreformennoi derevne," In A. A. Kondrashev, ed., *Sel'skoe khoziaistvo i krest'ianstvo severo-zapada RSFSR v dorevoliutsionnyi period.* Smolensk, 1979, 29–46.

Field, Daniel. "Peasants and Propagandists in the Russian Movement to the People of 1874," *Journal of Modern History* 59 (September 1987): 415–438.

———. *Rebels in the Name of the Tsar.* Boston, 1976.

Frank, Stephen P. "Popular Justice, Community and Culture among the Russian Peasantry, 1870–1900." *The Russian Review* 46/3 (1987): 239–65.

Freeze, G. L. *The Parish Clergy in Nineteenth-Century Russia: Crisis, Reform, Counter-reform.* Princeton, 1983.

Frieden, Nancy Mandelker. *Russian Physicians in an Era of Reform and Revolution, 1856–1905.* Princeton, 1981.

Frierson, Cathy A. "Crime and Punishment in the Russian Village: Concepts of Criminality at the End of the Nineteenth Century." *Slavic Review* 46/1 (1987): 55–69.

———. "*Razdel:* The Peasant Family Divided." *The Russian Review* 46 (January 1987): 35–51.

———. "Rural Justice in Public Opinion: The Volost' Court Debate, 1861–1912." *The Slavonic and East European Review* 64 (October 1986): 526–45.

———. "The Peasant Family Division and the Commune." In Roger Bartlett, ed., *Land Commune and Peasant Community in Russia: Communal Forms in Russia: Communal Forms in Imperial and Early Soviet Society.* London, 1990, 303–20.

Gagliardo, John G. *From Pariah to Patriot: The Changing Image of the German Peasant, 1770–1840.* Lexington, Ky., 1969.

Gessen, I. V. *Sudebnaia reforma.* St. Petersburg, 1905.

Gleason, Abbott. *Young Russia: The Genesis of Russian Radicalism in the 1860s.* New York, 1980.

Glickman, Rose. "An Alternative View of the Peasantry: The Raznochintsy Writers of the 1860s." *Slavic Review* 32 (December 1973): 693–704.

Glinka-Volzhskii, A. S. *Gleb Uspenskii v zhizni, po vospominaniiam, perepiske, i dokumentam.* Moscow, 1935.

Gol'dshtein, S. N. *Ivan Nikolaevich Kramskoi: Zhizn' i tvorchestvo.* Moscow, 1965.

Gomberg-Vershbenskaia, E. P. *Peredvizhniki.* Leningrad, 1970.

Gosudarstvennyi literaturnyi muzei. *Letopisi: Kniga Chetvertaia: Gleb Uspenskii.* Moscow, 1939.

Grant, Steven A. "Obshchina and Mir." *Slavic Review* 35 (December 1976): 636–51.

Grew, Raymond. "Picturing the People: Images of the Lower Orders in Nineteenth-Century French Art." In Robert I. Rotberg and Theodore K. Rabb, eds., *Art and History: Images and Their Meaning.* Cambridge, 1988, 203–31.

Guershoon, Andrew. *Certain Aspects of Russian Proverbs.* London, 1941.

Herlihy, Patricia, "Joy of Rus': Rites and Rituals of Russian Drinking," *The Russian Review* 50 (April 1991): 131–47.

Hilton, Alison. "Scenes from Life and Contemporary History: Russian Realism of the 1870s–1880s." In Weisberg, Gabriel P., Ed., *The European Realist Tradition.* Bloomington, 1982, 187–214.

Hourevich, I. A. *The Economy of the Russian Village.* 1892; New York, 1970.

Hubbs, Joanna. *Mother Russia: The Feminine Myth in Russian Culture.* Bloomington, 1988.

Itenberg, B. S. *Dvizhenie revoliutsionnogo narodnichestva: Narodnicheskie kruzhki i "khozhdenie v narod" v 70-kh godakh xix v.* Moscow, 1965.

Johns, Elizabeth. "The Farmer in the Works of William Sidney Mount." In Robert I. Rotberg and Theodore K. Rabb, eds., *Art and History: Images and Their Meaning.* Cambridge, 1988, 257–81.

Joravsky, David. *Russian Psychology: A Critical History.* Oxford, 1989.

Kingston-Mann, Esther. *Lenin and the Problem of Marxist Peasant Revolution.* New York, 1985.

Koni, A. F. *Otsy i dety sudebnoi reformy (k piatidesiatiletiiu sudebnykh ustavov).* Moscow, 1914.

Koz'min, B. P. *Russkaia zhurnalistika 70-kh i 80-kh godov xix veka.* Moscow, 1948.

Kropotkin, P. A. *Ideals and Realities in Russian Literature.* New York, 1916.

Kucherov, S. *Courts, Lawyers, and Trials under the Last Three Tsars.* New York, 1953.

Kuchumova, L. K. "Sel'skaia pozemel'naia obshchina Evropeiskoi Rossii v 60–70 gody xix-go veka." *Istoricheskie zapiski.* Moscow, 1981, 333–35.

Kurochkina, T. I. *Ivan Nikolaevich Kramskoi.* Moscow, 1980.

Lebedev, A. K., and A. V. Solodovnikov. *Vladimir Vasil'evich Stasov: Zhizn' i tvorchestvo.* Moscow, 1976.

LeBlanc, Ronald D. "Tenierism: Seventeenth-Century Flemish Art and Early Nineteenth-Century Russian Prose." *The Russian Review* 49 (1990): 19–41.

————. "Teniers, Flemish Art, and the Natural School Debate." *Slavic Review* 50 (Fall 1991): 576–89.

Leikina-Svirskaia, V. R. *Intelligentsiia v Rossii vo vtoroi polovine xix veka.* Moscow, 1971.

Leshchinskaia, G. I. *Emil' Zolia. Bibliograficheskii ukazatel' russkikh perevodov i kriticheskoi literatury na russkom iazyke 1865–1974.* Moscow, 1975.

Levin, Eve. *Sex and Society in the World of the Orthodox Slavs, 900–1700.* Ithaca, 1989.

Lewin, Moshe. *Russian Peasants and Soviet Power.* Translated by Irene Nove. Evanston, Ill., 1968.

————. "The *Obshchina* and the Village." In Roger Bartlett, ed., *Land Commune and Peasant Community in Russia: Communal Forms in Imperial and Early Soviet Society.* London, 1990, 20–35.

Lloyd, J. A. T. *Two Russian Reformers: Ivan Turgenev, Leo Tolstoy.* New York, 1911.

Lothe, Jean. *Gleb Ivanovich Uspenskii et le populisme russe: Contribution à l'histoire de la pensée et de la littérature populistes en Russie (1870–1890).* Leiden, 1963.

Lotman, Iu. M. and B. A. Uspenskii. "Binary Models in the Dynamics of Russian Culture (to the End of the Eighteenth Century)." In Iu. A. Lotman, L. Ia. Ginsburg, and B. A. Uspenskii., *The Semiotics of Russian Culture,* Alexander D. Nakhimovsky and Alice Stone Nakhimovsky, eds. Ithaca, 1985.

Mann, Jurij V. "The Natural School as a Stage in the Development of Russian Literature." *Neohelicon* 15/1 (1988): 89–99.

Markov, P. G. *A. Ia. Efimenko—istorik Ukrainy.* Kiev, 1966.

Mendel, A. P. *Dilemmas of Progress in Tsarist Russia: Legal Marxism and Legal Populism.* Cambridge, 1961.

Ministerstvo iustitsii. *Sudebnye ustavy 20 noiabria 1864 g. za piat'desiat' let.* 2 vols. Petrograd, 1914.

Mironov, Boris. "The Russian Peasant Commune after the Reforms of the 1860s," *Slavic Review* 44 (Fall 1985): 438–67.

Mirsky, D. S. *Contemporary Russian Literature, 1881–1925.* New York, 1926.

Mitrany, David. *Marx against the Peasant: A Study in Social Dogmatism.* Chapel Hill, 1951.

Naimark, Norman M. *Terrorists and Social Democrats: The Russian Revolutionary Movement under Alexander II.* Cambridge, 1983.

Obraztsov, G. A. *Estetika V. V. Stasova i razvitie russkogo iskusstva.* Leningrad, 1975.

Ouspensky, Leonid, and Vladimir Lossky. *The Meaning of Icons.* Edited by URS Graf-Verlag, Olten Switzerland. Boston, 1952.

Paramonov, A. *Illiustratsii I. E. Repina.* Moscow, 1952.

Pearson, Thomas S. *Russian Officialdom in Crisis: Autocracy and Local Self-Government, 1861–1900.* Cambridge, 1989.

Pipes, Richard E. "Narodnichestvo—a Semantic Inquiry." *Slavic Review* 23 (September 1964): 441–58.

Potter, Jack M., ed. *Peasant Society: A Reader.* Boston, 1967.

Pribyleva, A. P., and V. N. Figner. *Narodovolets Aleksandr Dmitrievich Mikhailov*. Leningrad, 1925.

Prutskov, N. I. *Gleb Uspenskii semidesiatykh-nachala vosmidesiatykh godov*. Gorkii, 1955.

———. *Tvorcheskii put' Gleba Uspenskogo*. Moscow, 1958.

Redfield, Robert. *Peasant Society and Culture: An Anthropological Approach to Civilization*. Chicago, 1956.

Robinson, G. T. *Rural Russia under the Old Regime*. New York, 1949.

Rogger, Hans. *National Consciousness in Eighteenth-Century Russia*. Cambridge, 1960.

Scott, James C. *The Moral Economy of the Peasant: Rebellion and Subsistence in Southeast Asia*. New Haven, 1976.

Semenkin, K. G. *N. N. Zlatovratskii: Ocherk zhizni i tvorchestva*. Iaroslavl', 1976.

Shanin, Teodor. ed. *Peasants and Peasant Societies: Selected Readings*. 1971; Hammondsworth, Middlesex, England, 1984.

———. *The Awkward Class: Political Sociology of the Peasantry in a Developing Society: Russia 1910–1925*. Oxford, 1972.

Shuvalova, I. N. *Miasoedov*. Leningrad, 1971.

Sokolov, N. I., ed. *G. I. Uspenskii v russkoi kritike*. Moscow, 1961.

———. *G. I. Uspenskii: Zhizn' i tvorchestvo*. Leningrad, 1968.

———. *Masterstvo G. I. Uspenskogo*. Leningrad, 1958.

———. *Russkaia literatura i narodnichestvo: Literaturnoe dvizhenie 70-kh godov xix veka*. Leningrad, 1968.

Spasibenko, A. P. *Pisateli-narodniki*. Moscow, 1968.

Teplinskii, M. V. *"Otechestvennye zapiski"* (*1868–1884*) *Istoriia zhurnala: Literaturnaia kritika*. Iuzhno-Sakhalinsk, 1966.

Thompson, James. *The Peasant in French Nineteenth-Century Art*. Dublin, 1980.

Thorner, Daniel, ed. *A. V. Chayanov on the Theory of Peasant Economy*. Homewood, Ill., 1966.

Todd, William Mills. *Literature and Society in Imperial Russia, 1880–1914*. Stanford, 1978.

Todes, Daniel P. *Darwin without Malthus: The Struggle for Existence in Russian Evolutionary Thought*. Oxford, 1989.

Tokarev, S. A. *Istoriia russkoi etnografii*. Moscow, 1966.

Utkina, N. F. *Positivizm, antropologicheskii materialism i nauka v Rossii* (*vtoraia polovina xix veka*). Moscow, 1975.

Valkenier, Elizabeth Kridl. *Ilya Repin and the World of Russian Art*. New York, 1990.

———. "The Peredvizhniki and the Spirit of the 1860s." *The Russian Review*, 34, (July 1975): 247–65.

———. *Russian Realist Art: The State and Society: The Peredvizhniki and Their Tradition*. Ann Arbor, 1977.

Venturi, Franco. *Roots of Revolution*. Translated by Francis Haskell. New York, 1960.

Vucinich, Alexander. *Darwin in Russian Thought*. Berkeley, 1988.

———. *Science in Russian Culture, 1861–1917*. Stanford, 1970.

————. *Social Thought in Tsarist Russia: The Quest for a General Science of Society, 1861–1917.* Chicago, 1976.

Vucinich, Wayne, ed. *The Peasant in Nineteenth Century Russia.* Stanford, 1968.

Walicki, Andrzej. *A History of Russian Thought from the Enlightenment to Marxism.* Translated by Hilda Andrew-Rusiecka. Stanford, 1979.

————. *Legal Philosophies of Russian Liberalism.* Oxford, 1987.

————. *The Controversy over Capitalism: Studies in the Social Philosophy of the Russian Populists.* Oxford, 1969.

Ware, R. J., "A Russian Journal and Its Public: Otechestvennye zapiski, 1868–1884." *Oxford Slavonic Papers* n.s., 14 (1981): 121–46.

Weber, Eugen. *Peasants into Frenchmen: The Modernization of Rural France, 1870–1914.* Stanford, 1976.

Wolf, Eric R. *Peasants.* Englewood Cliffs, N.J., 1966.

Woodhouse, Judy. "A Landlord's Sketches?: D. V. Grigorovič and Peasant Genre Fiction." *Journal of European Studies* 16 (1986): 271–94.

Worobec, Christine D. *Peasant Russia: Family and Community in the Post-Emancipation Period.* Princeton, 1991.

Wortman, Richard. *The Crisis of Russian Populism.* Cambridge, 1967.

————. *The Development of a Russian Legal Consciousness.* Chicago, 1976.

Zaionchkovskii, P. A. *Pravitel'stvennyi apparat samoderzhavnoi Rossii v xix v.* Moscow, 1978.

————. *Provedenie v zhizn' krest'ianskoi reformy 1861 g.* Moscow, 1958.

————. *The Russian Autocracy in Crisis, 1878–1882.* Translated by Gary A. Hamburg. Gulf Breeze, Fla., 1979.

Zakharina, V. F. *Golos revoliutsionnoi Rossii: Literatura revoliutsionnogo podpol'ia 70-kh godov xix v.* Moscow, 1971.

Zelenin, D. K., comp. *Bibliograficheskii ukazatel' russkoi etnograficheskoi literatury o vneshnem byte narodov Rossii, 1700–1910.* St. Petersburg, 1913.

Zyrianov, P. N. "Obychnoe grazhdanskoe pravo v poreformennoi obshchine." In P. A. Kolesnikov, ed., *Ezhegodnik po agrarnoi istorii,* vyp. 6. Vologda, 1976, 91–101.

————. "Sotsial'naia struktura mestnogo upravleniia kapitalisticheskoi Rossii (1861–1914 gg.)." *Istoricheskie zapiski* 107 (1982): 226–302.

Dissertations

Bondarevskii, A. V. "Volostnoe upravlenie i polozhenie krest'ian v tsarskoi Rossii (1861–1917 gg.)." Candidate diss., Kiev, 1950.

Clay, Catherine Black. "Ethos and Empire; The Ethnographic Expedition of the Imperial Russian Naval Ministry, 1855–1862." Ph.D. diss., University of Oregon, 1989.

Eklof, Arthur Benoit. "Spreading the Word: Primary Education and the Zemstvo in Moscow Province: 1864–1910." Ph.D. diss., Princeton University, 1976.

Grant, Steven Alan. "The Peasant Commune in Russian Thought." Ph.D. diss., Harvard University, 1973.

Macey, David Anthony James. "The Russian Bureaucracy and the 'Peasant Problem': The Pre-History of the Stolypin Reforms, 1861–1907." Ph.D. diss., Columbia University, 1976.

Minokin, M. V. "Problema krest'ianstve v tvorchestve L. N. Tolstogo (80–90-e gody xix veka)." Candidate diss., Moscow State Pedagogical Institute im. V. I. Lenin, Moscow, 1950.

Raeff, Marc. "The Peasant Commune in the Political Thinking of Russian Publicists: Laissez-faire Liberalism in the Reign of Alexander II." Ph.D. diss., Harvard University, 1950.

Taranovski, Theodor. "The Politics of Counter-reform: Autocracy and Bureaucracy in the Reign of Alexander III." Ph.D. diss., Harvard University, 1976.

Zyrianov, P. N. "Krakh vnutrennei politiki tret'eiiun'skoi monarkhii v oblasti mestnogo upraveleniia (1907–1914)." Candidate diss., Institute of History, Academy of Sciences, USSR, Moscow, 1972.

Index